Planning for Pregnancy, Birth, and Beyond

Second Edition

The American College of
Obstetricians and Gynecologists
409 12th Street, SW
Washington, DC 20024-2188

Planning for Pregnancy, Birth, and Beyond was developed by a panel of experts under the direction of the Division of Education of the American College of Obstetricians and Gynecologists (ACOG) :

Editors
Gerald B. Holzman, MD, FACOG,
    ACOG Director of Education
Rebecca D. Rinehart, Associate
    Director, Publications

Consultants
Leslie Bloss, RN
Nancy C. Chescheir, MD, FACOG
Ronald A. Chez, MD, FACOG
Mary E. D'Alton, MD, FACOG
Vivian M. Dickerson, MD, FACOG
Gay P. Hall, CNM
Gary D. V. Hankins, MD, FACOG
Deborah M. Smith, MD, FACOG

Publications Staff
Mary F. Mitchell, Managing Editor
Glenda Fauntleroy, Editor
Christine Draughn, Cover and Text Design
Thomas P. Dineen, Manager of Production
    and Design

Illustrators
Lydia V. Kibiuk
Russell Schofield
Lois Sloan
Terese Winslow
Wendy Wray
John Michael Yanson

Cover Photograph
Adam Auel

Editorial Consultant
Vicki Meade

Planning for pregnancy, birth, and beyond.
    Planning for pregnancy, birth, and beyond.
        p.   cm.
    Previously published in 1990 under the title: ACOG guide to planning for pregnancy, birth, and beyond.
    Includes index.
    ISBN 0-915473-27-5
    1. Pregnancy. 2. Childbirth. 3. Infants—Care. I. American College of Obstetricians and Gynecologists. II. Title.
RG525.A26   1995
618.2—dc20   95-6754
                                                                              CIP

Designed as an aid to patients, *Planning for Pregnancy, Birth, and Beyond* sets forth current information and opinions on subjects related to women's health and reproduction. The information does not dictate an exclusive course of treatment or procedure to be followed and should not be constructed as excluding other medical opinions or acceptable methods of practice. Variations taking into account the needs of the individual patient, resources, and limitations unique to the institution or type of practice may be appropriate.

345/9876

Contents

Preface

Planning for Pregnancy, Birth, and Beyond is a complete guide to preconceptional, prenatal, and postpartum care. The American College of Obstetricians and Gynecologists (ACOG)—the national medical organization devoted to women's health—has assembled in one volume everything a woman should know about her pregnancy—before, during, and afterward. It is designed to enable a woman to take an active role in her health care so she can work with her doctor and health care team toward having a healthy baby.

Planning for Pregnancy, Birth, and Beyond begins with the preconceptional period, that important time before pregnancy when a woman's health and life style can have a major impact on her baby. It continues with detailed explanations of changes that occur over the 9 months of pregnancy, and concludes with a step-by-step description of labor and delivery. There is detailed information on what a woman can expect after she and her baby go home. The latest advances in medical care are combined with practical information on general health and well-being in areas such as nutrition, exercise, work, and relationships.

Since it was first published, *Planning for Pregnancy, Birth, and Beyond* has become a classic, guiding over one million women through their pregnancies. The second edition has been completely revised and updated, with new information in every chapter and two additional chapters. One of the new chapters is devoted to techniques for assessing the well-being of the fetus, highlighting the latest methods for checking on the baby's health before birth. The other new chapter focuses on a less happy event, but one that cannot be ignored. Not all babies are born healthy, and when this occurs the parents grieve and need support. Advances in early detection of genetic disorders have been included to help parents be better informed of their risks. New art has been added to enhance the visual appeal and to describe complex events, particularly with regard to growth and development of the fetus.

Planning for Pregnancy, Birth, and Beyond is a reference to all aspects of pregnancy, including those that relate to special needs or problems. The information is organized to help readers turn to or skip a certain area, with cross-references to related subjects. The complete subject index can help locate topics of interest. Other features include an extensive glossary, which defines terms marked in ***boldface italic*** type at first mention, and a personal pregnancy diary that can be used to chart the progress of the pregnancy and to note key events. Questions at the end of each chapter reinforce key concepts and form the basis of a dialogue between a woman and her doctor.

The importance of the health care team is emphasized in this edition. As the health care system changes, doctors are more and more relying on the support of the other members of the team to provide care. Throughout the book the term "doctor" could in many cases also apply to other health care professionals. In today's health care environment, women continue to be able to exercise what is probably the most important choice they can make for the health of their babies—to have early and regular prenatal care throughout pregnancy.

Although advances in prenatal care have improved the outcome for mothers and babies, problems can arise during pregnancy. This book highlights areas where problems can occur, warning signs, and ways to prevent them. Pregnancy is a normal, natural process for most women, however, that has a profound impact on those it touches. A woman can work with her health care team toward the goal of pregnancy—the delivery of a healthy baby.

The information in this book represents the opinions of leading experts in the specialty of obstetrics and gynecology and related fields. It is drawn from educational materials developed by ACOG for practicing obstetrician–gynecologists and their patients. The views expressed here are not absolute, however, and should be considered flexible guidelines based on medical advice and local resources available.

Planning for Pregnancy, Birth, and Beyond

Second Edition

Preconceptional Care

Becoming a parent is a major commitment filled with challenges, rewards, and choices. By making some plans and changes now, before you conceive, you are more likely to have a healthy pregnancy later. Some aspects of pregnancy are part of a natural process you cannot control. You can have a big impact on other aspects, however—especially life style. A healthy life style adds greatly to your health and that of your baby. Planning for pregnancy can help you prepare for the events ahead and promote a healthy life style for your future.

Chapter 1

Planning Your Pregnancy

Pregnancy is a major event. If you plan for it, you can make wise decisions that will benefit both your health and that of your baby. Good health before pregnancy can help you cope with the stress of pregnancy, labor, and delivery. It can also help ensure that neither you nor your baby is exposed to things that could be harmful during pregnancy. Getting good health care before you become pregnant—sometimes called preconceptional care—will help you throughout your pregnancy. It also provides a chance to find any risks and treat any medical problems you may have.

Many women do not know they are pregnant until several weeks after they have conceived. These early weeks are some of the most crucial ones for the fetus—the baby growing inside you during pregnancy. It is during this time that the organs are formed. Certain substances such as cigarettes, alcohol, and some medications can interfere with normal growth, whereas healthy habits can help promote it. Preconceptional care can guide you in planning a healthy pregnancy.

A Preconceptional Visit

If you are planning to become pregnant, you may wish to schedule a preconceptional visit with your health care provider. As part of your visit, you will be asked questions about your family and medical history, medications you take, your diet and life style, and any past pregnancies. Your answers should be honest and open be-

3

cause they will help show whether you could need special care during pregnancy.

Your preconceptional visit is a time for you to ask questions. Don't hesitate to seek advice or discuss any concerns you might have. Your health care team is there to give information and guidance.

Family History

Some conditions occur more often in families. If a close member of your family has a history of a disorder, you may be at greater risk of having it, too. For example, you may be asked whether any member of your family has ever had diabetes, hypertension (high blood pressure), epilepsy (seizures), or mental retardation. You also may be asked if anyone in your family has a history of twin pregnancies.

Certain disorders can be inherited. These are called genetic disorders. Based on your age or family history, you may be advised to see a genetic counselor—someone with special training in inherited disorders. Genetic counseling can help couples be aware of their chances of having a child with an inherited disorder. It can also help pinpoint a pattern of inherited disorders, if one exists. Genetic counseling involves a detailed family history and sometimes a physical exam along with lab tests. Some genetic disorders can be detected by testing before you are pregnant; for further information about these disorders and the way they are inherited, see Chapter 7.

Medical History

Some women have medical conditions, such as diabetes, high blood pressure, and epilepsy, that call for special care

Genetic Disorders

The following diseases are inherited and, in some cases, can be detected before you are pregnant:

- Thalassemia
- Tay–Sachs disease
- Sickle cell disease
- Hemophilia
- Muscular dystrophy
- Cystic fibrosis
- Huntington chorea
- Fragile X (mental retardation)

This list changes as new information on how disorders are inherited is obtained. For further information, see Chapter 7.

during pregnancy. The condition may be an illness you had before pregnancy. Because pregnancy puts new demands on your body, a health problem that is normally under control can change while you are pregnant. If you have certain medical conditions, they should be brought under control before you become pregnant. They may require you to see your doctor more often or get other special care. Changes in your life style may also be necessary. The effects of these conditions during pregnancy are discussed in Chapter 11.

Questions you may be asked about your medical history include:

- Do you have diabetes, high blood pressure, or epilepsy? If so, when did it begin?
- Are you or have you ever been anemic? If so, for how long?
- How old were you when you had your first menstrual period?
- Have you ever had surgery? If so, what type?
- What type of birth control do you use?
- Have you had any accidents? What type?
- Do you have any allergies?

Past Pregnancies

Another part of preconceptional care is a review of your obstetric history. You will be asked about any previous pregnancies and if you had any complications.

If you had a problem in a past pregnancy, that doesn't mean the problem will recur or that you shouldn't try to get pregnant again. Some problems recur, but most do not. Previous problems can be a sign that you may need special attention before and during your current pregnancy.

Some women worry that they will have trouble having a baby if they have had a *miscarriage*. One in five women who become pregnant are known to have a miscarriage at some point in that pregnancy, and many more that are not detected are thought to occur. Most of these women go on to have normal pregnancies the next time they conceive. A few women have recurrent miscarriages (three or more pregnancy losses in a row). Most likely, though, if you have one miscarriage you will not have others and will be able to have a normal, healthy baby.

Most doctors agree that having a previous pregnancy terminated (induced abortion) does not make it harder to get pregnant again, nor will it affect the outcome of a future pregnancy. However, not much is known about the risk for women who have had more than one abortion. It is possible that more than one abortion might increase the risk for a low birth weight or a *preterm* baby.

Medications

You will be asked about any medications you are taking, including those bought over the counter (such as aspirin, antihistamines, and diet pills). Some medications could affect your fetus and should not be taken while you're pregnant. For example, a prescription medication for acne called isotretinoin can cause birth defects, and medications for high blood pressure called ACE inhibitors can cause kidney problems in the fetus. If you're taking certain medications, you may need to switch to others before you try to get pregnant. You will also be asked if you're still taking birth control pills. It's a good idea to take any medications you are using with you to the preconceptional visit.

Stopping Birth Control

Women who are planning pregnancy should stop using birth control several months in advance. Although methods vary, it can take a while for periods to resume and become regular. Because some methods are more effective than others, pregnancy can occur while a woman is using birth control. In most cases this does not pose a problem, although a woman should contact her doctor if she could be pregnant.

The birth control pill, or oral contraception, is the birth control method most commonly used by women. When you stop using birth control pills, your menstrual periods may be irregular for a while. This can make it hard to detect your fertile times, which means it may take longer for you to get pregnant. Irregular periods can also make it hard to tell your due date when you become pregnant. Using birth control pills before you become pregnant does not cause birth defects, no matter how close to conception you use them.

Other forms of hormonal birth control, such as implants and injections, may also cause a delay in getting pregnant. If you are using implants and want to become pregnant, have your doctor remove them.

If you have been using an intrauterine device (IUD) to prevent pregnancy, you should have it removed before you try to conceive. The IUD works by preventing sperm from fertilizing the egg. Even so, pregnancy can occur with an IUD in place. If this happens, your doctor should remove the device right away because the presence of an IUD during pregnancy is linked with infections and miscarriage.

Questions you may be asked about other medications include:

- Do you take sedatives or tranquilizers?
- Do you use illegal drugs?
- Do you drink alcohol? This includes beer and wine.
- Do you smoke? How many packs a day?

Life Style

Diet

Eating right before you become pregnant can help make sure that you and your fetus start out with the nutrients you both need. A balanced diet is a basic part of good health at all times in your life. During pregnancy, diet is even more important. The foods you eat are the main source of the nutrients for your fetus. As the fetus develops and places new demands on your body, you will need more of most nutrients. If you already follow a healthy diet, you can easily make changes during pregnancy to get the extra calories you need.

Special Needs

There may be needs in your diet that should be met before you become pregnant. Certain factors can affect how your body uses nutrients. If any of the following factors apply to you, consult your doctor, because you may need to make some changes in your diet.

■ Do you eat a strict vegetarian diet?

■ Do you commonly run long distances or do strenuous exercises?

■ Do you fast?

■ Are you following a diet to lose weight?

■ Do you have a history of anemia?

Folic acid may help prevent certain birth defects called *neural tube defects.* The U.S. Public Health Service has recommended that all reproductive-age women take 0.4 mg of folic acid daily to reduce the risk of neural tube defects. It can be taken as a vitamin or can be found in certain foods such as leafy, dark-green vegetables, citrus fruits, beans, and bread.

Women who have had a previous pregnancy that involved a neural tube defect have a higher risk of it recurring in a future pregnancy and should take 10 times more folic acid than the amount recommended routinely. Such women should take 4 mg daily for 1 month before pregnancy and during the first 3 months of pregnancy. These women should take folic acid alone, not as a part of a multivitamin preparation. To get enough folic acid from multivitamins, a woman would be getting an overdose of the other vitamins.

Weight

Maintaining proper weight is important for your good health. The right eating habits and moderate exercise are crucial to keeping a healthy weight and fit body—both before and during pregnancy. Weighing too much is a health hazard. During pregnancy, being overweight is linked to high blood pressure or diabetes. Extreme obesity puts a strain on the heart that becomes an added burden during pregnancy. Women who weigh too little tend to have low-birth-weight babies. These babies have more problems than other babies during labor and after birth.

About Your Weight

Fat is the form in which energy is stored. If a diet provides excess calories, they are stored as fat. To lose 1 pound you must lose 3,500 calories.

Body weight is not always a good measure of fat. A person who exercises loses fat and builds up muscle, which is heavier than fat. So a physically fit person can have a body weight that is above normal, but an amount of fat that is below normal. By contrast, a person who is not very active may weigh just as much as a physically fit person, but the inactive person will have more fat and less muscle. Generally, it is normal for a woman to have up to 20–25% of her total body weight in fat. The following table shows normal weights by height and age.

USDA Suggested Weights for Adults

Height*	Weight in pounds[†, ‡]	
	19–34 years	>35 years
5'0"	97–128	108–138
5'1"	101–132	111–143
5'2"	104–137	115–148
5'3"	107–141	119–152
5'4"	111–146	122–157
5'5"	114–150	126–162
5'6"	118–155	130–167
5'7"	121–160	134–172
5'8"	125–164	138–178
5'9"	129–169	142–183
5'10"	132–174	146–188
5'11"	136–179	151–194
6'0"	140–184	155–199

* Height is without shoes.

† Weight is without clothes.

‡ The higher weights generally apply to men, who tend to have more muscle and bone. The lower weights more often apply to women, who have less muscle and bone.

Adapted from the U.S. Department of Agriculture and U.S. Department of Health and Human Services. Nutrition and your health: dietary guidelines for Americans. 3rd ed. Washington, DC: U.S. Government Printing Office, 1990

It's best not to try losing weight while you are pregnant or trying to become pregnant. A weight-loss diet could deny you and your baby the nutrients you both need. It is best to try to reach a healthy weight well before you become pregnant.

Exercise

Good health at any time in your life involves proper diet and getting enough exercise. What you can do in sports and exercise during pregnancy depends on your health and, in part, on how active you are before you become pregnant (see Chapter 8 for specific guidelines).

Target Heart Rate

To check your heart rate, count your pulse by feeling the blood vessel at the side of your neck under your jaw or by feeling the pulse on the inside of your wrist. Count for the first 10 seconds after you stop exercising. Multiply this count by 6 to get the number of beats per minute. To find your target heart rate, look for the age category closest to your age and read the line across. These figures are averages to be used as general guidelines and do not apply to pregnant women.

Target Heart Rate for Nonpregnant Women

Age (years)	Target heart rate (beats per minute)	Average maximum heart rate (beats per minute)
20	120–160	200
25	117–156	195
30	114–152	190
35	111–148	185
40	108–144	180
45	105–140	175
50	102–136	170
55	99–132	165
60	96–128	160
65	93–124	155
70	90–120	150

National Heart, Lung, and Blood Institute. Exercise and your heart. NIH Publication No. 81-1677. Washington, DC: U.S. Government Printing Office, 1981

Ideally, you should be in shape and follow a regular exercise routine before you become pregnant. When starting an exercise program, decide whether you want to improve your heart and lung function, the tone of your body muscles, or both. Then, select exercises that will allow you to meet your goals. If you are not used to being active, you should start an exercise program gradually.

To get the best workout and strengthen your heart and lungs, you should exercise so your heart beats at a certain level called your target heart rate. Your target heart rate dictates how hard you should exercise.

Every time you exercise, you should begin with a 5- to 10-minute period of light activity, such as brisk walking, as a warm-up before each session. Once your body is warmed up, exercise for 20–30 minutes at your target heart rate. End with a cooldown period of at least 10 minutes by slowly reducing your activity to let your heart rate return to a normal level.

To tone your muscles or strengthen your heart you need to exercise at least three times a week. It does not have to be done daily—some people's muscles cannot withstand hard exercise every day. Every other day is fine. But it is important that you keep up your routine throughout the year. If you stop for 6–8 weeks, you will need to start again at a lower level of exertion.

Substance Use

Tobacco, alcohol, and illegal drugs are addictive and can harm both you and your fetus. They can have bad effects on the fetus at a time when organs are forming, causing damage that can last a lifetime or even result in death. The misuse of prescription medications can also harm the fetus.

Used in combination, as these substances often are, they are even more dangerous. For the sake of your own health and that of your baby, now is a good time to quit or at least cut down your use of tobacco, alcohol, and illegal drugs.

It takes time and patience to quit a habit. This is especially true if you've had that habit for a long time. Don't be embarrassed. Ask your doctor to suggest ways to get through the withdrawal stage of quitting and to refer you to support groups. Your decision to quit may be one of the hardest things you've ever done, but it will be one of the most worthwhile.

Environment

Some substances found in the environment or at the work place can make it harder for a woman to become pregnant or can harm the fetus. If you are planning to become pregnant, it's a good idea to look closely at your work place and surroundings. If you see that you could be exposed to a harmful substance, you can take steps to avoid it (see "Harmful Agents," Chapter 8). The effects of most chemicals in the environments are not known, however.

Before you accept a job, find out from your employer whether you might be exposed to toxic substances, chemicals, or radiation. After you start a job, discuss your level of exposure to specific substances with your employee health division, personnel office, or union representative.

Radiation, a form of energy transmitted in waves that you cannot see, is used in some jobs. It is also used, in the form of X-rays, to diagnose and treat disease. Exposure to high levels of some kinds of radiation can make men and women less fertile and can affect the fetus of a pregnant woman. Women planning a pregnancy who are exposed to radiation in industrial and medical settings should ask for monthly readings that show how much radiation they have been exposed to. The amount of radiation in a chest X-ray will not hurt fertility or a fetus. Radiation to treat diseases such as cancer, however, is used in much larger amounts and can be harmful.

Exposure to lead or certain solvents, pesticides, or other chemicals can reduce your partner's fertility by killing or damaging his sperm. Unlike women, who are born with a complete supply of eggs for their whole lifetime, men make new sperm daily for most of their lives. Unless the damage to a man's reproductive system is very serious, he will probably be able to make healthy sperm again a short time after his exposure to the harmful material stops.

Infections

Infections can prove harmful to both the mother and the fetus. Some infections during pregnancy can cause serious birth defects or illness in the fetus. Some can be prevented by vaccination. Ask your doctor if there are immunizations (vaccinations) you should have (eg, measles, mumps, tetanus, polio, and rubella). Even if you were vaccinated as a child, you may not be immune now. If you're vaccinated before you become pregnant, you will be protected. The vaccine should be given at least 3 months before you try to conceive. During that time you should use birth control.

If you plan to travel to areas where you may come in contact with infectious diseases not found in this country, you may need to be vaccinated against them. If you are not using birth control, consult your doctor regarding possible effects during pregnancy (see "Travel," Chapter 8, and "Vaccines," Chapter 13).

Other infections that are harmful during pregnancy are those passed on by sexual contact—sexually transmitted diseases (STDs). STDs come in many types and forms and not only can affect your ability to conceive but can also infect and harm your baby. Some common STDs are chlamydia, gonorrhea, genital herpes, and human immunodeficiency virus (HIV).

The use of some birth control methods, such as condoms and spermicides, can lower the risk of getting an STD. When a woman is trying to get pregnant, she will be at a higher risk of getting an STD because she will not be using any birth control. This is especially true if she has sex with more than one partner.

If you think you may have an STD, see your doctor right away to be tested and treated. Your partner should also be treated, and you both should not have sex until you have completed treatment.

Immunizations

Women in their reproductive years should have immunizations as a routine part of preventive care:

- Tetanus-diphtheria booster (every 10 years)
- Measles, mumps, rubella (once if not immune)
- Hepatitis B vaccine*
- Influenza vaccine*
- Pneumococcal vaccine*

* These immunizations are given as needed based on risk factors—check with your health care provider.

Later Childbearing

Most women in their mid-30s and older have healthy pregnancies and healthy babies. Even so, some questions arise for these women.

They may have concerns about whether their age will affect their ability to become pregnant, their health, and the health of their baby. Although there is no absolute age that is unsafe for older women who want to become pregnant, there are some special concerns that these women should consider.

A woman's fertility gradually declines as she reaches her mid-30s and beyond. Therefore, women at this age may find it takes longer to get pregnant. As women get older, certain medical and obstetric problems also occur more often. Because pregnancy puts new demands on a woman's body, the risk of complications during pregnancy is higher for women with these problems. They are more likely to need to visit the doctor more often, to stay in the hospital before the birth of the baby, and to need special tests.

Another concern for older women is the risk of birth defects. The likelihood of some birth defects increases with age, but it remains low well into a woman's 30s. Women 35 and older are usually offered testing for genetic disorders and other medical problems. (For more information on birth defects, see Chapter 7.)

Although these factors could be risks, an older woman can have a normal, healthy baby. It's important to be aware of these risks and discuss pregnancy plans with your doctor so that you are sure to get the proper medical attention that any special concerns require.

Questions to Consider...

- Do I or a member of my family have a disorder that could be inherited?
- Do I need to gain or lose weight to prepare for pregnancy?
- Should I make any changes in my life style?
- Could any medications I'm taking cause problems during my pregnancy?
- Can I continue my present exercise program?
- Does my work expose me to things that could be harmful during pregnancy?
- Do I need to be vaccinated for any infectious diseases before I try to get pregnant?

Chapter 2

How Reproduction Occurs

A finely tuned sequence of events must take place for reproduction to occur. A basic knowledge of how reproduction works will help you as you get ready for pregnancy. This knowledge will help you tell when you are most fertile—in other words, when you are most likely to get pregnant. It will also help you understand the rapid changes that take place during early pregnancy.

The Menstrual Cycle

A woman's fertility depends on her menstrual cycle. The changes during the menstrual cycle are caused by hormones—substances produced by the body to control certain functions. Each month, hormones cause the lining of the uterus to build up and an egg to mature in a follicle—tiny clusters of cells in the ovaries. When an egg is mature, it is released from the ovary. This process is called ovulation.

An average menstrual cycle lasts about 28 days, counting from the first day of one period (day 1) to the first day of the next. Although menstrual cycles typically last 28 days, cycles of 23–35 days are normal. Your own cycle will probably vary somewhat from month to month. It's a good idea to keep a diary of your cycle so you will know what is normal for you.

Ovulation occurs about 14 days before the next period. After ovulation, the egg moves down one of the fallopian tubes toward the uterus. If the egg is not fertilized by a sperm, it is absorbed by

---

Hormones: Key Players in Menstruation and Pregnancy

The menstrual cycle and pregnancy are caused by key hormones that interact at various stages:

- *Estrogen* and *progesterone.* Produced by the ovaries, these hormones trigger changes in the lining of the uterus (endometrium), causing it to thicken during each menstrual cycle and to be shed if pregnancy does not occur. Increases in these hormones when you are pregnant keep you from ovulating and having your period.
- *Follicle-stimulating hormone (FSH)* and *luteinizing hormone (LH).* These hormones are made by the *pituitary gland,* a small organ located at the base of the brain. One (FSH) causes eggs to mature, and the other (LH) causes them to be released by the ovaries.
- *Gonadotropin-releasing hormone.* This hormone, made by a part of the brain, tells the pituitary gland when to produce FSH and LH.
- *Human chorionic gonadotropin.* This hormone is made by cells that form the *placenta,* which nourishes the egg after it has been fertilized and become attached to the uterine wall. This hormone causes increases in estrogen and progesterone when you are pregnant. It is the hormone that is detected in a pregnancy test.

the body. Then, on the last day of the cycle, the lining of the uterus is shed as menstrual fluid. If the egg *is* fertilized, however, it becomes attached to the lining of the uterus. The fertilized egg then starts to grow as pregnancy begins. If you become pregnant, it will make it easier to set a due date for the baby if you kept a diary of your menstrual cycles.

Fertilization

The union of egg and sperm that results in pregnancy is called fertilization. Once an egg is released, it can be fertilized by a sperm.

Sperm cells are made in a man's testes, in the scrotal sac below the penis. When the sperm cells mature, they leave the testes through small tubes called the vas deferens. As sperm move from the testes, they mix with fluid made by the seminal vesicles and prostate gland, small organs located near the bladder. The mixture

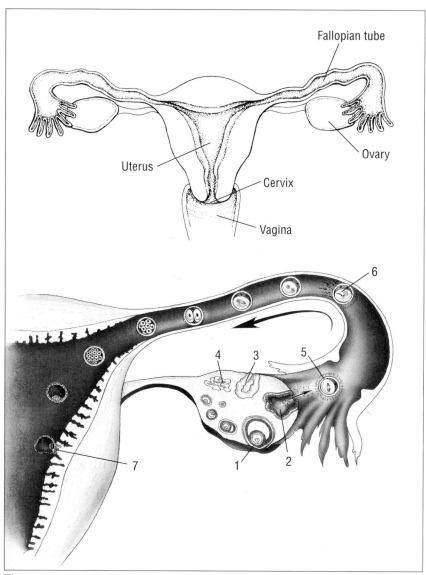

The egg matures in the follicle (*1*) and is released at ovulation (*2*). The follicle develops into the corpus luteum (*3*), which shrinks and disappears if pregnancy does not occur (*4*). If the egg (*5*) is fertilized by the sperm in the fallopian tube (*6*), it moves through the tube to the lining of the uterus (*7*), where it becomes implanted and grows.

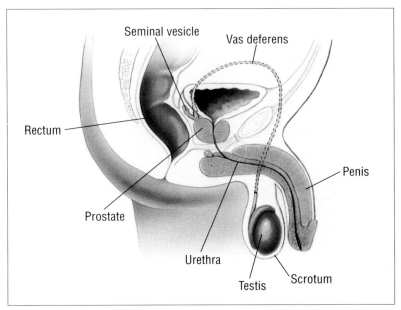

The male reproductive system.

of sperm and fluids is called semen. When the man ejaculates or climaxes during sex, semen moves through the urethra, a tube in the penis, into the vagina. A woman does not have to climax to become pregnant.

When a man ejaculates into the vagina, sperm move up through the cervix, into the uterus, and out into the fallopian tubes. Sperm live 2–3 days or longer. If a sperm joins with an egg in one of the tubes, fertilization occurs.

Sperm cells are made all the time. Some couples worry that having sex too often—such as every day—will reduce the number of sperm and make it harder for the woman to become pregnant. Daily intercourse should not be a problem if the man has produced enough sperm. The sperm count is the number of active sperm in a milliliter (less than a half teaspoon) of semen. A normal sperm count is between 20 million and 250 million per milliliter.

Detecting Ovulation

Eighty-five percent of women who have sex without using birth control will get pregnant within 1 year. Having sex near the time of ovulation increases a woman's chance of getting pregnant. There are several ways to detect ovulation. One way is to figure out when your next period will start and count back 14 days. For example,

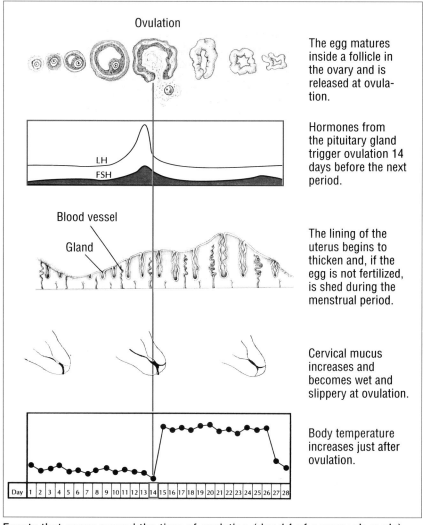

The egg matures inside a follicle in the ovary and is released at ovulation.

Hormones from the pituitary gland trigger ovulation 14 days before the next period.

The lining of the uterus begins to thicken and, if the egg is not fertilized, is shed during the menstrual period.

Cervical mucus increases and becomes wet and slippery at ovulation.

Body temperature increases just after ovulation.

Events that occur around the time of ovulation (day 14 of a woman's cycle).

in a 30-day cycle, ovulation takes place on day 16. To use this method, you must know how long your cycle usually lasts.

You can also detect ovulation by watching for changes in the amount and makeup of the cervical mucus, a fluid that is released from the vagina. It looks like the white of a raw egg. At the start of the menstrual cycle, the cervical mucus is sparse and dense. Around the time of ovulation the cervical mucus is plentiful and slippery. The fertile period starts with the first signs of slippery mucus and continues through the peak day.

Another way of detecting when you are likely to be ovulating is the basal body temperature method. Most women have a slight rise in their normal body temperature after ovulation. A woman using this method takes her temperature at the same time every morning of her cycle before getting out of bed. She records it on a graph. This method shows a pattern you can use to predict when you will ovulate in future cycles.

There are also kits that use chemicals to show the changes in hormones that come just before ovulation. These kits can be bought in a drugstore without a prescription. To be accurate, they must be used exactly according to the instructions.

Fertility

Most couples who want to have a child are able to do so. About 15 of 100 couples face fertility problems—they have tried to conceive but cannot. Couples who have not been able to conceive after 1 year of having regular sex without using any form of birth control should consider a fertility evaluation.

A fertility evaluation usually begins with a medical history and general physical checkup of the man and the woman. A medical history of the woman includes questions about past illnesses such as appendicitis or pelvic infections that might have harmed her reproductive organs. The couple will also be asked about their sexual relations to find out whether their infertility may be tied to factors such as timing or frequency of sex. Often a couple may simply need more information on the sexual techniques that are most helpful for getting pregnant.

These exams are then followed by more in-depth testing of both the man and the woman to detect the exact cause of the infertility and to find out whether it can be treated. Depending on the causes of the infertility, alternatives are available:

■ Medications to induce ovulation
■ Artificial insemination with sperm from the partner or a donor
■ Surgery to open blocked fallopian tubes
■ Assisted reproduction techniques

These methods are not suitable for everyone. Your doctor can tell you more about them and offer guidance on whether any of them would be right for you.

Questions to Consider...

■ How can I tell when I have ovulated?
■ If I'm trying to conceive, when is the best time to have sex?
■ Do we need an infertility evaluation?

Pregnancy

Pregnancy is a time of major change. From the very start, your baby-to-be alters your body and your daily life. For 40 weeks, your baby depends totally on you for its nutrients and life functions.

Most babies are born healthy. A few women, however, have problems during their pregnancy. If you are getting regular prenatal care, your doctor may be able to detect signs of problems early.

Advances in medicine have helped both to decrease the risk of childbirth and to improve the health of babies at birth. By planning your pregnancy, starting prenatal care early, making well-thought-out decisions, and having a healthy life style, you can take an active role in your pregnancy and can be assured that you're doing all you can to have a healthy baby.

Chapter 3

A New Life Begins

The process called fertilization, during which a man's sperm joins with a woman's egg, usually takes place in the fallopian tube. Once the egg is fertilized by the sperm, it travels down the fallopian tube and into the uterus. Here, the egg attaches to the wall of the uterus and starts to grow. This fertilized egg is called an embryo for the first 8 weeks; after that it is called a fetus. Inside the uterus, between the uterine wall and the developing embryo, an organ called the placenta grows. The placenta nourishes the fetus by taking oxygen and other products from the mother's blood and passing them to the fetus. During the 40 weeks of pregnancy, which are divided into three *trimesters*, the fetus grows very quickly. It changes from a single cell that carries the blueprint for the baby's entire physical makeup to a fully formed baby. Term babies weigh an average of 7 pounds and are about 20 inches long. Babies grow at different rates, however, and some may be larger or smaller than average.

Early Signs of Pregnancy

The first sign that most women relate to being pregnant is a missed menstrual period. Not all women have regular periods, though. Menstrual periods can be affected by stress or illness, so it is best to watch for a number of other signs and symptoms:

- Light menstrual period or spotting
- Tender breasts
- Being very tired
- Upset stomach or nausea

■ Feeling bloated
■ Needing to urinate often

If you have one or more of these symptoms along with a missed period, you could be pregnant, even if you have been using birth control.

Diagnosis of Pregnancy

Pregnancy can be confirmed by the time you've missed a period. During early pregnancy, the hormone called human chorionic gonadotropin (hCG), which is made by the developing placenta, is in the mother's urine and blood. You can be tested by your doctor or at a clinic, or you can test yourself with a home pregnancy test kit.

You can buy most home pregnancy test kits without a prescription. If your body has made enough hCG, a chemical in the test kit will react with the hCG in your urine. The tests show the presence of the hCG in different ways. In some, a ring forms in a liquid or a bead changes color. They can easily give a wrong result if the directions are not followed. Therefore, it is important to follow all the directions on the kit carefully. If a home test shows that you are pregnant, you should make plans to begin prenatal care.

Home pregnancy tests can be very accurate, but no test is 100% foolproof. False-negative results (results showing that you are not pregnant when you really are) can occur in a small number of cases. If you think there is even a small chance that you could be pregnant despite getting negative results from a home pregnancy test, see your doctor as soon as possible. He or she may choose to confirm the results with more accurate tests.

Growth and Development

During pregnancy the fetus grows in the mother's uterus, a muscular organ located between the bladder and the rectum. The lining of the uterus thickens and its blood vessels enlarge to nourish the growing fetus. Throughout pregnancy, the uterus expands as the fetus grows.

The placenta begins to form the moment the fertilized egg attaches to the lining of the uterus. Also known as the afterbirth, the placenta is the channel through which oxygen, nutrients, drugs, hormones, and other substances pass from mother to fetus. In the opposite direction, waste products from the fetus cross through the placenta to the mother and are disposed of by the mother's kidneys. The placenta is attached to the **umbilical cord,** which connects to the fetus at the spot that will become its navel.

The placenta starts as small fingerlike projections growing from the wall of the fertilized egg. In these projections, called **chorionic villi,** fetal blood vessels form. The tips of the vessels enter the wall of the uterus and tap the mother's blood vessels. The maternal and fetal blood systems are in close contact, but the blood

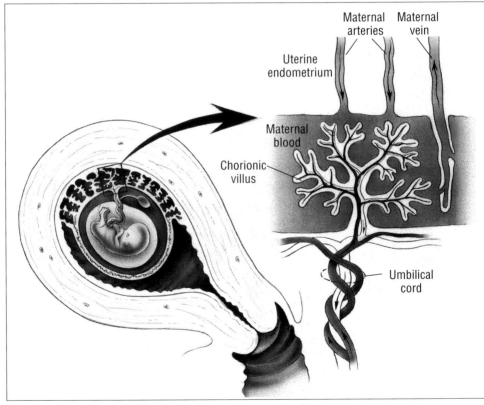

The placenta is composed of many lobes of chorionic villi, which contain fetal blood vessels. One of these lobes is shown magnified at right.

Growth and Changes During Pregnancy

0–14 Weeks (First Trimester)

Woman

- Your period stops or is light.
- You may have nausea and vomiting. These usually go away by the end of this time.
- Your breasts become larger. They may be tender.
- Your nipples may stick out more.
- You may have to urinate more often.

Fetus

- The heart begins to beat.
- Bones appear; the head, arms, fingers, legs, and toes form.
- The major organs and nervous system form.
- The placenta forms.
- Hair starts to grow.
- 20 buds for future teeth appear.
- By the end of this time, the fetus is about 4 inches long and weighs just over 1 ounce.

Week 4
(actual size)

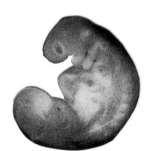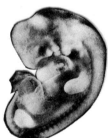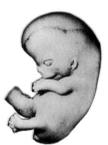

The embryo develops rapidly during the first 8 weeks of pregnancy.

Photos courtesy of Carnegie Institution of Washington.

14–28 Weeks (Second Trimester)

Woman

- Your abdomen begins to swell. Your uterus will be near your ribs by the end of this time.
- The skin on your abdomen and breasts stretches. You may see stretch marks.
- At about 16–20 weeks, you may start to feel the fetus move.
- You may get a dark line from the navel down the middle of the abdomen, or you may get brown, uneven marks on your face. Your *areolas*, the brown area around your nipples, may darken.

Fetus

- The fetus grows quickly from now until birth.
- The organs develop further.
- Eyebrows and fingernails form.
- The skin is wrinkled and covered with fine hair.
- The fetus moves, kicks, sleeps, and wakes. It can swallow, hear, and pass urine.
- By the end of this time, the fetus is about 11–14 inches long and weighs about 2–2 $\frac{1}{2}$ pounds.

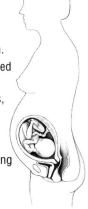

28–40 Weeks (Third Trimester)

Woman

- You can feel the movements of the fetus more strongly.
- You may have abdominal pains. These may be false or true labor pains.
- You may feel short of breath as the uterus pushes against the diaphragm, a flat, strong muscle that aids in breathing. Toward the end of this time the baby's position may drop lower in your abdomen, which will make it easier for you to breathe.
- When the baby drops, you may need to urinate more often.
- Yellow, watery fluid called *colostrum* may leak from your nipples.
- Your navel may stick out.
- Your cervix may begin to thin out and open slightly.

Fetus

- The fetus kicks and stretches, but as it gets bigger it has less room to move.
- Fine body hair disappears.
- Bones harden, but bones of the head are soft and flexible for delivery.
- The fetus usually settles into a good position for birth.
- At 40 weeks, the fetus will be full term. It is about 20 inches long and weighs 6–9 pounds.

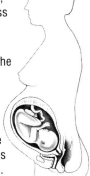

The Growth and Development of the Fetus

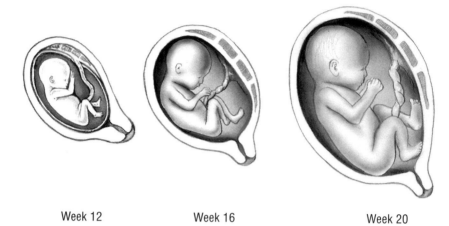

Week 12   Week 16   Week 20

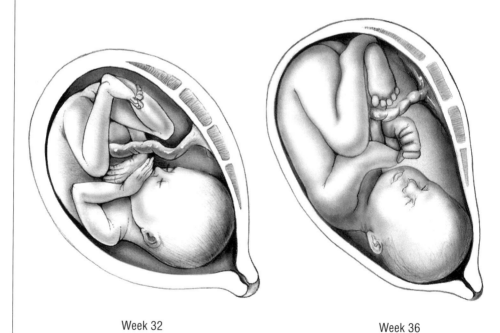

Week 32   Week 36

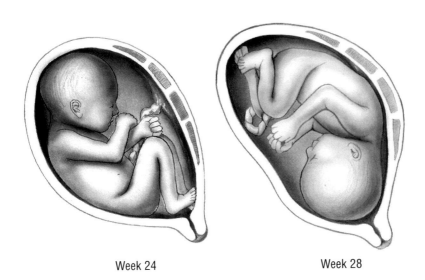

Week 24   Week 28

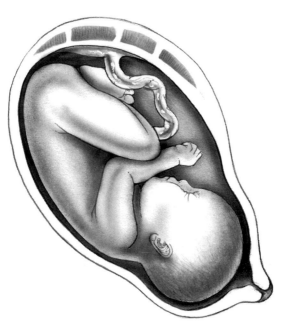

Week 40

from the mother and the blood from the fetus do not mix. The placenta is expelled from the uterus minutes after the baby is born.

A pregnancy usually lasts about 280 days from the beginning of a woman's last normal menstrual period, although it can range from 266 to 294 days. This is equal to 40 weeks, or about 9 calendar months—each month made up of about 4½ weeks.

The developing fetus has a dramatic effect on a pregnant woman. Although most women undergo many of the same physical changes, other changes may be unique to each woman. No two pregnancies are alike. Even for the same woman, a second or third pregnancy may be very different from the first. Understanding the changes that take place in your body and in the growing fetus during pregnancy will help you prepare for the weeks to come.

Questions to Consider...

■ Do I have any symptoms that mean I might be pregnant?

■ Did I perform my home pregnancy test correctly?

■ Should the results of my pregnancy test be confirmed?

■ Where will I get prenatal care?

Chapter 4

Decisions, Decisions

Pregnant women have many choices to make. You need to decide where you want the baby to be delivered, who will deliver it, and how best to prepare for childbirth. You'll want to explore choices regarding breast-feeding and other aspects of your care. These important decisions will affect how comfortable you will be with your care and how confident you will feel as you approach the birth of your baby. It's important to think over your options early and discuss them with your partner and your health care provider so you can make the best decisions possible.

Planning Your Obstetric Care

Choosing who will care for you during your pregnancy and delivery may be one of your first decisions. Ideally, you saw your health care provider before you became pregnant and discussed your medical history and other preconceptional issues. Many women ask friends or relatives who have children to recommend a health care provider. Some women decide on a hospital where they would like to deliver their baby and ask the staff there for a referral. Keep in mind that your health insurance policy may have restrictions that can affect your choices.

Babies can be delivered by three types of health care providers: certified nurse–midwives, doctors in family practice, or obstetrician–gynecologists. Sometimes a doctor and a nurse–midwife work as a team.

Certified nurse–midwives are registered nurses who are also educated to care for women and their babies from early pregnancy through labor, delivery, and the period after birth. They have graduated from an accredited nursing program and have a graduate degree in midwifery. To be certified, they must pass a national exam and maintain an active nursing license. Nurse–midwives must have an arrangement with a doctor to provide backup support. They care for healthy women with normal pregnancies and consult with or refer patients to a doctor if medical problems occur.

Doctors in family practice provide general care for most conditions, including pregnancy. These doctors have completed medical school and received special training in family practice. They are certified to practice medicine by passing an exam.

Obstetrician–gynecologists are doctors who specialize in the general medical care of women as well as care related to pregnancy and the reproductive tract. After graduating from medical school, obstetrician–gynecologists go through a 4-year course of specialized training called a residency. Then, they are eligible to be certified by the American Board of Obstetrics and Gynecology. To be certified, a physician must pass written and oral tests to show that he or she has obtained the special knowledge and skills required for the medical and surgical care of women.

If an obstetrician–gynecologist is certified, he or she is eligible to become a Fellow of the American College of Obstetri-

cians and Gynecologists. This group champions women's health care issues and represents the specialty on both a national and a local level. It also offers a wide range of continuing medical educational programs to help physicians stay up with the latest scientific and clinical practice advances.

Board-certified obstetrician–gynecologists may become further specialized. One of these subspecialty areas is maternal–fetal medicine. These specialists have extra training and experience in caring for women whose pregnancies are complicated by medical or obstetric problems. Patients are usually referred to them by another doctor.

Many obstetrician–gynecologists coordinate a team of health care professionals to provide various types of care based on a woman's special needs during pregnancy. Some may be employed by the doctor's office or the facility where the doctor works, such as a collaborative practice or a teaching hospital. Others may be consulted as needed about your care. The following health care professionals may be members of the health care team:

- *Registered nurses* assist obstetricians in providing patient care, patient education, and counseling. *Labor and delivery nurses* help care for patients in labor and for babies right after birth, *postpartum nurses* help care for the mother after birth, and *neonatal nurses* help care for the newborn. All have studied in accredited nursing programs and passed a licensing exam.

- *Residents* are doctors in training at a teaching hospital.

- *Physician assistants* handle many types of medical duties and work under the supervision of doctors. They go through a 2-year education program after college and must pass a licensing exam.

The health care team may also include childbirth educators, who teach parents-to-be about pregnancy, childbirth, and family life; dieticians, who give advice on nutrition and any special needs; social workers, who provide counseling and information about community services for families; and genetic counselors, who evaluate the baby's risk of having inherited disorders and provide counseling.

Other doctors may be a part of the health care team depending on the care provided and any special needs. The team may include maternal–fetal medicine subspecialists; neonatologists or pediatricians, who provide special care for the newborn; and anesthesiology teams, doctors or nurses who provide pain relief during labor and delivery.

The qualifications of each member of the health care team may differ. However, each one has an important role in making sure your pregnancy and birth go well.

Many women like to visit and interview different health care providers before making a final decision. Feel free to raise questions about areas of concern to you or your partner. A number of points could affect your choice:

- Is the practice close to your home or work?
- Where does the health care provider have hospital privileges?
- How do you get emergency care outside normal office hours?
- Do you have any problems that may require special care?
- What are the provider's fees, and how are they covered by your health insurance plan, if you have one? If you need advice on insurance or a payment plan, the health care staff may be able to help.
- Does your insurance plan limit your choice to certain providers?
- What is the health care provider's attitude about questions of concern to you, such as breast-feeding, pain relief, having fathers in labor and delivery rooms, and using birthing rooms?

Another factor to consider is whether the doctor is in a group, collaborative, or solo practice. In a group practice, constant coverage is provided by two or more doctors. You may have a primary doctor but on occasion receive care from the others. It is possible that one of the other doctors will deliver your baby. This also is true for collaborative practice, in which a doctor and a nurse, certified nurse–midwife, or other health professionals work as a team to provide care before, during, and after pregnancy. With a solo practice, one doctor provides complete care for all of his or her patients. If the doctor gets sick or goes on vacation, another doctor will step in to care for you.

Each type of practice has benefits and drawbacks. The solo practice allows you to see the same doctor each time, but could involve delays or canceled appointments if the doctor is called away when someone else's baby arrives unexpectedly, as babies often do. The group and collaborative practices have the efficiency of shared resources, but you will receive care from more than one provider.

After birth, the baby will need his or her own physician. You may want a family doctor to care for your baby or you may prefer a pediatrician—a doctor who specializes in children's health care. Whichever you choose, try to meet with the doctor before the baby is born to discuss matters that are important to you. When you choose the baby's doctor in advance, he or she can be notified if the baby has any health problems and can examine the baby in the hospital. (If you do not choose the baby's doctor ahead of time, your own doctor or the hospital will select someone.)

The Setting

The areas for labor and delivery vary from one hospital to another. Your options depend not only on what the hospitals in your area offer but also on your health insurance. You will be given information about the choices available. You can tour the hospitals in your community to see which types of settings appeal to you.

Many hospitals have responded to the desires of parents-to-be by offering birthing rooms where the family can take part. Birthing rooms share the staff and services of a more traditional labor and delivery suite, which may be needed if a problem occurs. They provide a comfortable setting for labor, delivery, and, usually, postpartum recovery. Some enable the entire birth process, including the postpartum stay, to happen in one room. These rooms are called LDRs (labor/delivery/recovery) or LDRPs (labor/delivery/recovery/postpartum).

There are also freestanding birthing centers that are not in a hospital. These centers may not offer all the services you may need if an emergency arises. Because of this, a hospital is thought to be the safest place to give birth.

When selecting your care, you may wish to ask about policies regarding fathers or others in the delivery room. Most hospitals permit support people in both labor and delivery rooms. It is wise to know the hospital's policy in advance so you can plan.

If you have health problems during your pregnancy or complications are likely during birth, you may have to deliver at a specific hospital. It is possible that the hospital, which must be equipped to handle complex procedures, may not be near where you live.

Childbirth Preparation

Preparing for childbirth means knowing what to expect and learning how to help labor and delivery go as smoothly as possible. Classes are available to help you get ready for the demands of childbirth, as well as teach you about proper diet and exercise. They can ease your fears and teach you techniques for coping with the discomfort that most women have during childbirth. It is not possible to know in advance how much pain you will feel, how long your labor will last, or how you will deal with childbirth.

Parents-to-be often attend childbirth preparation classes
to learn relaxation techniques for labor and delivery.

Childbirth preparation classes can help you feel more in control of the situation. To find a childbirth educator or learn about the types of childbirth preparation, ask your doctor or a member of the health care team.

The most common methods of preparation—Lamaze, Bradley, and Read—are based on the theory that much of the pain of childbirth is caused by fear and tension. Although specific techniques vary, classes usually seek to relieve discomfort through the general principles of education, support, relaxation, paced breathing, focusing, and touch.

Some childbirth education classes may help you set up a birth plan. This plan might include the setting you want to deliver in, the people you want to have with you, and the pain medications you want, if any. Be sure to check your plan with the hospital in which you'll be delivering your baby, in case parts of it do not fit the hospital's policy.

Your Childbirth Partner

One of your early decisions will be selecting your childbirth partner to help you through pregnancy, labor, and delivery. Support by a partner from the beginning can ease the stress of a woman's pregnancy and help labor and delivery go more smoothly. This person may go with you on prenatal care visits and will attend childbirth classes to help with your breathing and relaxation exercises. During labor, your partner will take an active role as a coach, helping you carry out what you learned and practiced in childbirth class.

The father of the baby is usually, but not always, the partner. If for some reason the father is not involved in the pregnancy, others can give support and play an active role. A support person can be any family member or friend who will help you and be there for you.

The concept of family-centered care, now widely embraced in modern obstetric practice, focuses on the physical, social, and psychological needs of the family unit, no matter who makes up that unit. Family-centered care can extend to family members and loved ones who wish to take part in the birth process.

Options

Many decisions need to be carried out soon after the baby is born. It's best to think about your options and resolve as much as you can in advance. For example, you need to consider whether to breast-feed, whether to circumcise the baby if it's a boy, and what you want to do about birth control after the baby is born. (Work and travel considerations, which also require preplanning, are discussed in Chapter 8.)

Breast-Feeding

Should you feed your baby with breast milk or with formula? This is one basic decision you must make about the care of your infant. During pregnancy, your body prepares to make milk whether or not you plan to breast-feed. Breast milk, including the colostrum that appears in the first 2–4 days, is designed by nature to nourish and protect newborns. It contains *antibodies*, which help the baby's immune system fight off disease. It has the right amount of all the nutrients the baby needs. Infants who are breast-fed have fewer feeding problems, tend to be less constipated, and have fewer infections and allergies. Breast-feeding also releases hormones that contract the uterus, helping it return to its normal size more quickly. Many women find breast-feeding to be a loving, natural, convenient, and inexpensive way to nourish their babies.

Some women choose not to breast-feed. Babies can also be well nourished by commercially available formulas. These typically contain nonfat cow's milk and fat from soy, coconut, or corn. They also include vitamins, minerals, and trace elements. Formulas that use soy protein in place of cow's milk are available for babies with milk allergy or intolerance. Infant formulas do not contain antibodies to help protect the baby from illness.

Before you choose either breast-feeding or bottle-feeding, talk with others. Find out your partner's feelings. Ask all the questions you may have. Talk with women who have breast-fed their babies and others who have decided against it. Expense may be an important factor, so look into the costs. If you bottle-feed, you'll need to buy bottles and formula. Whatever decision you make, be sure you feel comfortable with it. (More information on breast-feeding appears in Chapter 17.)

Circumcision

A layer of skin (the foreskin) covers most of the sensitive end of the penis of a male who has not been circumcised. Circumcision involves cutting away this foreskin. When parents choose to have their son circumcised it is usually done soon after birth, before the baby leaves the hospital.

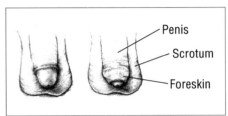

Much has been written about circumcision— both positive and negative—by people who have very strong feelings. Circumcision is an elective procedure. It is a matter of choice, and in most cases there is no medical reason to perform the surgery. Although more than half of newborn boys in the United States are circumcised, the procedure is much less common in Northern Europe and other parts of the world. Some parents have their sons circumcised for religious or cultural reasons. Moslems and Jews, for example, have circumcised their male babies for centuries.

Two views of the penis—circumcised (*left*) and uncircumcised. The scrotum is the pouch that contains the testes.

Some people support circumcision for hygiene's sake. Smegma —a cheesy discharge containing dead cells—can build up under the foreskin of uncircumcised males and can lead to odor or infection. A boy can be taught to wash his penis to get rid of the smegma as part of his daily bathing routine.

In rare cases baby boys are born with either no opening in the foreskin or a very small one, which impedes urination. Circumcision corrects this problem. Researchers have debated whether circumcision brings about a lower risk of sexually transmitted diseases and cancer of the penis, but evidence is scanty. Circumcised infants appear to have less risk of infections of the urinary tract than uncircumcised infants, but the risk in both groups is low. The circumcision surgery itself can cause complications in rare cases.

Personal, emotional, and religious preferences come into play when making decisions about circumcision. It is not required by law or by hospital policy. Circumcision is no longer offered routinely to parents in some hospitals—they must request it.

Talk with your doctor about circumcision early so you have enough time to make an informed decision. You can ask for written material about the procedure and the care necessary for both circumcised and uncircumcised boys.

Birth Control and Sterilization

Family planning is more than preventing unwanted pregnancy—it means deciding how many children you want and how to space them. A key factor in planning your family is the type of birth control you will use between pregnancies. You can usually start having sex about 3–4 weeks after giving birth. You should choose a form of birth control ahead of time, so you can have intercourse safely when you feel ready. Talk with your doctor or nurse about the methods available, and ask which are best suited to your future childbearing plans.

Couples who decide they do not want more children may consider sterilization of either the man or the woman. Many women who choose sterilization have it done postpartum. It is often performed within a day after delivery, while the woman is still in the hospital.

Sterilization is permanent. Therefore, you and your partner must think about it carefully and figure out well before your baby's birth if it is the right choice for you. It is not a decision to make at times of stress or near the end of pregnancy. If the procedure will be paid for by a government program, you must sign a consent form at least 30 days before delivery. Because you probably do not know the exact day you will deliver and cannot be positive that you will not deliver before your expected due date, your doctor will ask you to sign the consent a number of months before your expected date.

You may wish to wait until the health of your newborn is ensured before making a decision about sterilization. If at any time you have doubts—even after you've signed papers giving your consent—let your doctor know. You can cancel the operation. For further details about family planning and sterilization, see Chapter 17.

Getting Ready for the Baby

Many couples are so excited at the prospect of a new baby—especially if it's their first—that they start shopping right away. It can be hard to resist all the cute outfits, cuddly toys, and baby gear sold today. But what do you really need?

Among the basics are clothes, diapers, a crib where your infant can sleep, an infant car safety seat, and a carrier seat, front pack, or backpack for carrying the baby. You can wait until the baby is a little older to get most other items.

The most important guideline when choosing clothing for your newborn is to be practical. What you need right away will depend on the time of year your baby is born. For example, you probably won't need a thick blanket sleeper if your baby arrives in midsummer.

A good rule of thumb is to buy clothes a bit too big. If they fit just right, the baby could outgrow them in a few weeks or less.

Diapers

Your baby will go through about 65 diapers a week during the first year—that's more than 3,000 diapers. Cost and convenience are two important considerations when choosing among the options available:

- *Disposables.* Try different brands until you find one you like. Brands that do not allow plastic to touch the baby's skin are better for preventing diaper rash. Don't use brands that shred when wet—your baby could swallow loose pieces.
- *Cloth diapers.* These come in two styles—flat and prefolded. Flat ones are more absorbent and can be adjusted more easily to fit your growing baby, but they are sometimes hard to find. Many stores carry only diapers in which the folds are stitched in place. Start with at least three dozen diapers. Waterproof pants—about three pairs to start—help keep bedding and clothing dry. The snap-on kind are easier to use and allow more air movement. Use diaper pins with safety locks that snap down over metal latch sections. Throw away pins when they get dull or start to rust.
- *Diaper services.* This option is cheaper than disposables but more costly than buying and washing your own cloth diapers. The services usually pick up and drop off diapers once or twice a week. They give you a choice of diaper sizes and often provide a diaper pail or bags in which to store dirty diapers.

Choosing an Infant Car Safety Seat

It's important to get an infant car safety seat ahead of time so your baby can ride home from the hospital safely. These seats can be purchased or rented.

Infant car safety seats are specially designed to protect babies and small children if a car crash occurs. They come in various models, but are typically made of plastic and are strapped onto the back seat or front passenger seat using the car's lap belt. Infant seats should be installed facing backward. A plastic infant carrier is not a car safety seat, even if a seat belt is placed around it. It can shatter in an accident.

Car seats are required by law in every state. Many hospitals will not allow the baby to be discharged unless the parents have a car seat in which to take him or her home. Check with your hospital, local car dealers, or baby stores to determine the best type of infant car safety seat for you.

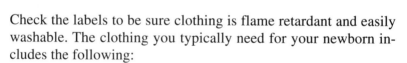

Check the labels to be sure clothing is flame retardant and easily washable. The clothing you typically need for your newborn includes the following:

- Diapers
- Cotton undershirts
- Newborn gowns
- Footed stretch suits that snap at the crotch
- Sweaters
- Socks or booties
- Bonnets or hats
- A bunting (a quilted or knitted sleeping bag with a zipper and a hood)
- Blankets
- Baby washcloths and towels

Only a few items are essential while your child is still an infant. Whether you buy them new or get hand-me-downs, it's important to be sure they are safe and sturdy. Recommended equipment includes a crib. Cribs manufactured since 1985 must meet current safety standards. If you use an older one, make sure it has these features:

- Spaces that are no more than $2^3/8$ inches apart between slats.
- No missing or cracked slats.
- No cutouts in the headboard or footboard (where the baby's head could get trapped).
- Corner posts that are no higher than $^1/_{16}$ of an inch.
- Latches that hold securely and cannot be released easily by a baby.
- No rough edges, sharp points, or loose screws or bolts.
- A mattress that fits snugly. You should not be able to slip more than two fingers between the mattress and the crib on all four sides.
- A crib bumper that goes all the way around and ties or straps securely to the crib.
- A waterproof mattress cover. Flannel-backed covers are more comfortable for the baby than plain rubber or plastic ones.

A bassinet or cradle can also be used for sleeping, but the baby will outgrow it quickly. If you use one, make sure it has a sturdy bottom and a wide base so it stays stable. It should have smooth surfaces—no staples that stick out or other hardware that could hurt the baby. The mattress should be firm and should fit snugly. If the bassinet or cradle has folding legs, make sure they lock firmly in place.

Other items to consider:

- Bedding, such as fitted sheets and a soft quilt or blanket
- A changing table with safety straps
- A large diaper pail that can be closed securely

■ An infant carrier that is appropriate for the baby's size and weight

■ A comfortable chair, such as a rocking chair, to sit in while feeding the baby

■ A large plastic tub for bathing the baby

■ An infant car safety seat

All baby gear should be kept clean and in good repair. Making sure your equipment meets existing federal safety codes is a big step toward ensuring your baby will be free from harm.

Questions to Consider...

■ Who will be my health care providers during pregnancy, labor, and delivery?

■ Where can I enroll in a childbirth preparation class?

■ Where can I obtain further information on breast-feeding, circumcision, and birth control or sterilization?

■ What clothing and supplies will I need for my newborn?

Chapter 5

Prenatal Care

Prenatal care is an important part of making sure you and your growing baby are as healthy as possible. Regular prenatal visits give you a chance to ask questions, be informed about your pregnancy, and make decisions that are best for you. It also allows your progress and that of your fetus to be checked throughout pregnancy.

Most pregnancies proceed normally, but there are some risks. Assessing these risks is a key part of prenatal care. At each visit, you will be examined and the course of your pregnancy charted. Tests or studies of the fetus may be done to help point out problems that may arise. Your prenatal care will be guided by all members of the health care team.

Even if you had a problem-free pregnancy in the past, you should receive prenatal care as early as possible in pregnancy. No two pregnancies are alike, and problems can come up without warning.

Prenatal care is not just medical care. It also includes childbirth education, counseling, support of the family, and taking good care of yourself every day. All members of the health care team will provide care throughout your pregnancy. They can also direct you to services in your community that may be helpful.

Your first visit for prenatal care will be longer and more involved than later visits. It will include a history of your health, a physical exam and laboratory tests, and setting the estimated date of delivery (your due date). A schedule will be made for future visits and any special tests you may need. During these visits, you should discuss all aspects of your care, and you should feel free to ask questions.

Informed Care

The better informed you are, the better you can make decisions about your health care. During your prenatal visits, many concepts and procedures will be described to you. The process of learning what a medical test or treatment involves before you grant permission for it is called informed consent. This process begins with a discussion of the treatment you might expect and the possible risks, benefits, and alternatives. It is important that you understand this information. Don't be afraid to ask questions about anything that isn't clear to you. It will be noted in your record that the treatment and risks have been explained to you and what you decided to do. Sometimes you may be asked to sign forms saying that you received certain information or that you agreed to have a procedure done.

Partners in Health Care

As partners in your medical care, both you and your health care provider have rights and responsibilities. You have the right to:

- Get quality care without discrimination
- Be given privacy
- Know the professional status of your health care providers and their fees
- Be advised of your diagnosis, treatment, options, and the expected outcome
- Be given the chance to be actively involved in decisions about your care
- Refuse treatment
- Agree or refuse to participate in any research that affects your care

You have the responsibility to:

- Provide accurate and complete health information
- Let your providers know that you understand the medical procedures and what you are expected to do

If you do not follow the suggested plan, or if you refuse treatment, you must take responsibility for your actions. Your provider has the right to stop treating you as long as you have time to find other care. While you are in his or her care, your health care provider is responsible for giving you quality medical treatment.

History

One of the first things you'll be asked for is details about your health, the health of your family and that of the baby's father, and any past pregnancies. This information can help in detecting future problems. You are the only one who can provide these facts, so it is important that your answers be honest, complete, and accurate.

The medical history covers your general health. This includes whether you are taking any medications, have any allergies or medical conditions, or have been exposed to infections. It also covers your menstrual history, including the date of your last menstrual period and use of birth control. You'll be asked about life style habits such as use of alcohol, illegal drugs, or cigarettes and exposure to harmful agents that may put your pregnancy at risk.

The history of past pregnancies includes details about all former pregnancies: the baby's weight at birth, how long labor lasted, the method of delivery, and if you had any complications. It focuses on any problems that may come up again, such as preterm labor. You'll also be asked about any pregnancy losses.

Your family history includes questions about any genetic disorders that may be inherited. If you had a previous child with a birth defect, you may need genetic counseling and further tests. You'll also be asked about your ethnic origin and general life style to determine whether there are any factors that might pose a risk. Chapter 7 has more details on genetic disorders.

Physical Exam

After your health history, your height, weight, and blood pressure will be measured. The next step is usually a physical exam, which can include:

- Ears, eyes, nose, throat, and teeth
- Thyroid
- Breasts, heart, lungs, back, and abdomen
- Arms and legs
- Lymph nodes
- Skin

Your reproductive organs—cervix, vagina, ovaries, fallopian tubes, and uterus—are checked during a pelvic exam. The first pelvic exam is often more detailed than one done at any other time. In addition to the usual exam, the size of the inside of your pelvis is also checked. Although it may be slightly uncomfortable, this exam is important to check for changes in your cervix (opening of the uterus) and the size of your uterus and pelvis.

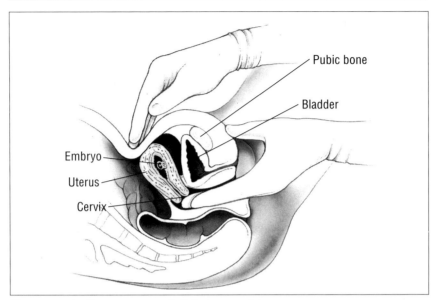

Your reproductive organs are felt during a pelvic exam.

Early in pregnancy, the size of the uterus is used as one guide to estimate your due date. Until 12 weeks of gestation, your uterus fits inside your pelvis. At 20 weeks of gestation, its top reaches your navel. At term, when the fetus is full grown, the uterus will be under your rib cage.

When Is the Baby Due?

The average length of pregnancy is 280 days, or 40 weeks, from the first day of the last period. However, a normal full-term pregnancy can last anywhere from 37 to 42 weeks. Only about 1 in 20 babies are born on the due date. Most women deliver within 2 weeks before or after their due dates.

Estimated Date of Delivery

Your due date will be calculated based on the information from your first visit. The due date is also called the estimated date of delivery, or EDD. (It's also known as the estimated date of con-

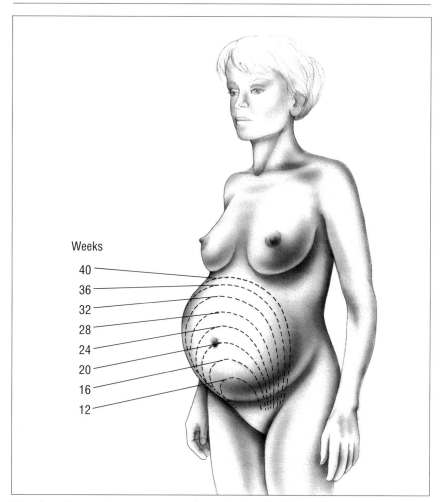

Weeks
40
36
32
28
24
20
16
12

The size of your uterus corresponds to the length of gestation early in pregnancy. It fits inside the pelvis until the 12th week; by the 36th week, the top of the uterus is under your rib cage.

finement, or EDC). The date of ovulation is the most reliable way to determine the age of the fetus, but this is not usually known exactly. Calculating the due date on the basis of your period is not always exact. Menstrual cycles differ from one woman to another, and the pattern of cycles affects the due date. Also, it's easy to forget when your last period started. You can help by recording your periods and sharing this information with your doctor.

The method used most often is based on conception occurring 14 days after the start of the last period. The approximate date may be figured out by taking the date your last period began, adding 7 days, and then counting back 3 months. For example, if the first day of your last period was May 5, add 7 days to get May 12, then count back 3 months—the estimated due date is February 12.

Because it can be hard to predict the exact date, more than one method may be used:

- Throughout pregnancy, but especially early on, the size of the uterus can provide useful information.
- Fetal heart tones can usually be heard at 12 weeks by using a **Doppler** device, a form of **ultrasound** that converts sound waves into signals you can hear, or at 18–20 weeks by using a special stethoscope.
- You can usually first feel fetal movements, or **quickening,** by 16–20 weeks.
- In the first half of pregnancy, ultrasound can be used to estimate the age of a fetus within 7–10 days. Later, this method is not as accurate.

The Importance of Accuracy

The due date is important because some tests must be done at a certain time in pregnancy, and the accuracy of the results depends on the stage of the pregnancy. The due date is also used as a guide for gauging the growth of the fetus and the progress of your pregnancy. Setting an accurate due date puts your provider in a better position to detect and manage problems, should they occur. It also helps to know when a patient is overdue.

Tests

Several laboratory tests will be done early in your prenatal care:

- *Blood tests* to identify your blood type and Rh factor, check for anemia (lack of iron) and sexually transmitted diseases (syphilis), and to find out whether you have had German measles (rubella) or mumps

■ *Urine tests* to check levels of sugar and protein (ketones) and detect possible urinary infections

■ *Pap test* to check for cervical cancer

The results of these tests will be noted in your medical record. Other tests may be suggested depending on your medical history, family background, race, or the results of your first exam. For example, you may be checked for diabetes, which can develop during pregnancy. In general, people who are obese, have high blood pressure, or have a family history of diabetes have a higher risk of getting the disease. Older women also have a higher risk. Because it is hard to predict which women will develop diabetes during pregnancy, sometimes women are tested even if they don't have any risk factors.

Screening tests are available that give information about a pregnant woman's risk of having a baby with certain birth defects such as **Down Syndrome** and **spina bifida**. A screening test is a blood test performed when a patient has no symptoms or known risk factors. It is not a diagnostic test. (See Chapter 7 for more information on screening and diagnostic tests.)

Future Visits

After your first prenatal visit, the following visits are usually shorter. The time during these visits is generally used to find out how you are doing and how the baby is growing and to respond to any concerns you may have. If you had a previous baby by cesarean delivery, your history and record will be reviewed to see whether the baby can be delivered vaginally. (More information on vaginal birth after cesarean delivery appears in Chapter 14.)

You and your health care team will work out the timing of your visits, depending on your risk factors. Women with medical or obstetric problems need more attention, and women who have no known risk factors may need less. You may follow a schedule somewhat like this one:

From the first visit to 28 weeks .... Every 4 weeks

From 28 to 36 weeks .... Every 2 weeks

From 36 weeks to delivery (at about 40 weeks) .... Weekly

You will be seen more often if you have a problem or the potential to develop one. During these visits, your weight, blood pressure, and urine are checked. Your abdomen is measured to check the growth and position of the fetus. The fetal heartbeat is also checked. Lab tests and pelvic exams may not be done each time.

Throughout your pregnancy, you will receive advice and counseling on leading a healthy life style. Many women find that writing down questions ahead of time helps them remember things they wanted to ask during the visit. You should also make a note of any unusual signs or symptoms that may appear between visits. The diary at the back of this book can be used as a handy way to chart the course of your pregnancy.

Risk Factors

A pregnancy is considered to be at increased risk when a problem is more likely than usual to occur. Such a problem could be caused by a health condition the mother had before she was pregnant. It could also arise during pregnancy or at delivery. The small number of women who have known risks account for a large number of the problems that occur. However, not all problems can be predicted. About one in five infants who have serious problems are born to mothers who did not have any signs of risk during pregnancy.

Factors That Can Complicate Pregnancy

Medical

- High blood pressure
- Heart, kidney, lung, or liver diseases
- Sexually transmitted diseases, urinary tract infections, or other viral or bacterial infections
- Diabetes
- Severe anemia
- Seizure disorders

Obstetric

- Problems in past pregnancies
- Mother's age younger than 15 or older than 35 years old
- Previous birth defects
- Multiple gestation (eg, twins or triplets)
- Bleeding, especially during the second or third trimester
- Pregnancy-induced high blood pressure (*preeclampsia*)
- Abnormal fetal heartbeat
- Intrauterine growth restriction (fetus not growing adequately for age)

Life Style

- Smoking and drinking alcohol
- Taking drugs not prescribed by a doctor
- Poor nutrition, including inadequate weight gain
- Lack of prenatal care
- Multiple sexual partners

Because problems can arise at any time, risks will be assessed throughout the pregnancy. Regardless of when problems occur, they can threaten the health of the mother, the fetus, or both. For this reason, a woman with an increased risk of complications will require special care.

Special Procedures

Depending on your history and the results of your routine tests, it may be suggested that you have more tests to check the growth and health of the fetus. Some tests, such as ultrasound, produce an image of the fetus. This can be especially helpful for seeing whether your fetus has grown and developed as expected for its age. Other tests result in a sound or recording of the fetal heartbeat. Chapter 6 has more details on special techniques used to check the well-being of the fetus.

Questions to Consider...

- Is there anything in my history that could pose a problem in pregnancy?
- When is my due date?
- What are the dates of my future visits?

Testing for Fetal Well-Being

Many techniques are used to check the well-being of your fetus. Those described in this chapter are generally used in the second half of pregnancy. However, they will be used only if there is a need to check the health of the fetus. Most of the time, these tests offer reassurance that all is going well. They may be done to confirm other test results or to provide further information. When problems arise, the tests can help pinpoint them early.

These tests cannot cure a problem, nor can they guarantee a healthy baby. What they can do is draw attention to the need for special care. When they show no signs of trouble, these techniques help you feel more secure about your baby's health.

Depending on the results of routine tests or risk factors, other tests may be needed to diagnose a problem. These tests may include *amniocentesis* or *chorionic villus sampling.* They are detailed in Chapter 7.

Ultrasound

Ultrasound, which creates pictures of the baby from sound waves, can be found today in every major hospital and in many doctors' offices. This technology is useful for the general health care of women, but it is especially valuable during pregnancy and childbirth. No harmful effects to either the mother or the baby have been found in over 30 years of use of ultrasound.

Ultrasound is energy in the form of sound waves produced by a small crystal. The sound waves move at a frequency too high to be heard by the human ear. They are directed into a specific area of the body through a device called a ***transducer***. The transducer is moved across the skin. The sound waves bounce off tissues inside the body, like echoes. They are changed into sounds of the fetus's heartbeat or pictures of the internal organs and the fetus that appear on a screen similar to a television. Real-time ultrasound quickly combines still pictures one after another to show movement, somewhat like the single frames that make a motion picture.

Ultrasound is often used to help find a possible problem or check a known condition. It is an important diagnostic tool that gives information other tests do not. It is not designed to take pictures of the fetus for mementos. Ultrasound should not be done only to try to determine the baby's sex, although the images sometimes show whether the fetus is male or female.

In a way, ultrasound is a limited physical exam of a

An ultrasound exam creates a picture of the fetus called a sonogram from sound waves.

fetus. It can provide valuable information about the fetus's health and well-being, such as:

- Age of the fetus
- Rate of growth of the fetus
- Placement of the placenta
- Fetal position, movement, breathing, and heart rate
- Amount of *amniotic fluid* in the uterus
- Number of fetuses
- Some birth defects

To prepare for an ultrasound exam, wear clothes that allow your abdomen to be exposed easily, such as a top and a skirt or slacks. Some hospitals may ask you to wear a hospital gown. You may need a full bladder for your exams done early in pregnancy.

A doctor or another team member specially trained in doing ultrasound exams will conduct the test. As you lie on the table with your abdomen exposed from the lower part of the ribs to the hips, mineral oil or a gel is applied to the abdomen to improve contact of the transducer with the skin surface. The transducer is then moved along the abdomen. The sound waves sent out from the transducer enter the body and are reflected back when they make contact with the internal organs and the fetus.

Another style of transducer may also be inserted in the vagina to help view the pelvic organs. Ultrasound with a vaginal probe is a painless exam that may feel like the exam you had for a Pap test.

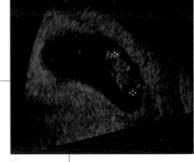

A vaginal ultrasound exam is done with a probe inserted into the vagina.

Kick Counts

You may be asked to keep track of your fetus's movements—called kick counts. Various methods are used. A common one is to record the length of time it takes for the fetus to make 10 movements. You can pick any time of day to count movements, but a good time is late evening after dinner, when the fetus is generally most active. Each fetus has its own level of activity, and most have a sleep cycle of 20–40 minutes. If you have been asked to monitor your baby's kick counts, your doctor or nurse will instruct you in what to do and when to call.

Fetal Heart Rate Monitoring

Ultrasound can be used not only to make images, but also to listen to the fetal heartbeat. When used this way, it is called fetal heart rate monitoring. A small device that transmits sound waves is pressed against the mother's abdomen or is attached with belts. When the fetal heartbeats are reflected, they make sounds you can hear. Monitoring the fetal heart gives helpful information before labor. It also can show how the fetus is responding to labor (see "Monitoring," Chapter 14).

There are two ways to monitor the fetal heart rate before labor starts—the *nonstress test* and the *contraction stress test.* Both of these tests measure the fetal heart rate in response to some form of stimuli.

Nonstress Test

The nonstress test measures the fetal heart rate in response to the fetus's own movements. Usually the fetal heart rate quickens when the fetus moves, just as your heart beats faster when you exercise. Changes in the fetal heart rate are considered a sign of good health. During the nonstress test, you lie on a bed or examining table with a belt around your abdomen. You push a button each time you feel the baby move, which causes a mark to be made on a paper recording. (The nonstress test also can be done with a device that

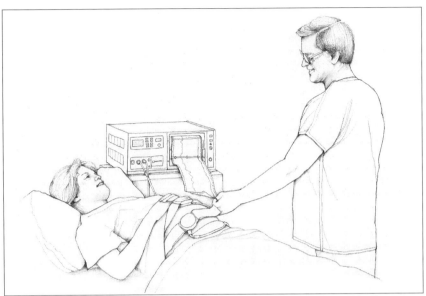

Electronic fetal monitoring can be used to check the heart rate of the fetus.

senses fetal movement.) The length of the test usually ranges from 10–20 minutes to a half hour or more.

If the fetus does not move for a time during the nonstress test, it may be asleep. A device like a buzzer may be used to produce sound and vibration to wake the fetus and cause it to move. This test is called ***vibroacoustic stimulation.***

Contraction Stress Test

The contraction stress test measures how the fetal heart rate reacts to the uterus when it contracts. When the uterus contracts, the blood flow to the placenta decreases temporarily. Normally, contractions do not affect the fetal heart rate. If the placenta isn't working right or the baby has a problem, however, the contraction can decrease the oxygen flow and cause the fetal heart rate to drop. The contraction stress test is often used if the nonstress test shows no change in the fetal heart rate when the fetus moves.

To make the woman's uterus contract mildly, she is either given a drug called ***oxytocin*** or is told to rub one of her nipples lightly, which causes her body to release oxytocin naturally. (In a small number of cases the woman's uterus may contract on its own, especially if the test is done late in pregnancy.) The response of the fetal heart rate to the contractions is then recorded. For results to be obtained, three contractions must take place over about 10 minutes, and each must last about 40 seconds. The test can take up to 2 hours. An abnormal response means that further testing or, possibly, treatment is needed.

Biophysical Profile

The *biophysical profile* is a nonstress test combined with ultrasound. The biophysical profile examines the fetal heart rate, muscle tone, body movement, and the amount of amniotic fluid (the liquid surrounding the fetus inside the uterus). It also checks breathing movements. Although the fetus does not really breathe air, it does make chest wall movements with muscles used for breathing after birth. The fetus gets oxygen directly through the placenta.

Each of these items is given a score, and a total is obtained. The test takes about a half hour. A score of 8–10 is normal; if the score falls below that range, you may need to have the test redone the next day. As with *electronic fetal monitoring*, the biophysical profile does not cause any harm to the fetus, so it can be repeated as needed to check the progress of your pregnancy. The score will help determine whether you need special care or whether your baby should be delivered sooner than planned.

Percutaneous Umbilical Cord Blood Sampling

Percutaneous umbilical cord blood sampling (PUBS), also called cordocentesis, is a special test that allows the blood of the fetus to be checked for problems such as chromosome defects or infections. The blood can also be measured for acidity and levels of oxygen, carbon dioxide, and other substances. If the right amount of these substances is found, it's a strong sign that the fetus is healthy. This method can also be used to inject the fetus with blood cells if it needs transfusions, such as when it has anemia caused by Rh incompatibility (see Chapter 12).

For the test, the doctor punctures the umbilical cord with a needle and withdraws a small amount of blood. Ultrasound is used to guide the needle, which is inserted through the abdomen and uterine wall into the cord. It is performed with local anesthesia. The test is usually done after the 18th week of pregnancy because the umbilical cord's blood vessels are very narrow before that time.

Questions to Consider

- ■ What information can an ultrasound exam provide?
- ■ If my baby's heartbeat speeds up during the nonstress test is it a good sign?
- ■ How should I monitor my baby's kick count?
- ■ What tests does my health care provider recommend?

Chapter 7

Genetic Disorders and Birth Defects

Genetics is the study of how traits are passed from parents to a child. Many personal traits, such as height and eye color, are inherited this way. Unfortunately, some diseases can be conveyed in the same way. These genetic—or hereditary—diseases may be obvious at birth, or they may not develop until later. Another term often used is *congenital disorder.* This means that a baby is born with a defect that may or may not be genetic.

Most children in the United States are born healthy. Of each 100 babies, about two to three are born with some type of major birth defect. Some birth defects may be inherited from the parents. Others may result from exposure to something harmful during pregnancy, such as an infection or a drug or medications. Often, the reason for the defect is unknown.

Most babies with birth defects are born to couples with no special risk factors. Each pregnancy is different, and each baby has its own genetic makeup. A birth defect can occur even if you've had normal children and have no history of genetic problems. However, the risk of birth defects—including genetic disorders—is higher when certain risk factors are present. In some couples these factors can be identified in advance through tests done before or during pregnancy. These tests, combined with counseling, give information about the risk of having a baby with certain birth defects. The decision to have these tests is a personal one. Prospective parents should know what the tests can and cannot do and what the results mean when making decisions.

Genes and Chromosomes

Traits are passed from parents to their children through ***genes*** and ***chromosomes***. Each cell in the body contains pairs of genes and chromosomes that control the person's makeup. Normally, a man's sperm and a woman's egg contain 23 chromosomes each. All other cells in the body have 46. When an egg is fertilized by a sperm, the 23 chromosomes from the mother's egg and the 23 chromosomes from the father's sperm join to form the 46 chromosomes of the fetus.

One pair of chromosomes—one each from the sperm and the egg—are the sex chromosomes. There are two types of sex chro-

DNA: The Key to the Genetic Code

Cells are the basic building blocks of the body. Inside each cell is a nucleus. Inside each nucleus are the chromosomes. All cells in the body have 46 chromosomes, except for the eggs and sperm, which have 23 each. The chromosomes are made up of DNA (deoxyribonucleic acid) molecules. The DNA molecule is double stranded. The two strands are in the shape of a double helix that resembles a spiral stair. The double strands are connected at what are called base pairs. Each chromosome contains anywhere from 50 million to 250 million base pairs, depending on the size of the chromosome. There are approximately 3 billion base pairs of DNA in the human body. DNA contains the genetic code for the entire body.

A gene is a segment of a DNA molecule that is coded to pass along a specific characteristic. In humans, there are approximately 50,000–100,000 genes. Each one has a specific position on the chromosome and a specific function.

The human genome is the full set of genes of an individual. Together they control all aspects of human growth, development, and function. Scientists know the role of only a small number of human genes. The Human Genome Project is an international effort now under way to map the entire human genome—to locate each gene to a specific place on a chromosome. By knowing the role of genes and their placement in the genome, scientists can better understand how they affect the body in both health and disease.

mosomes, which are labeled by the letters X and Y. A normal sperm will carry either an X or a Y chromosome; a normal egg always has an X chromosome. If a man's sperm with a Y chromosome joins with the woman's egg, the fetus will be male (XY). If the man's sperm with an X chromosome joins with the woman's X egg, the fetus will be female (XX). Thus, the sex chromosome in the sperm decides the sex of the child.

Each chromosome carries many genes. Genes also come in pairs. Half of the genes of each pair come from the mother, and the other half come from the father. Some traits are controlled by a single gene pair. Some traits, including eye and hair color and height, are the result of many pairs of genes working together.

A gene is either *dominant* or *recessive*. If one gene in a pair is dominant, the trait it carries—such as brown hair—will override the trait carried by the recessive gene—such as blond hair. The recessive gene must be inherited from both parents for its trait to appear. Genetic diseases can also be dominant or recessive.

Genetic Disorders

There are several types of genetic disorders. Besides those caused by dominant or recessive genes, disorders can result from a problem in the chromosomes. These problems can be either be X-linked (located on the X chromosome) or caused by an abnormal number of chromosomes. Genetic disorders can also be multifactorial (tied to a mix of factors). Genetic disorders are usually grouped by these types.

Certain disorders can be detected with tests done during pregnancy. These tests can show whether the fetus has a particular genetic disorder (birth defect). There are also tests that show whether the mother or father is a **carrier** for a certain disorder. For some of these disorders, there are no risk factors, so testing may be offered to everyone. In other cases, a personal or family history may point to a risk that can be assessed with counseling and special tests.

Dominant Disorders

Some genetic disorders are dominant—only one gene from either parent is needed to cause it. When a parent has the gene, there is a one-in-two chance that any child (male or female) will inherit the disorder.

Huntington Disease

The nerve disorder Huntington disease leads to uncontrollable movements and mental decline. It usually is diagnosed in middle age and is followed by death in about 15 years. It affects about 1 in 100,000 people. Each child of either parent with Huntington

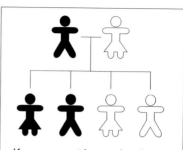

If one parent has a dominant gene disorder, there is a one-in-two chance that it will be passed to each child.

disease has a one in two chance of developing it. In families with Huntington disease, a test can be done to find out which family members have inherited the gene and will later develop the disease.

Polydactyly

With the disorder polydactyly, a baby is born with extra fingers or toes. This disorder is fairly common and can be corrected easily by surgery.

Recessive Disorders

Some genetic disorders are recessive—a pair of genes, one from each parent, is needed to cause them. Everyone carries a few abnormal recessive genes. In most people, no defect appears because the abnormal recessive gene is overruled by the normal gene. If you have only one abnormal gene of a recessive disorder, you are a carrier. A carrier shows no signs of the disorder but can pass the gene to his or her children.

If both parents are carriers of a recessive disorder, there is a one in four chance that their children will be affected with the disorder. If one parent has the disorder and the other does not and is not a carrier, all their children will be carriers.

Recessive disorders are more common in some ethnic groups. Some common ones are sickle cell disease and Tay–Sachs disease. A recessive disorder occurs more often among family members. This is one reason why marriages between first cousins and other close relatives are discouraged.

Sickle Cell Disease

Sickle cell disease is a disorder in which the red blood cells take on a crescent, or "sickle," shape, rather than the normal doughnut shape. These sickle cells can get caught in the blood vessels. Oxygen is then cut off to tissues, causing pain. Because the body destroys these abnormal cells faster than it can make normal ones to replace them, anemia often occurs. Sickle cell disease occurs most often in African Americans, although it can occur in other groups. In the United States, about 1 in 625 African Americans has sickle cell disease. About 1 in 10 are carriers of the trait that causes the disorder but do not have it. For a couple to have an affected child, both parents must be carriers of the trait or affected with the disease.

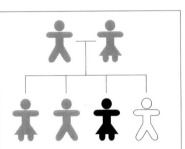

If both parents are carriers of a recessive disorder, there is a one-in-four chance that a child will have the disorder and a one-in-two chance that a child will be a carrier like the parents.

Tay–Sachs Disease

Tay–Sachs disease is caused by the lack of an chemical needed for normal brain function. Symptoms first occur at about 6 months of age. It causes severe mental retardation, blindness, seizures, and death usually before age 5–7 years. Tay–Sachs disease is found mostly in people of eastern European Jewish descent (Ashkenazi Jews). In this group, the disease occurs in 1 in 3,600 births. It is more common in French Canadians as well. The chance of being a carrier is 1 in 30 for Ashkenazi Jews and French Canadians but 1 in 300 for others.

Cystic Fibrosis

Cystic fibrosis is the disorder that most often affects whites, particularly those of northern European descent. It strikes in childhood—sometimes right after birth. The lungs produce thick, sticky mucus that clogs the bronchial tubes and leads to lung infections. Most people with cystic fibrosis are infertile. In the United States, the chance of whites having the disease is about 1 in 2,500, and the chance of being a carrier is 1 in 25. For African Americans, the risk of having the disease and the chance of being a carrier is much lower. By testing a person suspected of having the cystic fibrosis gene and his or her relatives, it is possible to find most carriers of the gene and also fetuses who have the disease.

Thalassemia

Thalassemia causes anemia and can lead to liver and heart problems. One type, beta-thalassemia, is more likely to occur in persons of Mediterranean descent, such as people from Italy or Greece. The chance of being a carrier is about 1 in 250. Another type, alpha-thalassemia, tends to occur in people of Asian descent. Carrier testing of the parents and prenatal testing of the fetus can be done.

X-Linked Disorders

Genetic disorders that are determined by genes on the X chromosome are referred to as X-linked or sex-linked. In most X-linked disorders, the abnormal gene is recessive. A woman can carry such a gene yet not have the disorder because her normal gene on the other X chromosome protects her from the disease. Her male child who inherits that X chromosome, however, could get the disorder because he does not have another X chromosome to override the abnormal recessive gene. Color blindness is a common X-linked trait. Hemophilia and muscular dystrophy are common X-linked disorders.

If the mother is a carrier for an X-linked disorder and the father is not, there is a one-in-two chance that a son will have the disorder and a one-in-two chance that a daughter will be a carrier. Very rarely, a daughter will have a certain X-linked recessive disorders. In this case, her father has the disease and her mother is a carrier.

Hemophilia

People with hemophilia lack a substance that helps blood clot. When they are injured, bleeding stops very slowly, which can be life-threatening. Hemophilia affects almost only males. Females are carriers. It occurs in about 1 in 10,000 boys. Testing can be done to identify carriers and affected male fetuses.

Duchenne Muscular Dystrophy

Duchenne muscular dystrophy is the most common severe form of the muscular dystrophies, diseases that cause muscles to weaken. It affects almost only boys, usually around age 2 years, because it is X-linked. As the muscles weaken, the child has difficulty standing and walking and by the age of 10 or 12 may be confined to a wheelchair. This disorder usually causes death in early adulthood. Carriers of the disorder can often be detected by testing, and there are tests available for prenatal diagnosis.

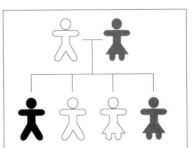

If a woman is a carrier of an X-linked (or sex-linked) disorder, there is a one-in-two chance that a son will have the disorder and a one-in-two chance that a daughter will be a carrier.

Fragile X

Fragile X syndrome is the most common inherited cause of mental retardation. The gene for this disease is on the X chromosome. Normal women may be carriers of the fragile X gene. It affects 1 in 1,250 boys and 1 in 2,000 girls. Boys with the disorder have a long, triangular face and ears that stick out. The disorder cannot be diagnosed on the basis of appearance, however. Tests can be done to find out if a woman carries the fragile X gene and if a fetus has the disorder.

Chromosomal Disorders

Some chromosomal problems are inherited, but most are caused by an error when the egg or sperm was developing. Extra, missing, or incomplete chromosomes usually cause serious health problems. The risk of having a child with this type of disorder rises with the age of the mother. The chance that a 35-year-old woman will have a child with any type of chromosomal disorder is about 1 in 200; for a 40-year-old woman, the chance is about 1 in 60.

How Common Are Chromosomal Disorders?

Chromosomal disorders can occur when there are too few or too many chromosomes. The following table shows the overall risk of having a baby with an abnormal number of chromosomes and the risk of having a baby with Down syndrome (extra chromosome 21).

Risk of Having a Baby with an Abnormal Number of Chromosomes

Mother's Age	Risk of Down Syndrome	Risk of Total Chromosomal Disease
20	1/1,667	1/526
25	1/1,250	1/476
30	1/952	1/385
35	1/378	1/192
40	1/106	1/66
41	1/82	1/53
42	1/63	1/42
43	1/49	1/33
44	1/38	1/26
45	1/30	1/21

Most children born with chromosome disorders have lower-than-average intelligence and physical defects. Down syndrome is one of the more common problems. Persons with Down syndrome have three number 21 chromosomes instead of the usual two. This is called trisomy 21. Down syndrome causes mental retardation to varying degrees. About a third of persons with Down syndrome also have heart defects. Affected people have certain facial features: a flat face, slanting eyes, and low-set ears.

Down syndrome occurs in about 1 in 800 births. The risk of having a live baby with Down syndrome increases with age, although it can occur in women of all ages. Most babies with Down syndrome (8 in 10) are born to younger women with no risk factors. This is because most babies are born to younger women. The risk of having a child with Down syndrome is increased 1–3% if the couple previously had one baby with Down syndrome. Of 100 couples who have a child with Down syndrome, more than 95 have no family history of the disorder.

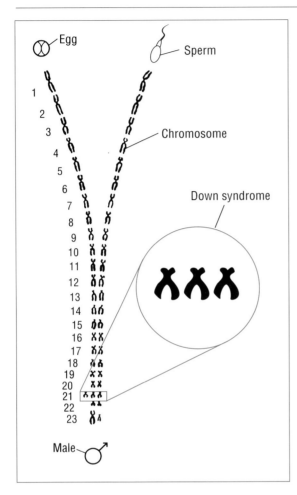

Chromosomes carry genes, the basic units of heredity that determine a person's physical features, such as eye and hair color. Normally, each cell carries 46 chromosomes arranged in 23 pairs. When the 23 chromosomes from the woman and the 23 from the man join to form the 46 of the baby, something may go wrong.

In the case of Down syndrome, there is an extra copy of chromosome 21. This is called trisomy 21.

Other disorders can occur when a person has too many or too few sex chromosomes. For example, about 1 in 800 boys have Klinefelter syndrome. They have an extra X chromosome—that is, two X chromosomes and one Y chromosome for a total of 47 chromosomes. Men with Klinefelter syndrome may be infertile and some have lower intelligence. Slightly less common is having one X and two Y chromosomes, which can cause a man to grow taller than normal.

Some girls have just one X chromosome. This condition is called Turner syndrome. These girls tend to be short and are almost always infertile. The risk for Turner syndrome is about 1 in 3,000 liveborn girls.

Multifactorial Disorders

Many disorders are thought to come from a mix of genetic and environmental factors. This is called multifactorial inheritance. How often these disorders happen may vary in different parts of the world. Some can be detected during pregnancy. A couple who has a child with one of these disorders usually has a 1–5% chance that the disease will affect future children. These defects often can be corrected with surgery. Birth defects also may be caused by being exposed to toxic substances like mercury or lead. These substances may play a role in some disorders of the brain. Infections like German measles, or rubella, if active during pregnancy, can cause birth defects. Environmental agents that can cause birth defects are called teratogens (see Chapter 8).

Congenital Heart Defects

Congenital heart disease is the most common congenital disorder. It occurs in about 1 in 125 births. The outcome for babies with congenital heart disease depends on the type of the defect and whether other problems are present. Usually the defects are the result of multifactorial inheritance. Chromosomal disorders are responsible for about 1 in 10 cases of congenital heart disease in newborn infants. After the birth of an affected child, the risk that this disorder will recur is 2–5%. In families who have two affected children, the risk of recurrence may be 1 in 10. If a parent has a congenital heart defect, there is an increased risk for his or her children.

It is possible but difficult to detect congenital heart disease prenatally with a general ultrasound exam. It has been estimated that only 1 in 10 cases of congenital heart disease are detected by this method. If you already are known to be at risk for having a baby with a congenital heart defect, a special ultrasound exam of the fetal heart can be done. This exam usually is performed by a doctor skilled in diagnosing congenital heart disease. This type of ultrasound is much more accurate in finding heart problems.

Neural Tube Defects

Neural tube defects occur when the fetal brain, spinal cord, or their coverings do not form normally during the early stages of pregnancy. Most neural tube defects are open, meaning they are not covered by skin. There are two major types of neural tube defects—spina bifida and ***anencephaly:***

■ Spina bifida occurs in North America in 1–2 of 1,000 births. The effects of spina bifida vary and depend on where the defect is located. In general, when the defect is low in the spine, the problems may be mild. If the defect is higher in the spine, it may cause leg paralysis, loss of feeling, lack of bladder and bowel control, hydrocephalus (water on the brain), mental retardation, and even death.

■ Anencephaly occurs when the brain and head do not develop normally. Babies with this disorder may be stillborn or die soon after birth.

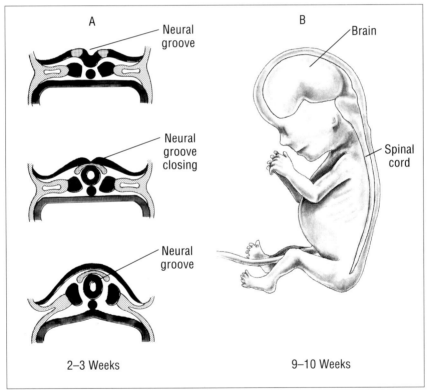

Formation of the neural tube and the fetal brain and spinal cord. Panel A shows a cross-section of the developing fetus in very early pregnancy. The neural tube forms from a groove that deepens and normally closes. Panel B shows the brain and spinal cord of a fetus later in pregnancy.

The cause of neural tube defects is unknown. About 9 in 10 babies with neural tube defects are born to parents who have no family history of it. When parents have already had a child with a neural tube defect, the risk of having another is about 3%.

Folic acid can help prevent neural tube defects. Taking 0.4 mg of the vitamin folic acid each day before getting pregnant and during the first three months of pregnancy may help prevent neural tube defects. Women can take vitamins containing folic acid and eat foods that contain the nutrient: leafy, dark-green vegetables, citrus fruits, bread, beans, and fortified cereal. Women who have had a previous pregnancy affected by a neural tube defect should take a much larger amount—4.0 mg of folic acid a day—preferably starting 1 month before they plan to become pregnant and through the first 3 months of pregnancy.

Cleft Lip and Palate

Cleft lip and cleft palate refer to a gap or space in the lip or a hole in the palate (roof of the mouth). Cleft lip is sometimes referred to as a harelip. Most cases of cleft lip or cleft palate are multifactorial. Cleft lip can also occur with certain chromosome problems or can be inherited as a dominant trait. When parents have already had a child with both a cleft lip and palate, they usually have about a 4% chance of having another affected child. If they have had a child with only a cleft palate, they have a 2% chance of having another affected child. This is one of the most common congenital defects, occurring in more than 1 in 1,000 births. Sometimes it can be detected during pregnancy by ultrasound. After birth it can be corrected by surgery.

Clubfoot

Clubfoot is the term used when a baby is born with one or both feet twisted at the ankle. It occurs in about 1 in 1,000 births. If the defect is slight, it may be possible to correct it through exercises. For more severe cases, the baby can wear splints or casts for a year or more, or surgery may be needed.

Pyloric Stenosis

Pyloric stenosis is a condition in which the opening from the stomach to the intestine is blocked. It usually causes problems between the second week and second month after birth. It can cause vomiting that will not go away, constipation, or failure to gain weight. It is usually easily treated by surgery. Most of the children with pyloric stenosis are boys, but girls can be affected.

Other Defects

Some defects can occur that are sometimes, but not always, linked to a chromosome problem. These defects do not have a pattern of being inherited. An example is abdominal wall defects. With such defects, the skin does not completely form over the abdomen, leaving it open. This problem can sometimes be detected by testing during pregnancy. There are two major types of abdominal wall defects—omphalocele and gastroschisis:

- *Omphalocele* is the absence of the usual muscle and skin covering of the wall of the abdomen of the fetus. The abdominal contents are covered only by a membrane. The disorder can vary in size from a small defect to a very large defect where most of the abdominal wall is missing. This is a rare problem, occurring in about 1 in 5,000 births. Other defects may occur along with this disorder. The outcome for babies born with omphalocele depends on whether there are other defects.

- *Gastroschisis* is a defect in the abdominal wall, usually to the right of the navel, through which the bowel protrudes. Unlike omphalocele, this defect is not covered by a membrane and also is usually not linked with other abnormalities. Gastroschisis occurs in about 1 in 8,000 births. Babies with this type of defect usually do very well after having corrective surgery.

Genetic Counseling

A genetic counselor (someone who has special training in genetics) can give you expert advice about the types of genetic disorders and your risk of having a baby with an inherited disorder. Counseling often helps couples make choices about whether to become pregnant, have carrier testing, or have prenatal testing of the fetus. Counseling can give you a realistic outlook about your risk, can provide information about your options, and may calm undue fears. You may be given a questionnaire that deals with risk factors. If you answer "yes" to any of the questions, your doctor will discuss with you what these answers mean. Genetic counseling is strongly advised for couples with an increased risk of having a child with a birth defect, as signaled by the following factors:

- Mother being 35 years old or older when the baby is due
- Family or personal history of birth defects, genetic diseases, or certain medical disorders
- Having a previous child with a birth defect or genetic disease
- Certain ethnic backgrounds—African–American, Mediterranean, Asian, French Canadian or Jewish descent
- Three or more consecutive miscarriages

During counseling, the couple will be asked to recall family medical histories as far back as they can. Blood tests and physical exams may also be done. If a family member has had a problem, the counselor may ask to see that person's medical records. Genetic tests that might be helpful, as well as the couple's concerns, are discussed. A counselor will use all the information available to figure out the chance of the fetus having a birth defect and explain these risks to you.

It is the parents' decision whether to have genetic testing. Some feel that is reassuring. Others would rather not know. The results of genetic tests can help some women make decisions about their options and prepare for a child with a birth defect if one is found. If you learn information that might affect other family members, it will be helpful to them if you share this information.

If you learn before getting pregnant that you have a strong chance of having a child with a genetic defect, you may choose to have your family by adoption. Another option is to use a sperm or egg donor. A woman can have artificial insemination with sperm from a male donor. With a female donor, the egg is fertilized in a lab with the husband's sperm and is implanted in your uterus.

Genetic Tests

Some genetic tests are offered to all pregnant women. Others are offered when the results of your personal medical history, family history, and physical exam indicate they would be of value. These tests cannot find all problems and are not 100% accurate. Your fetus may have a birth defect even if the test for it is negative (does not show a problem). Your fetus may also be free of that defect even if the test is positive (does show a problem). The counselor can help you understand what the test results mean and tell you what the chance is that the result is incorrect.

A screening test is performed when there are no symptoms or known risk factors present. It is performed on samples of blood from the mother. It can assess your risk of having a baby with a certain birth defect, but it is not used for diagnosis. A diagnostic test can usually show with a high degree of accuracy whether your baby has the birth defect. If your screening test shows a higher-than-average risk for having a baby with a certain defect, further tests may be used for diagnosis. If a woman is already at an increased risk of having a baby with a disorder, she may be offered the diagnostic test first rather than the screening test. Diagnostic tests include amniocentesis, chorionic villus sampling (CVS), and ultrasound.

Maternal Serum Screening Tests

Maternal serum screening tests are blood tests used to find out if a woman has a higher-than-average risk of having a baby with certain birth defects. These tests measure substances in the mother's blood that may be changed when certain disorders are present. These tests are performed in women without risk factors, followed by other tests if the results are abnormal. The most common problem found through maternal serum screening tests is a higher-than-normal risk for open neural tube defects, Down syndrome, and abdominal wall defects. Maternal serum screening tests include *alpha-fetoprotein (AFP)* and multiple marker screening (MMS).

Alpha-fetoprotein
Alpha-fetoprotein is a protein produced by a growing fetus. It is present in fetal blood and in amniotic fluid, which surrounds the

Tests Used to Detect Genetic Disorders

Test	What It Is	What It Looks For	Who Should Have It	When
Maternal serum screening	A blood test for substances produced by the fetus and placenta that are also in the woman's blood	Signs of birth defects such as open neural tube defects (NTDs) or Down syndrome	Every woman should be offered maternal serum screening	15–18 weeks
Ultrasound	Test that creates an image of the fetus from sound waves by either moving an instrument across the abdomen or placing a small device in the vagina	Information about the fetus such as age; rate of growth; placement of the placenta; fetal position, movement, and heart rate; number of fetuses; some, but not all, fetal problems	Women whose doctors want to tell how old the fetus is, confirm a condition, or check a suspected problem	Depends on the reason for performing ultrasound
Amniocentesis	A sample of amniotic fluid (the liquid around the fetus inside the uterus) is drawn through a thin needle that is inserted through the abdomen into the uterus; ultrasound is used to guide the needle	Certain conditions, such as Down syndrome and NTDs; other tests may be run on amniotic fluid depending on woman's risk factors; may be used late in pregnancy to see if baby's lungs are likely to work if the birth occurs soon	Test may be offered to women who already have a child with certain birth defects, who have a family history of birth defects, who will be 35 or older on their due date, or if they or their partner are at risk for certain genetic diseases	14–18 weeks
Chorionic villus sampling	A sample of the chorionic villi is taken from the placenta, either through a needle passed through the abdomen and uterus or through a thin tube passed through the vagina and cervix	Certain conditions, such as Down syndrome; other tests may be run depending on woman's risk factors	If available, test is offered to women who already have a child with certain birth defects, who have a family history of birth defects, who will be 35 or older on their due date, or if they or their partner are at risk for certain genetic diseases	10–12 weeks

fetus inside the mother's uterus. A smaller amount crosses the placenta into the mother's blood. Abnormal levels of AFP at certain times during pregnancy can be a sign of an open neural tube defect or Down syndrome. Maternal serum AFP testing may pick up 8 in 10 cases of open spinal defects and almost all cases of anencephaly.

The test is performed at 15–18 weeks of pregnancy. A small amount of blood is taken from a vein in the woman's arm. Results are usually available in about 1 week. At 15–18 weeks of pregnancy, AFP levels are higher than normal in the blood of 8 in 10 women who are

Amniotic Fluid

The fetus develops inside a sac formed by two membranes, the amnion and the chorion. Inside the sac, a liquid called amniotic fluid collects to support and protect the fetus.

Amniotic fluid begins forming at 4–5 weeks of pregnancy. New fluid forms all the time, and some of the fluid is swallowed by the fetus. At first the fluid is made almost entirely of fluid from the mother. As early as 11 weeks, the kidneys of the fetus start to put out a weak urine. After 20 weeks, the urine from the fetus is the main source of fluid.

Amniotic fluid cushions the fetus. Because the fluid puts pressure on the walls of the uterus, the fetus has room to grow. In this safe, temperature-controlled environment, the fetus can practice the movements it will need after birth. It can exercise its muscles by moving around. As it breathes in and swallows the fluid, it develops both a swallowing and a breathing mechanism. Amniotic fluid also prevents the growth of some kinds of bacteria. This helps protect the fetus from infection.

carrying fetuses with open defects. Other causes of high AFP levels are that the fetus is older than was thought or that the mother is carrying twins. Lower-than-normal levels of AFP may mean that the fetus has Down syndrome or is younger than was thought. Diagnostic tests are then done to rule out other causes of abnormal AFP levels. Only a small number of patients whose maternal serum screening tests shows abnormal AFP levels have a baby with a birth defect.

Multiple Marker Screening

Doing certain tests in addition to the AFP test can give more information about the risk of having a baby with Down syndrome than the AFP test does alone. These tests, called MMS tests, measure levels of the hormones human chorionic gonadotropin (hCG) and estriol in the mother's blood, in addition to AFP. In most pregnan-

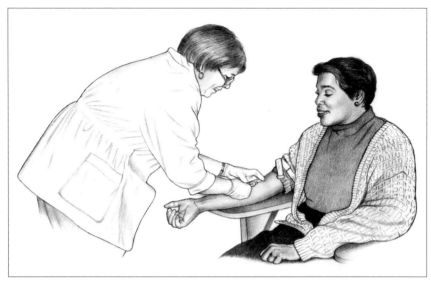

A blood test can be used to check for substances that might be linked with some birth defects.

cies, levels of hCG (a hormone made by the placenta) are higher than normal when the fetus has Down syndrome. Levels of estriol (made in the placenta and the fetal liver) are lower than normal when the fetus has Down syndrome. These screening tests are offered to women under age 35 years who do not have any special risk factors for Down syndrome. Women over 35 already have a higher risk for Down syndrome because of their age. It is suggested that these women consider diagnostic testing.

Multiple marker tests are performed on samples of the mother's blood taken at 15–18 weeks of pregnancy. Usually, the same blood sample is used for all the tests.

You can get results of these tests within 1–2 weeks. If the levels of the three substances measured in these tests do not fall in the low-risk range, your doctor will offer you further testing. This testing might include ultrasound and amniocentesis. Only about 1–2 of 100 women whose MMS tests show an increased risk for Down syndrome will have a baby with the disorder.

Ultrasound

The first diagnostic test you may have after finding a high level of AFP is ultrasound (see Chapter 6). Ultrasound can confirm that the fetus has a heartbeat. It can also help show whether the estimated age of the fetus is correct. If the pregnancy is not as far along or is further along than was thought, your screening test results will be explained differently. Ultrasound can often show whether the fetus has an open neural tube defect. It can also show whether you're carrying twins. In about half the cases, ultrasound explains why AFP levels are high. If no reason for high AFP levels is found with ultrasound, you may be offered amniocentesis.

Ultrasound is also used to assess abnormal MMS results. However, it cannot confirm that the fetus does not have Down syndrome. Amniocentesis is done to confirm the diagnosis of Down syndrome.

Amniocentesis

In amniocentesis, a sample of amniotic fluid is withdrawn and tested for certain genetic disorders. Amniocentesis is usually done at 15–18 weeks of pregnancy, although it can be done earlier or later than this period.

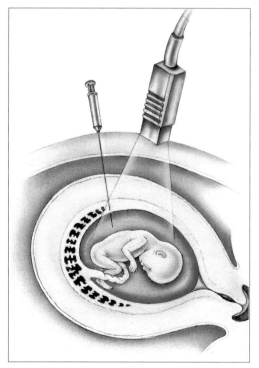

During amniocentesis, a small sample of amniotic fluid is withdrawn to be studied.

For this test, you lie flat on an examining table. With sterile instruments and the aid of ultrasound, a thin needle is guided through your abdomen into the uterus and *amniotic sac.* A small amount of fluid is withdrawn through the needle and sent to a lab for testing.

Cells from the fetus are shed into the amniotic fluid. They are grown in a special culture and analyzed. It can take up to 3 weeks for enough fetal cells to grow to allow a diagnosis. The chromosomes in these cells are studied under a microscope to see whether there is an extra one (as in Down syndrome) or whether there are other chromosomal abnormalities. Because amniocentesis shows whether the fetus is male or female, it can help determine the risks of an X-linked disorder. Testing the AFP level in the amniotic fluid can help determine the chances that the fetus has certain problems such as neural tube defects.

Amniocentesis can be done in a doctor's office or a hospital's outpatient department. Complications are not common, but some risk is involved. Some side effects may include cramping, vaginal bleeding, and leaking of amniotic fluid after the test. Injury to the fetus is rare. When amniocentesis is done, 1 in 200 women will have a miscarriage they would not otherwise have had.

Chorionic Villus Sampling

Chorionic villi (the plural form of villus) are tiny, fingerlike projections of tissue that make up the placenta. Because villi come from the same fertilized egg as the fetus, they have the same genetic makeup. In CVS, some villi are withdrawn, grown in a culture, and analyzed. The villi can be drawn through a catheter that goes through the vagina and cervix into the placenta. They can also be obtained through a needle inserted into the abdomen and placenta. Ultrasound is used to guide the instruments for the test.

Chorionic villus sampling detects some of the same chromosome problems as amniocentesis, but CVS can be done earlier— usually at 10–12 weeks of pregnancy. The results are available within up to 3 weeks.

Chorionic villus sampling is performed in a hospital or doctor's office. It is newer than amniocentesis and is not available in all areas. It also carries some risks. The most common one is miscarriage. The risk is still fairly low, however. One in 100 women who

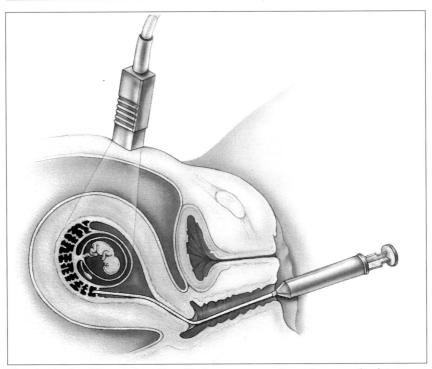

The chorionic villi contain cells with the same genetic makeup as the fetus that can be tested early in pregnancy.

have CVS will have a miscarriage they would not normally have had. There has been some limited evidence of limb deformities with CVS, although this risk is very low.

Abnormal Test Results

An abnormal screening test may mean that the fetus is older or younger than was thought or that there is more than one fetus. Sometimes there is no explanation for an abnormal screening test, and amniocentesis will show that your baby does not have a birth defect. Most women with abnormal screening test results have normal babies. If diagnostic testing shows that your baby has a birth defect, however, you will receive counseling about what this problem will mean for your family. This is a time of great stress for couples.

You should discuss the facts and your feelings with your partner, doctors, and genetic counselors. Decisions need to be made, often within a short time. It may be hard to predict how severely the child will be affected. Sometimes when a problem is found, the parents decide to end the pregnancy. In deciding what to do, your values and resources will come into play. A decision that is right for one couple may not be right for another.

If the baby has a problem, you may find it helpful to use the time left in the pregnancy to prepare yourself and your family. It is best to seek special care with medical and surgical experts. They can give you reading material about the condition your child may have and also suggest support groups that may be useful. With help from your doctor and family, you may start to plan your child's future so that he or she has the best possible care from the beginning.

Questions to Consider...

- ■ Could my partner or I be a carrier of a genetic disorder?
- ■ What is the chance of my baby having a genetic disorder?
- ■ Should I have amniocentesis or CVS?

Chapter 8

A Healthy Life Style

Many of the choices you make in your daily life affect your fetus. This is true of the things you do—exercise, rest, and work—as well as the things you don't do—drink, smoke, or abuse drugs. Some women may need to change their life style during pregnancy. This change may not be easy, but your doctor and the health care team can give you information and support. Even better is the daily support of your family and friends—especially your partner. Together, you can build a healthy life style that will benefit you and your baby.

Nutrition

During pregnancy it's important to eat a healthy, balanced diet to make sure your fetus gets enough nutrients. The food you eat supplies energy for both you and your fetus. You also need to eat more than you did before you became pregnant. Chapter 9 provides guidelines to help you eat right during pregnancy. Combining good nutrition with regular exercise is one of the best ways to stay fit.

Rest

During pregnancy, the growing fetus puts demands on your body that make you get tired more easily than usual. At times, you may feel drained of energy. This fatigue is normal but can be hard to handle.

Try to get all the rest you need. Go to bed earlier, if you can, and get up later. Take mini-breaks during the day to relax. At work, find a couch or quiet room where you can put your feet up. Short naps are fine if they don't prevent you from sleeping well at night. Take brisk walks or do other exercises to release tension and feel more refreshed.

Housework and child care duties don't stop during pregnancy and can be hard work. These duties can result in you feeling tired and stressed. You may need to share more duties with your partner or others to ensure you are getting enough rest. Careful planning and enough sleep are very important.

Exercise

Regular exercise during pregnancy can make you look and feel better, help your posture, and lessen discomforts such as backaches and fatigue. The goal of exercise during pregnancy should be to reach or keep a level of fitness that is safe. You should not exercise to lose weight during pregnancy. Some exercises provide aerobic conditioning of the heart and lungs; others relieve stress and tone muscles. For total fitness, an exercise program should include exercises that provide both conditioning and strengthening.

Pregnancy causes many changes in your body, some of which affect your ability to exercise. The hormones produced during pregnancy cause the ligaments that support joints to become stretched. This makes the joints more mobile and prone to injury. The extra weight gained in pregnancy, as well as its uneven distribution, shifts your center of gravity. This places stress on joints and muscles, especially those in the lower back and pelvis, and can make you less stable and more likely to fall. For these reasons, you may wish to modify your form of exercise during pregnancy.

Almost any form of exercise is safe if it is done with caution and if you don't do too much of it. Here are some general guidelines for a safe and healthy exercise program geared to the special needs of pregnancy:

■ Get regular exercise (at least three times a week). Avoid spurts of heavy exercise followed by long periods of no activity.

■ Avoid brisk exercise in hot, humid weather or when you are sick with a fever (such as the flu).

■ Avoid jerky, bouncy, or high-impact motions. Activities that call for jumping, jarring motions, or quick changes in direction may strain your joints and cause pain. Low-impact exercise is best. A wooden floor or a tightly carpeted surface reduces impact and gives you sure footing.

■ Wear a bra that fits well and gives lots of support to help protect your breasts.

■ Wear the proper shoes for the activity to be sure your feet are well cushioned and to give your body good support. There are shoes designed just for walking, running, aerobics, or tennis.

■ Avoid deep knee bends, full sit-ups, double leg raises (in which you raise and lower both legs together), and straight-leg toe touches.

■ After 20 weeks of pregnancy, avoid exercises that require lying with your back on the floor for more than a few minutes.

■ Always begin with 5 minutes of slow walking or stationary cycling with low resistance to warm up your muscles. Intense exercise should not last longer than 15 minutes.

■ Follow intense exercise with 5–10 minutes of gradually slower activity that ends with gentle stretching in place. To reduce the risk of injuring the tissue connecting your joints, do not stretch as far as you possibly can.

■ The extra weight you are carrying will make you work harder as you exercise at a slower pace. Measure your heart rate at peak times of activity (see "Exercise," Chapter 1).

■ Get up from the floor slowly and gradually to avoid feeling dizzy or fainting. Once you are standing, walk in place briefly.

■ Drink water often before, during, and after exercise to be sure your body gets enough fluids. Take a break in your workout to drink more water if needed.

■ If you did not exercise two or three times a week before getting pregnant, start with physical activity of very low intensity and, bit by bit, move to higher levels.

■ Stop exercising and consult your doctor or nurse if you get any of these symptoms, and they are unusually severe:
  —Pain
  —Vaginal bleeding
  —Dizziness or feeling faint
  —Shortness of breath
  —Irregular or rapid heart beat
  —Difficulty walking
  —Pain in your back or pubic area

The sports and exercises you can do during pregnancy depend on your own health and, in part, on how active you were before you became pregnant. Pregnancy is not a good time to take up a new, strenuous sport. If you were active before your pregnancy, however, you should be able to keep it up, within reason.

Here are some sports you may have done before pregnancy:

■ *Walking* is always good exercise. If you were not active before you became pregnant, walking is a good way to start an exercise program. Try to walk briskly for 20–30 minutes, three times a week.

■ *Swimming* is great for your body because it uses many different muscles while the water supports your weight. It is best not to dive in the later months of pregnancy, however.

Scuba diving is not recommended at any time during pregnancy.

■ *Jogging* can be done in moderation. Avoid becoming overheated, stop if you are feeling uncomfortable or unusually tired, and drink plenty of water to replace what you lose through sweating.

■ *Aerobics* is good to strengthen the heart and lungs. It is safest to do only the low-impact version. Water aerobics combines the advantages of swimming and aerobics.

■ *Tennis* is generally safe during pregnancy, but be aware of your change in balance and how it affects rapid movements.

■ *Body building* or *strength training* can make your muscles stronger. It can also help prevent the muscle aches and pains that are common during pregnancy. Strength training should be done under the supervision of an expert to avoid muscle and joint injuries. Use slow, controlled movements and do short sets of strength exercises (10 or fewer repetitions).

■ *Golf* and *bowling* are fine for recreation but don't really strengthen the heart and lungs. With either of these sports, you may have to adjust to your change in balance.

■ *Snow skiing* can be okay if you are careful, but be aware that several possible hazards are beyond your control. Two such hazards are the risk of injury to yourself and the effects of exercising at an altitude that you are not used to. At very high altitudes the air is thinner, which makes it harder to breathe. Because of the danger of serious injuries and hard falls while downhill skiing, stay on safe slopes. You may have problems with balance, although some skiers find the shift in their center of gravity helps their balance during skiing. Cross-country skiing is safer than downhill skiing during pregnancy, and it is also better for strengthening your heart. Ski machines are acceptable to use.

■ *Water skiing and surfing* should be avoided completely. You can hit the water with great force, and taking a fall at such fast speeds could harm you or possibly your fetus.

The added weight and changes in your posture caused by pregnancy can make your back hurt. Certain exercises can ease back pain by strengthening and stretching muscles. You should also take special care to avoid injury and ease discomfort.

A Healthy Back

Following are exercises that strengthen and stretch muscles that support the back and legs and promote good posture—muscles of the back, the abdomen, the hips, and the upper body. These exercises not only will help ease back pain but also will help prepare you for labor and delivery.

Upper Body Bends

This exercise strengthens the muscles of your back and torso.

- Stand with your legs apart, knees bent slightly, with your hands on your hips.
- Bend forward slowly, keeping your upper back straight. You should feel a slight pull along your upper thigh.
- Repeat 10 times.

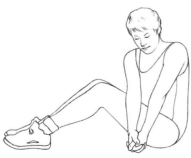

Diagonal Curl

This exercise strengthens the muscles of your back, hips, and abdomen. If you have not already been exercising regularly, skip this exercise.

- Sit on the floor with your knees bent, feet on the floor, and hands clasped in front of you.
- Twist your upper torso to the left until your hands touch the floor.
- Do the same movement to the right.
- Repeat on both sides 5 times.

Forward Bend

This exercise stretches and strengthens the muscles of your back.

- Sit in a chair in a comfortable position. Keep your arms relaxed.
- Bend forward slowly, with your arms in front and hanging down.
- If you feel any discomfort or pressure on your abdomen, do not push any further.
- Hold this position for a count of 5, then get up slowly without arching your back.
- Repeat 5 times.

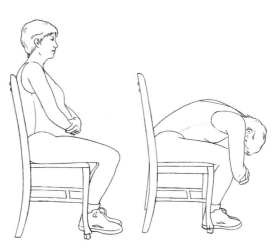

Trunk Twist

This exercise stretches the muscles of your back, spine, and upper torso.

- Sit on the floor with your legs crossed, with your left hand holding your left foot and your right hand on the floor at your side for support.
- Slowly twist your upper torso to the right.
- Do the same movement to the left, after switching your hands (right hand holding right foot and left hand supporting you).
- Repeat on both sides 5–10 times.

Backward Stretch

This exercise stretches and strengthens the muscles of your back, pelvis, and thighs.

- Kneel on hands and knees, with your knees 8–10 inches apart and your arms straight (hands under your shoulders).
- Curl backward slowly, tucking your head toward your knees and keeping your arms extended.
- Hold this position for a count of 5, then come back up to all fours slowly.
- Repeat 5 times.

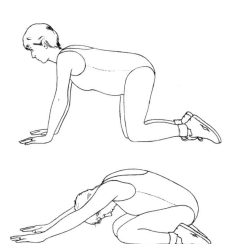

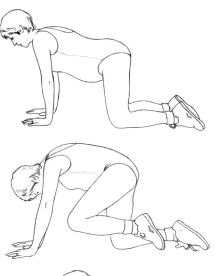

Leg Lift Crawl

This exercise strengthens the muscles of your back and abdomen.

- Kneel on hands and knees, with your weight distributed evenly and your arms straight (hands under your shoulders).
- Lift your left knee and bring it toward your elbow.
- Straighten your leg without locking your knee.
- Extend your leg up and back.
- Do this exercise to a count of 5. Move slowly; don't fling your leg back or arch your back.
- Repeat on both sides 5–10 times.

Rocking Back Arch

This exercise stretches and strengthens the muscles of your back, hips, and abdomen.

- Kneel on hands and knees, with your weight distributed evenly and your back straight.
- Rock back and forth, to a count of 5.
- Return to the original position and curl your back upward as much as you can.
- Repeat 5–10 times.

Back Press

This exercise strengthens the muscles of your back, torso, and upper body and promotes good posture.

- Stand with your feet 10–12 inches away from a wall and your back against it.
- Press the lower part of your back against the wall.
- Hold this position for a count of 10, then release.
- Repeat 10 times.

Work

Today more than two thirds of the women of childbearing age have jobs outside the home. More than 1 million of these working women become pregnant each year. Many work until a short time before delivery and return to work within weeks or months of the baby's birth. This trend, along with a growing awareness of on-the-job health and safety, has prompted women, health care providers, and employers to ask a number of questions that have no easy answers: Is it safe for a pregnant woman to work? How long, under what conditions, and with what effects can she continue to work?

Pregnant women can usually keep doing the physical activities they were used to doing before. Heavy lifting, climbing, carrying, and other efforts that require agility and stamina may cause discomfort for some.

The first few months of pregnancy may bring periods of dizziness, nausea, fatigue, and heat sensitivity that can increase the risk of accidents. Toward the end of pregnancy, your greater weight and bigger abdomen throw off your balance, increasing the risk of falling. Also, because women tire more easily when pregnant, even those in the best physical shape find work more tiring than usual.

If your job is strenuous, requires physical effort, or requires a lot of standing or walking, you may need to cut back on work hours, transfer to less demanding work, or stop working a few weeks before delivery. You may also be advised to stop working if you have certain diseases, have given birth to more than one premature baby, have a history of miscarriages, or are expecting more than one baby. Otherwise, if you and your fetus are healthy and you work in a job that presents no greater hazards than those in daily life, you can usually work until your due date.

Agencies that protect the rights of workers are the Occupational Safety and Health Administration in Washington, DC, and the National Institute of Safety and Health in Atlanta, Georgia. At the request of an employee, union, or health care provider, these agencies will inspect possible hazards in the workplace.

Pregnancy-Related Disability

Having a disability means that you are not able to work because of physical problems that could keep you from doing your usual duties. Your pregnancy may be partly or totally disabling. A disability may be one of three types:

1. *Disability of the pregnancy itself.* Some women suffer side effects such as nausea, vomiting, indigestion, dizziness, and swollen legs and ankles. These problems are usually minor.

2. *Disability due to complications.* More serious problems such as infection, bleeding, early labor, or early rupture of the amniotic sac that surrounds the fetus may cause disability. Medical conditions you had before getting pregnant such as heart disease, diabetes, or high blood pressure may become disabling in pregnancy.

3. *Disability due to job exposures.* Some disabilities may be linked with exposure to high levels of toxic substances at work that could affect the fetus.

If your doctor decides that your pregnancy is disabling, you may request a letter to verify to your employer that you are eligible for disability benefits. Likewise, if you are told that you are able to keep working, your employer may request a letter from your doctor stating so.

Disability Benefits for Pregnant Employees

Employee maternity policies vary widely from company to company and state to state. Only about 4 in 10 employed women in the United States are entitled to paid 6-week disability leave for childbirth. Others must use sick leave and vacation time or take time off without pay. The Family and Medical Leave Act protects a woman's right to be able to take time off from her job for childbirth. To be eligible, an employee must have worked for the employer for at least 12 months and a minimum of 1,250 hours during the past 12-month period.

Your Rights As an Employee

Several federal laws protect the rights of pregnant women in the workplace. If you are deprived of your rights, contact the agencies involved for further information.

Pregnancy Discrimination Act

The 1978 Pregnancy Discrimination Act requires your employer to offer the same medical disability compensation for pregnancy-related disabilities that is offered for other disabilities.

Occupational Safety and Health Act

The Occupational Safety and Health Administration (OSHA) requires employers to provide a workplace free from recognized hazards that cause, or are likely to cause, death or serious physical harm and to give employees information about dangerous chemicals and substances. State and municipal laws also give employees and unions the right to ask for the names of chemicals and other substances used in the workplace.

The National Institute for Occupational Safety and Health identifies hazards, figures out ways to control them, and suggests ways to limit the dangers.

Family and Medical Leave Act

The Family and Medical Leave Act (FMLA) requires both public and private employers with 50 or more employees to give employees 12 work weeks of unpaid leave in the following circumstances:

1. Upon the birth, adoption, or foster care of a child.
2. When needed to care for a spouse, child, or parent who has a serious health condition, such as an illness, injury, or physical or mental condition.
3. When an employee is unable to perform his or her job due to the employee's own health condition, including a maternity-related disability.

An employer may require that an employee use accrued paid vacation, personal, sick, or medical leave for any part of the 12-week period. Employers are not required to provide paid leave if they would not otherwise do so. An employer providing health care benefits under a group health plan must continue to provide such coverage during leave at the same level. An employee is entitled to the same or equal position and the same benefits upon return to work. A few states have more liberal family and medical leave laws than the federal FMLA. For information on family and medical leave, contact the Work and Family Clearinghouse, U.S. Department of Labor at 1-800-827-5335.

The Pregnancy Discrimination Act, passed by Congress in 1978, requires employers offering medical disability compensation to treat pregnancy-related disabilities the same way as other disabilities. This means that if you can't work for a few weeks or months because of pregnancy, your employer must give you the same rights as other employees temporarily disabled by illness or accident. If you are partly disabled by pregnancy and your employer normally gives lighter work to other partly disabled workers, the same must be done for you. Unfortunately, many employers offer no disability benefits at all and therefore do not have to provide paid leave.

If no disability plan is offered where you work, you may qualify for unemployment or temporary disability benefits from your state. To find out whether your state offers benefits and how to qualify, contact your local unemployment office.

Travel

Most women can travel safely until close to their due date if they follow a few simple guidelines. The most comfortable time for most pregnant women to travel is mid-pregnancy. By this time your body has adjusted to pregnancy and you probably have more energy. Morning sickness is usually no longer a problem, and complications are less likely. Toward the end of your pregnancy, it may be harder for you to move around and sit comfortably for long periods.

The best rule of thumb is to follow your body's signals. Your own physical feelings are among the best guides to your well-being and safety—on the road as well as at home. When choosing how to travel, think about how long it will take for you to reach your destination. The quickest way may be the best. Whether you go by car, bus, train, plane, or ship (motorcycles aren't recommended), take extra steps to ensure your comfort and safety. Here are some hints that apply no matter what type of transportation you choose:

■ Walk around often—every 2 hours or so. This will decrease swelling and help make you more comfortable.

- Wear comfortable shoes and clothing that doesn't bind.
- Take some crackers, juice, or other light snacks with you to help prevent nausea.
- While you are away, take time to eat regular meals. Make sure they are balanced and nutritious; you'll have more energy and feel better. Add fiber to your diet to ease constipation, which can be a problem during travel.

Foreign Travel: Let the Traveler Beware

If you are thinking about a trip out of the country, discuss your plans with your doctor. She or he can help you decide whether foreign travel would be safe for you and, if so, what steps you should take in advance. Plan ahead to allow time for any shots you may need, and be prepared to take a copy of your prenatal record with you.

The Centers for Disease Control and Prevention has an International Travelers Hotline for information on disease and world travel. The number is (404) 332-4559. There may be other international medical travel services near you that can help you prepare for your medical needs during a trip.

Contaminated Food and Water

Traveling to other countries exposes you to diseases that are not common in the United States. Natives of a country are used to the organisms found in the food and water, but the same organisms can make a visitor ill. This is true whether you travel to cities or rural areas.

Although traveler's diarrhea may be a minor nuisance to someone who is not pregnant, it is a greater concern for pregnant women. Talk with your doctor about using medication to prevent diarrhea. The best way for you and your fellow travelers to avoid getting diarrhea is to avoid contaminated food and water. Be sure to:

- Drink only pure bottled water, bottled soft drinks, hot tea, or broth. Iodine used to purify water may not be safe for pregnant women.
- Don't use ice in your drinks, and don't use glasses that could have been washed in impure water. Drink out of the bottle or use paper cups.
- Avoid fresh fruits and vegetables unless they have been cooked or can be peeled.
- Stay away from raw or undercooked meat. It can contain organisms that cause toxoplasmosis, a disease that may harm the fetus.
- Make sure the milk you drink has been pasteurized.

If you do get diarrhea, drink plenty of fluids. Do not take any medication without checking with a doctor first. A doctor can arrange for medication that is safe for use during pregnancy.

- Drink extra fluids
- Although traveling can upset your stomach or disrupt your sleep, do not take any prescription or over-the-counter medications before checking with your doctor or nurse. These include motion-sickness pills and laxatives.
- Try to get more sleep, and rest often so you won't feel tired and irritated.

Malaria

Malaria is a tropical infection passed on by mosquito bites. It produces anemia and symptoms similar to flu and can result in miscarriage, stillbirth, small babies, and other problems. To avoid mosquito bites in areas where malaria may be a problem, wear long-sleeved clothing and use mosquito netting and bug repellant or lotion.

No drug fully protects against malaria. A drug called chloroquine can help prevent and treat malaria, however, and is safe for use during pregnancy. You must start taking it before you travel and keep taking it for a few weeks afterward. You should not travel to areas where there are mosquitoes that carry types of malaria resistant to chloroquine because there is no other safe drug that prevents malaria.

Immunizations

Some countries require that people be vaccinated so they will be immune to certain diseases before they travel there. Requirements for immunization vary; find out which immunizations are needed for the countries you plan to visit. Ideally, vaccines should be given before you become pregnant, but some can be given during pregnancy. You and your doctor will need to decide whether the risks of a disease are greater than the risks of its vaccine. In some cases it may be best to delay a trip until after you have given birth.

Foreign Medical Facilities

Find out where medical facilities and doctors are located in the countries you plan to visit. If you have to see a doctor who doesn't speak English, it may be helpful to have a foreign language dictionary with you.

Register with an American embassy or consulate when you arrive. This will help if you need an emergency evacuation. The safety of blood transfusions varies from country to country.

There are groups that can help you find a doctor or hospital. One is the International Association for Medical Assistance to Travelers (Lewiston, New York). Another is International SOS Assistance (Philadelphia, Pennsylvania), which requires you to be a member. Contact them in advance of your trip for further details.

■ Take a copy of your medical record with you if you will be far from home.

■ You may want to schedule a prenatal visit before you leave.

■ If you plan to be away for more than a few weeks, ask your doctor to give you the name of another doctor in the area where you will be staying in case of an emergency.

■ If you plan to travel very late in your pregnancy, check with your doctor. Going into labor away from home can pose problems.

■ Keep your travel plans flexible. Problems can come up before you leave that could force you to cancel your trip.

Travel during pregnancy is safe for most women, but it is not recommended for women who have serious health problems that need special medical care. If you are planning a trip out of the country, you may need to take special precautions. If you are not sure whether travel is safe for you, ask your doctor.

By Land

A car can be a good way to travel, especially for short distances. Make each day's drive short enough to be fun. Ten hours on the road is tiring even when you aren't pregnant. No more than 5 or 6 hours of driving each day is a good target.

Always wear a seat belt. Some women worry that the belt will hurt the fetus if the car stops quickly or if there is an impact. The fetus is not likely to be harmed unless the mother has a serious injury. The fetus is cushioned in a fluid-filled sac inside the uterus, which, in turn, is protected by muscles, organs, and bones. Studies have shown that in nearly 100% of car crashes, the fetus recovers quickly from any pressure the seat belt exerts and suffers no lasting injury. If you don't wear a seat belt you can be thrown from the car or get a concussion (an injury to the brain caused by a hard blow). These risks are much more serious than any risk from wearing a seat belt.

Air bags do not replace seat belts. If your car has an air bag, you should still wear your seat belt. (The gas used in air bags is harmless.) If you get in an accident, you should see your doctor to make sure you and your fetus are okay.

You may also choose to travel by bus or train. Buses have narrow aisles and small bathrooms. Trains have more space for

The Right Way to Wear a Safety Belt

For the best protection, you should wear a lap and shoulder belt throughout your pregnancy every time you travel in a car, including during your ride to the hospital for the birth of your baby. Some cars have only lap belts in the back seat. If a lap belt is all there is, use it.

Place the lower part of the lap part of the belt under your abdomen, as low as possible, and against your upper thighs. Never place the lap belt above your abdomen, because this could cause major injuries in a crash. Position the upper part of the belt between your breasts. Adjust both the upper and lower parts of the belt as snugly as possible.

The upper part of the belt should cross your shoulder without chafing your neck. Never slip the upper part of the belt off your shoulder. Safety belts worn too loosely or too high on the abdomen can cause broken ribs or injuries to your abdomen. But, more damage is caused when they aren't used at all.

walking around but are wobbly, so balance might be a problem. Don't worry that bumpy rides could induce labor: they don't.

By Air

Flying is generally safe during pregnancy. Airlines in the United States usually allow pregnant women to fly up until 36 weeks of pregnancy. Commercial planes are pressurized (the air in the cabin is not as thin as the air outside), but many private planes are not. It is best to avoid altitudes higher than 7,000–9,000 feet in unpressurized planes. Metal detectors and airport security checks do not harm the fetus. Here are some tips for a comfortable flight:

■ Try to get an aisle seat so you can walk around and get to the bathroom easily. The forward part of the plane usually has a more stable ride. You may wish to avoid a seat near an exit, where you may be expected to assist others in an emergency.

■ Cabin temperature can change even on a short flight. Wear a few layers of light clothing that will allow you to bundle up or remove a layer or two. You can also ask the flight attendant for a blanket. Pillows may also make your seat more comfortable.

■ Eat lightly to avoid being airsick. You can get special meals on many flights if you order in advance. Because the air in the cabin is dry, drink plenty of fluids.

■ Allow for extra rest after long flights to recover from jet lag.

By Sea

Ship cruises can be a relaxing way to travel. However, sea travel can upset your stomach. If you've never been on a ship before, this is not a good time to try it. If you think your stomach can stand the ship's motion, check on the cruise line's regulations for pregnant women. Your doctor can tell you about medicine you can take for seasickness and what to do about medical care while the cruise is on the open sea.

Sex

Most couples can have sex until shortly before the baby is born. Sometimes couples are afraid that sex will harm the fetus—this is usually not true. The fetus is well cushioned by amniotic fluid. Other couples may find sex less enjoyable now because of the changes in the woman's body during pregnancy (see "Your Partner and Family," Chapter 10).

For your comfort, you and your partner may want to try different positions for sex. For example, if the man and woman lie on their sides it puts less pressure on the woman's abdomen.

The basic guide to sex during pregnancy is your own comfort. You may be advised to limit or avoid having intercourse if any of the following have occurred in a previous pregnancy:

■ Past preterm birth (born before 37 weeks)

■ Infection

■ Bleeding

■ Breaking of the amniotic sac or leaking amniotic fluid

Intercourse is not the only form of sexual expression. Other ways can be equally satisfying. This is an area that you may wish to discuss with your doctor or nurse and your partner.

Whatever form of sexual expression you choose, it's best to stay with one steady partner. A monogamous relationship, in which both partners are faithful to each other, is more important now than ever. Having more than one sexual partner greatly increases the risk of getting a sexually transmitted disease. These diseases can be dangerous for the mother and the fetus (see "Sexually Transmitted Diseases," Chapter 13).

Harmful Agents

Teratogens are agents that can cause birth defects when a woman is exposed to them during pregnancy. Hazards can be posed by some prescription drugs, chemicals in the environment or workplace, or infections (see Chapter 13). These agents can prevent the fetus's normal development, causing physical and mental defects. Their effect depends on how much of the substance the mother came into contact with and at what point in her pregnancy she was exposed to it. Other substances, such as tobacco, alcohol, and illegal drugs, are harmful in different ways. They should be avoided for the sake of your health and that of your baby.

Work-Related Hazards

The risks that come from being exposed to many substances in the workplace are not known. Scientific information is either lacking or conflicting. A few substances that can be found in the workplace, however, are known to cause harm. You also may come in contact with these agents through a hobby.

Heavy metals such as lead and mercury are teratogens. Lead is used in industries such as brass foundries, ship building, paint manufacturing, pottery glazing, and printing. Tollbooth attendants

Agents That Can Harm the Fetus

Agent	Reasons Used	Fetal Effects
Alcohol	Social reasons, dependency	Growth restriction and mental retardation
Androgens	To treat *endometriosis*	Genital abnormalities
Anticoagulants (eg, warfarin [Coumadin, Panwarfin] and dicumarol)	To prevent blood clotting; used to prevent or treat thromboembolisms (clots blocking blood vessels)	Abnormalities in bones, cartilage, and eyes; central nervous system defects
Antithyroid drugs (eg, propylthiouracil, iodide, and methimazole [Tapazole])	To treat an overactive thyroid gland	Underactive or enlarged thyroid
Anticonvulsants (eg, phenytoin [Dilantin], trimethadione [Tridione], paramethadione [Paradione], valproic acid [Depakene])	To treat seizure disorders and irregular heartbeat	Growth and mental retardation, developmental abnormalities, neural tube defects
Chemotherapeutic drugs (eg, methotrexate [Mexate] and aminopterin)	To treat cancer and psoriasis (skin disease)	Increased rate of miscarriage, various abnormalities
Diethylstilbestrol (DES)	To treat problems with menstruation, symptoms of menopause and breast cancer, and to stop milk production; previously used to prevent preterm labor and miscarriage	Abnormalities of cervix and uterus in females, possible infertility in males and females
Isotretinoin (Accutane)	Treatment for cystic acne	Increased rate of miscarriage, developmental abnormalities
Lead	Industries involving lead smelting, paint manufacture and use, printing, ceramics, glass manufacturing, and pottery glazing	Problems in development of the fetal central nervous system
Lithium	To treat the manic part of manic–depressive disorders	Congenital heart disease
Organic mercury	Exposure through eating contaminated food	Brain disorders

Agents That Can Harm the Fetus (continued)

Agent	Reasons Used	Fetal Effects
Streptomycin	An *antibiotic* used to treat tuberculosis	Hearing loss
Tetracycline	An antibiotic used to treat a wide variety of infections	Underdevelopment of tooth enamel, incorporation of tetracycline into bone
Thalidomide	Previously used as a sedative and a sleep aid	Growth deficiencies, other abnormalities
X-ray therapy	Medical treatment of disorders such as cancer	Growth restriction and mental retardation

and others who work on heavily traveled roads may be exposed to high levels of lead from car exhaust.

Ionizing radiation is used to take X-rays of the internal organs to diagnose health problems. It can also be used in larger doses for treatment. In larger doses, such as those used to treat cancer, it can harm a fetus. Most women who work around radiation, however, are protected from exposure.

A common question during pregnancy is whether you can still color or perm your hair. Experts agree that using these products is okay when you're pregnant.

There is no evidence that working at a computer causes any harm to the fetus. Women, however, should be aware of the risk of repetitive wrist and hand motion and should remember to move about at least once an hour.

If you think you may be exposed to a harmful agent at work, talk to your employer about it. You may be able to be moved to another job on a temporary basis. If you have questions about whether a substance could be harmful, ask your doctor. You may also be able to call one of several hot lines that track reproductive hazards.

Medications

Many types of medication can affect the fetus, and some can cause severe birth defects or other problems for the baby. Don't stop taking any medication prescribed by a doctor—the lack of treatment could be more harmful than the drug—but do seek medical advice. Certain medications have been linked with birth defects.

Be sure that your health care provider during your pregnancy knows about any medical problems you may have. Tell him or her about medications prescribed to you and whether you have any drug allergies. You may need to change the kind or amount of drug you take.

Some prescription medications can also be abused and can be harmful during pregnancy. They include tranquilizers and sleeping pills (also called "downers") and amphetamines (also called "uppers" or "speed"). Tranquilizers are used to produce a calm feeling and relieve stress. If the mother takes these drugs, her baby can be inactive, have poor muscle tone, and have trouble breathing and feeding. The effects of these medications can last longer in newborns than in adults. For the woman, addiction and overdose are possible. Amphetamines can cause agitation, insomnia (inability to sleep), and loss of appetite. Pregnant women who use them may not get enough nutrients for their growing fetus. Users can come to depend on them and can overdose.

Not all medications require a prescription. Pain medicines (aspirin, acetaminophen, and ibuprofen), cold and allergy medicines, and some skin treatments are medications, even though you can buy them in a drug store without a prescription. You should not take over-the-counter medications during pregnancy without checking first with your health care provider. Instructions that come with these over-the-counter medications are usually not meant for pregnant women.

Smoking

When you smoke before, during, or after birth, you risk not only your own health but that of your baby. Each puff subjects you and the fetus to harmful chemicals such as nicotine, tar, and carbon monoxide. Carbon monoxide travels to the fetus's blood and lowers the amount of oxygen to both the mother and fetus. Nicotine crosses the placenta (which connects mother and fetus) and can cause the fetal blood vessels to constrict so that less oxygen and nourishment reach the fetus. If you or your partner smoke around the baby after he or she is born, the baby is exposed to the harmful effects of the smoke.

Smoking may make it harder for you to have a normal pregnancy. If you smoke, you are more likely to have vaginal bleeding during pregnancy. You are also more likely to have an ***ectopic pregnancy,*** miscarriage, ***stillbirth,*** or preterm baby. There may be problems with the way the placenta attaches to the uterus. You may have a low-birth-weight baby. On the average, a smoker's baby weighs ¹/₂ pound less than a nonsmoker's baby and is about ¹/₂ inch shorter in body length. Low birth weight raises the baby's chances of being born early and needing special care. ***Sudden infant death syndrome*** occurs more than twice as often among babies of smoking mothers.

The sooner you quit, the better it will be for your baby. If you stop smoking during the early months of your pregnancy, your chance of having a low-birth-weight baby is the same as that of a nonsmoker. Almost one fourth of all pregnant women who smoke quit while they are pregnant. If you can quit during pregnancy, you may be able to quit for a lifetime, and it will be a healthier one for both you and your family.

If you can't quit, it's important to cut back to as few cigarettes as possible. Cutting down or stopping smoking at any time while you are pregnant is better than not stopping at all. Tell your doctor if you need help in quitting. If you are a heavy smoker and have not been able to quit or cut down, try using a nicotine substitute in the form of chewing gum or a skin patch. There are risks to using the patch during pregnancy, but the risk of heavy smoking may be greater. It is a good idea to encourage your partner and other family members to quit too. Even if *you* don't smoke, the smoke from other people's cigarettes (secondhand smoke) can endanger you and your baby.

Caffeine

Caffeine is a stimulant and diuretic found in coffee, tea, colas and some other soft drinks, chocolate, and a few over-the-counter medications. Caffeine crosses the placenta into the fetal blood, but it does not appear to be linked with birth defects. Very high amounts may be linked to some complications of pregnancies, however.

Alcohol

About 6 in 10 American women drink alcoholic beverages. There is a difference between alcohol use and alcohol abuse. Some people have one or two drinks on occasion—this is alcohol use. Others may drink daily or in binges (drinking a large amount of alcohol in a short time once in a while)—this is alcohol abuse. The amount of alcohol that sets use apart from abuse is not clearly defined.

Alcohol slows down body functions, such as the beating of the heart and breathing. When a pregnant woman drinks alcohol, it quickly reaches the fetus through the bloodstream. The same level of alcohol that goes through your bloodstream also goes through your fetus's. Women who drink heavily while pregnant have a higher risk of miscarriage than women who don't drink. The more a woman drinks while pregnant, the greater the danger to the fetus. The risk is greatest in early pregnancy.

A number of studies have been done on infants born to women who drank heavily during pregnancy. Many of the infants were born with a strong pattern of physical, mental, and behavioral problems called *fetal alcohol syndrome.* This syndrome is the most common cause of mental retardation in babies.

Babies with the syndrome are shorter and weigh less than normal babies and do not catch up, even after special care is provided. They also have small heads; abnormal features of the face, head, joints, and limbs; heart defects; and poor control of movements. Most are mentally retarded and have a number of behavioral problems, including hyperactivity, extreme nervousness, and a poor attention span. Some are born with all of these problems. Others show signs of only some of them.

Other factors—cigarette smoking, use of other drugs, poor diet, problems handling stress—may well play a role in fetal alcohol syndrome. But alcohol itself appears to be the one common agent in all cases. Other factors alone cannot account for the damage.

One of the questions asked most often about alcohol and pregnancy is whether there is a safe level of alcohol intake. Does the woman who drinks only once in a while put her baby in danger? Women who have an occasional drink seem to have babies with

Do You Have a Drinking Problem?

Sometimes it can be hard to tell the difference between alcohol use and alcohol abuse. The "T-ACE" questions below can help you determine whether you have a drinking problem:

T How many drinks does it take to make you feel high? (TOLERANCE)

A Have people ANNOYED you by criticizing your drinking?

C Have you felt you ought to CUT DOWN on your drinking?

E Have you ever had a drink first thing in the morning to steady your nerves or get rid of a hangover? (EYE OPENER)

If your answer to the TOLERANCE question is more than two drinks, give yourself 2 points. Give yourself 1 point for every "yes" response to the other questions. If your total score is 2 or more, you may have a problem with alcohol. Talk to your health care provider about your drinking habits. He or she can give you more information and refer you for counseling or treatment. You may wish to contact Alcoholics Anonymous to talk with someone about your problem. Check your telephone directory for the chapter in your area.

Modified from Sokol RJ, Martier SS, Ager JW. The T-ACE questions: practical prenatal detection of risk drinking. Am J Obstet Gynecol 1989; 160:865

no more problems than those women who do not drink. However, moderate drinking—having one or two drinks a few times a week—may cause problems. Studies suggest that children whose mothers drank moderately during pregnancy may have some of the same problems found in children with fetal alcohol syndrome, although the problems may be less severe. For instance, they may have problems with learning, speech, attention span, and language, and they may be hyperactive.

It's hard to know how much alcohol puts the fetus at risk. Each fetus may be affected differently. The best course is not to drink at all during pregnancy. If you can, cut down your drinking gradually over the 6 months before you become pregnant. Try to find other ways to relax, such as warm baths, taking a long walk, listening to soothing music, or talking with a friend.

If you choose to drink, keep it to an occasional drink. Avoid binges and daily drinking, which are more dangerous for the fetus. Even if you don't binge and you think of yourself as a light drinker, it's still best to cut back. Reducing your alcohol intake anytime during pregnancy can be helpful. It's just one more change in your life style that boosts your chances of having a healthy, normal baby.

Illegal Drugs

The life style that often goes along with using illegal drugs can make it hard to pinpoint their effects during pregnancy. It is known, however, that drug users are more likely to have problems during pregnancy that place their babies at risk. As many as 1 in 10 babies may be exposed to illegal drugs before birth. The effects of drugs can be so harmful that even women who only use them once in a while are at risk. They have the greatest effect early in pregnancy, so if you are using these drugs you should stop before you get pregnant.

Most drugs cross the placenta. Some can cause direct toxic (poisonous) effects and addiction in the fetus. After birth, some drugs can be passed to the baby through breast-feeding. If drugs are taken together, it can be hard to predict the effects. Sometimes the drugs add to each other's effect.

Drugs can cause problems throughout your pregnancy. For example, the early part of pregnancy is the most critical because this is when the main body systems form. Using drugs during this time can cause severe damage. During the last 12 weeks of pregnancy, drug use poses the greatest risk for stunting fetal growth and causing preterm birth.

Drug use may have long-term effects. For example, using needles that have been used by others can cause infection and increase the risk of getting hepatitis B virus or human immunodeficiency virus (HIV), the virus that causes acquired immunodeficiency syndrome (AIDS). These viruses can then be passed to the fetus through the placenta.

Marijuana

Marijuana (also called grass or pot) can be smoked or eaten. It changes your moods and sense of reality. Marijuana can stay in the body for a long time, leading to prolonged fetal exposure. When it is smoked, marijuana releases carbon monoxide, a gas that could keep the fetus from getting enough oxygen.

Cocaine

Cocaine is a highly addictive drug that can be snorted, injected, or smoked in a highly purified and addictive form known as crack. Pregnant women who use cocaine have a 25% higher chance of having a preterm birth. The fetus may also have withdrawal symptoms. Babies born to mothers who use cocaine may:

- Grow more slowly
- Have smaller heads
- Have brain injury
- Be more irritable and fussy

Cocaine may cause the placenta to detach from the uterus too soon—a condition called placental abruption or ***abruptio placentae.*** This can cause bleeding, preterm birth, and fetal death. If you've heard that cocaine can bring on labor *safely*, don't believe it. It can lead to high blood pressure in the mother or sudden death from heart attack or stroke. Recent studies suggest that even babies who survive being exposed to cocaine during pregnancy will have long-lasting physical, behavioral, and emotional problems.

Heroin and Other Narcotics

Heroin is smoked or injected. It can cause preterm birth or fetal death, addiction in the fetus, and low birth weight. Studies of children whose mothers used heroin showed that some children were smaller, had trouble thinking clearly, and had behavioral problems.

Women who use heroin often become addicted to it. They may die from overdose. Sudden withdrawal can harm the woman and the fetus. Methadone is often used to replace heroin in drug treatment centers. This replacement should be done only under a doctor's supervision.

"T's and blues" is the street name for a mix of a prescription narcotic drug and an over-the-counter antihistamine medication. It is often used as a cheap substitute for heroin. Babies of mothers who use T's and blues are more likely to grow more slowly before they are born. They may also suffer withdrawal symptoms.

PCP and LSD

PCP, or angel dust, is usually smoked but also can be eaten, snorted, or injected. It has unpredictable effects and can cause a user to lose touch with reality. Use during pregnancy can lead to small babies and babies with poor control of their movements. The mother can have flashbacks, seizures, heart attacks, and lung failure leading to death. Violent acts are common.

LSD, or acid, is swallowed. It can cause hallucinations, such as hearing and seeing things when nothing is there. Use of LSD during pregnancy may lead to birth defects in the baby. Users may act violently and have flashbacks.

Glues and Solvents

Glues and solvents like toluene are sometimes inhaled or sniffed to give a temporary "high" feeling. They can make the user lightheaded and dizzy and can even cause death. They may also damage the liver, kidneys, bone marrow, and brain. The sniffing of these fumes by a pregnant woman may cause birth defects in the baby similar to those caused by alcohol.

Getting Help

Addictions can be hard to overcome. Pregnancy may give you extra incentive to try. If you need help to stop using illegal drugs, talk to your doctor or nurse. He or she can give you more information about the effects of these drugs on your fetus and can refer you to a treatment program.

The Battered Woman

Abuse of women by their male partners—physical, sexual, or emotional abuse—is one of America's most common health problems. It can occur no matter how much money you have or what your race, age, or religion is. The effects of this abuse are serious. About one in five visits made by women to emergency rooms are for injuries related to abuse. More than one third of female murder victims are killed by their male partners.

Children may also be affected, because men and women in abusive relationships often abuse their children too.

Abuse often starts or gets worse during pregnancy, putting both the mother and the fetus at risk. During pregnancy, the abuser is more likely to aim blows at the woman's breasts and abdomen. Dangers to the fetus include miscarriage, low birth weight, and direct injury from blows to the mother. Sometimes, though, abuse lessens during pregnancy. In fact, some women feel safe only when they are carrying a child. They may get pregnant as a way to escape abuse.

There are better ways of dealing with abuse. First, realize that you are not to blame for your partner's actions. Abusers blame their victims, but it is not your fault. He and he alone is the cause of his actions. Second, tell someone you trust—a close friend, doctor or nurse, counselor, or clergy member—about your dilemma. Letting someone else know can be a relief, and the person you tell can help you get in touch with support services such as crisis hot lines, domestic violence programs, legal aid services, and shelters for battered women and children. These services offer counseling that can help you understand the situation and decide what to do.

The next step is making sure you and any children you have are safe. Make a fast-action plan so you and your children can leave quickly if you ever need to. Here are key steps in an exit plan:

- Pack a suitcase to store with a friend or neighbor. Include a change of clothes for you and your children and an extra set of keys to the house and car.
- Keep important items in a safe place so you can take them with you on short notice. These include prescription medications; identification such as birth certificates, social security cards, and driver's license; cash, a checkbook, savings account book, and credit cards; and a special toy for each child.
- Know exactly where you will go and how to get there at any time of the day.
- Know what you will do if you can't escape the violence— go to the doctor or emergency room, tell the doctor how you were hurt, and ask for a copy of your medical record in case you want to file charges later.

■ Call the police—physical abuse is a crime, even if you are living with or married to the abuser.

Learn to recognize danger signs so you can use your exit plan to avoid being hurt. Signs can include your partner having a weapon or threatening to use one, threatening or hurting children or other members of the family, forcing you to have sex, or showing less guilt and remorse after a violent act.

No one deserves to be abused: not you, not your fetus, and not your children. If your partner has begun or continues to abuse you, talk to someone and start taking steps to end the violence.

Questions to Consider...

■ Can I start or continue an exercise program during pregnancy?

■ Is it safe for me to work while I'm pregnant?

■ Should I change my travel plans while I'm pregnant?

■ Do my partner and I need to change our sexual practices during pregnancy?

■ What can I do to protect myself and my fetus from harmful agents or situations?

Chapter 9

Nutrition

Eating habits and choices are personal. What you eat is influenced by your likes and dislikes, your family, your attitudes and beliefs, the price of foods, and what's available. It's hard to start a new diet if other family members are not sharing it, if you don't like it, or if it means giving up lifelong traditions and habits.

Pregnancy is an important time to examine the foods in your daily diet. You should consider what you eat, how it provides nutrition to your fetus, and how it gives you the calories for your own needs and energy. Women all over the world with many different food habits have healthy babies. The total number of calories and the content of what you eat are the key factors.

A Healthy Diet

The Food Guide Pyramid

A way to be sure you are eating a balanced diet is to follow the Food Guide Pyramid developed by the U.S. Department of Agriculture. The pyramid offers guidelines to help you eat foods that give you the nutrients you need and the right amount of calories to stay at a healthy weight. It stresses a diet that is low in fat, sugar, and cholesterol and high in vegetables, fruits, and grain products. The food pyramid contains six food groups:

■ *Bread, cereal, rice, and pasta.* This group provides complex carbohydrates (starches), which are an important source of energy, and vitamins, minerals, and fiber. One serving equals 1 slice of bread; 1 ounce of cold cereal; or ½ cup of cooked cereal, rice, or pasta. Choose whole-grain products

117

such as whole-wheat bread. Look for foods made with less fat or sugar such as bread, English muffins, rice, and pasta.

■ *Vegetables.* This group provides vitamins A and C, folate, and minerals such as iron and magnesium. Vegetables are low in fat and contain fiber. One serving equals 1 cup of raw, leafy vegetables; ½ cup of other cooked or raw vegetables; or ¾ cup of vegetable juice. Choose a variety:

—Dark-green leafy vegetables (spinach, romaine lettuce, broccoli)
—Deep-yellow vegetables (carrots, sweet potatoes)
—Starchy vegetables (potatoes, corn, peas)

■ *Fruits.* This group provides vitamins A and C, potassium, and fiber. One serving equals 1 medium apple, banana, or orange; ½ cup of chopped, cooked, or canned fruit; or ¾ cup of fruit juice. Choose fresh fruits, fruit juices, and frozen, canned, or dried fruit. Eat vitamin C-rich citrus fruits, melons, and berries often. Choose fruit juices instead of fruit drinks.

■ *Milk, yogurt, and cheese.* This group is a major source of protein, calcium, phosphorus, and vitamins. Calcium is especially important in pregnancy and while you are breast-feeding. One serving equals 1 cup of milk or yogurt, 1½ ounces of natural cheese, or 2 ounces of processed cheese. If you don't like milk, choose items made from milk such as yogurt, cottage cheese, sliced cheese, or ice cream. Choose low-fat, skim, or part-skim items whenever possible.

■ *Meat, poultry, fish, dry beans, eggs, and nuts.* These foods provide B vitamins, protein, iron, and zinc. Protein and iron are important during pregnancy because the fetus needs enough of each to develop normally. One serving equals 2–3 ounces of cooked lean meat, poultry, or fish. For the other foods in this group, count ½ cup of cooked dry beans, 1 egg, or 2 tablespoons of peanut butter as 1 ounce of lean meat. Choose lean meats and trim off fat and skin before cooking. Use low-fat cooking methods such as baking, poaching, or broiling.

■ *Fats, oils, and sweets.* These contain calories, but few vitamins or minerals. Fat should make up no more than 30% of

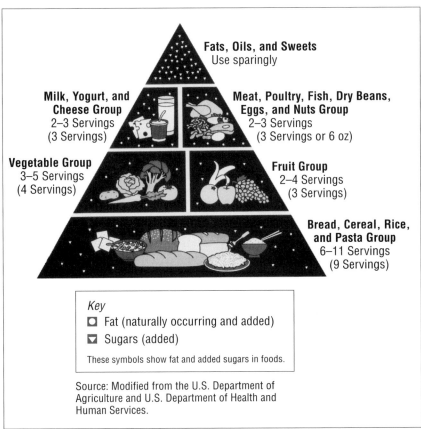

Fats, Oils, and Sweets
Use sparingly

Milk, Yogurt, and Cheese Group
2–3 Servings
(3 Servings)

Meat, Poultry, Fish, Dry Beans, Eggs, and Nuts Group
2–3 Servings
(3 Servings or 6 oz)

Vegetable Group
3–5 Servings
(4 Servings)

Fruit Group
2–4 Servings
(3 Servings)

Bread, Cereal, Rice, and Pasta Group
6–11 Servings
(9 Servings)

Key
◻ Fat (naturally occurring and added)
◥ Sugars (added)
These symbols show fat and added sugars in foods.

Source: Modified from the U.S. Department of Agriculture and U.S. Department of Health and Human Services.

This is a guide to help men and nonpregnant women choose foods that will give them the nutrients they need. Because a pregnant woman needs extra calories, she should get at least the number of servings shown in parentheses after the standard servings.

your daily calories. Try to choose low-fat foods and limit your use of butter, margarine, salad dressings, and gravies. Eat fewer foods that are high in sugar such as candies, sweet desserts, and soft drinks.

Essential Nutrients

Every diet should include proteins, carbohydrates (sugars and starches), fats, vitamins, and minerals. Your body uses these nutrients for growth and repair. To be sure your diet gives you the right amount, you need to know which foods are good sources of each.

When you look at the labels on boxes, cans, and bottles, you'll often see the initials RDA. This stands for Recommended Daily Allowance. RDAs are the levels of nutrients almost every healthy person needs on a daily basis. If you consume less than the daily RDAs, it does not necessarily mean you have a poor diet. But if your diet provides nutrients in amounts equal to the RDAs, it is very likely that you are eating right. You do not need to get 100% of the RDA in one serving of food. During pregnancy, the RDAs are higher for most nutrients. If you eat a variety of foods and eat enough servings of foods from the Food Guide Pyramid, you will be eating a very good diet.

Recommended Daily Dietary Allowances for Adolescent and Adult Nonpregnant, Pregnant, and Lactating Women

Nutrient (unit)	Nonpregnant			Pregnant	Lactating
	15–18 yr	19–24 yr	25–50 yr		
Protein (g)	44	46	50	60	65
Calcium (mg)	1,200	1,200	800	1,200	1,200
Phosphorus (mg)	1,200	1,200	800	1,200	1,200
Magnesium (mg)	300	280	280	320	355
Iron (mg)	15	15	15	30	15
Zinc (mg)	12	12	12	15	19
Iodine (µg)	150	150	150	175	200
Selenium (µg)	50	55	55	65	75
Vitamin A (µg)	800	800	800	800	1,300
Vitamin D (µg)	10	10	5	10	10
Vitamin E (mg)	8	8	8	10	12
Vitamin C (mg)	60	60	65	65	65
Thiamin (mg)	1.1	1.1	1.1	1.5	1.6
Riboflavin (mg)	1.3	1.3	1.3	1.6	1.8
Niacin (mg)	15	15	15	17	20
Vitamin B_6 (mg)	1.5	1.6	1.6	2.2	2.1
Folic acid (µg)	180	180	180	400	280
Vitamin B_{12} (µg)	2	2	2	2.2	2.6

Adapted from *Recommended Dietary Allowances,* © 1989, by the National Academy of Sciences National Academy Press, Washington, DC.

Protein

Protein is made of long strings of chemicals called amino acids. The body can produce all but 8 of the 22 amino acids it needs for health and growth. The eight amino acids the body can't produce are called the essential amino acids, because they must be provided by what you eat.

Protein gives you nutrients needed to grow, maintain, and repair body tissues such as muscles. It is also needed to make hemoglobin, the chemical that carries oxygen in the blood and gives blood its red color. Antibodies are proteins that fight infection.

Adults and all but the youngest children should eat 45 grams of high-quality protein each day, and pregnant women should eat 60 grams. High-quality protein comes from animals—meats, fish, poultry, and milk and other dairy products. Animal foods rich in protein include beef, pork, ham, and canned tuna (3-ounce servings each provide 27 grams of protein), broiled chicken (3 ounces provides 22 grams of protein), and low-fat milk (1 cup provides 11 grams of protein).

Plant products such as grains and legumes can also be good sources of protein. Because they don't contain all the needed amino acids, however, they must be carefully paired with other foods to provide a complete source of protein. Grains or legumes can be paired with animal proteins (cheese pizza, meat chili with beans, or milk and cereal) or with each other (black-eyed peas or beans and rice, peanut butter sandwich, or lima beans and corn) to give you a more complete source of protein.

Carbohydrates

Sugars provide the body's main source of energy. There are two types of sugar. The simple sugars, like **glucose**, are ready to be used by the body right away and thus provide the quickest form of energy. Sources of this type of sugar are table sugar, honey, syrup, fruit juices, and hard candies. Simple sugars are often found in processed foods.

The other type of sugar is starches. They are the storage form of simple sugars and are a long-lasting energy source. Examples of foods that contain starches are grains, fruits, and vegetables. Good sources are bread, rice, pasta, and starchy vegetables such as potatoes, yucca, or corn.

Foods rich in starch also provide fiber, the tough part of plants that gives them support. Fiber speeds your digestion and helps keep you "regular." Fiber can also help your body rid itself more quickly of extra amounts of cholesterol and fats. You should eat about 20–30 grams (about 1 ounce) of fiber each day.

Carbohydrates should make up more than half of your total diet. Simple sugars do not provide many nutrients, so they should be just a small part of your diet. Rely more on starches, which provide both energy and fiber.

Fats

Fats are either saturated or unsaturated. Saturated fats, which are often solid at room temperature, come from meat and dairy products and some vegetable fats. They should make up less than one third of the total fat in your diet, or no more than 10% of your daily calories. Palm oil and coconut oil are vegetable fats that are high in saturated fats. Unsaturated fats tend to be liquid at room temperature and come mostly from plants and vegetables, such as olive oil, canola oil, peanut oil, and sunflower oil. Fish oil is also unsaturated.

Fats provide a very concentrated source of energy. This also means they are high in calories. For example, while a gram of protein or carbohydrate provides 4 calories, a gram of fat provides 9 calories. In addition to giving you energy, fats help the body use vitamins A, D, E, and K (the fat-soluble vitamins), proteins, and carbohydrates. Any extra fat not used by the body is stored as fat tissue, to be used later when energy is needed.

Obvious sources of fat are the butter, margarine, lard, shortening, and oil that you cook with or put on your food. However, fat is a part of many other foods as well—meats, baked goods, and even nondairy coffee creamer. Choose unsaturated fats more often and saturated fats less often. For example, choose corn oil margarine instead of butter. Remember, though, that even if a package is labeled "no cholesterol" or "contains no animal fat," it could still contain saturated fats such as palm oil.

Water

Water is not often thought of as a nutrient, but life cannot exist without it. It is used to build new tissue, carry nutrients and waste products, aid digestion, and help chemical reactions. One half to three fourths of your body's weight is water. In addition to the water that is used by your body, some is lost through sweat and urine and even breathing. To be sure your body is getting enough water, you should drink six to eight glasses of liquids each day. Because they often contain simple sugars and caffeine, choose coffee, tea, and sodas less often than water.

Nutritional Needs During Pregnancy

During pregnancy your body has special nutritional needs that must be met. Because you are providing all of the food for your fetus, you must eat more calories. Your body also needs to produce more blood to be able to circulate some through the placenta. This means you will need more iron, protein, and folic acid. These nutrients also build bones and muscles. The fetus's growing bones need minerals such as calcium and phosphorus. If you already have a balanced diet, it is a simple matter to add the extra nutrients the fetus needs.

Calories and Weight Gain

Both your weight before you get pregnant and the amount of weight you gain during pregnancy determine the baby's birth weight. For example, women who are underweight should gain up

Where Does the Weight Go?

In pregnancy, your body must store nutrients and increase the amount of blood and other fluids it produces. Here is where the weight will go:

7 pounds	Maternal stores (fat, protein, and other nutrients)
4 pounds	Increased fluid
4 pounds	Increased blood
2 pounds	Breast growth
2 pounds	Uterus
7½ pounds	Baby
2 pounds	Amniotic fluid
1½ pounds	Placenta

to 40 pounds, but women who are very overweight need only gain 15 pounds. Recommended weight gains are based on your overall body mass, which is a calculation of weight for height (see Chapter 1 for a list of recommended weights by height).

Women who are underweight during pregnancy are more likely to have small babies. Babies who have a low weight at birth (less than 5½ pounds) have a harder time adjusting to life outside the uterus. Proper eating and weight gain will help reduce the chance of having an underweight baby. Labor is not made easier because your baby is small or underweight. You should never gain less weight than is expected to try to have a smaller baby or more weight to have a cute, plump baby.

Recommended Weight Gain in Pregnancy

Condition	Weight gain (pounds)
Underweight	28–40
Normal weight	25–35
Overweight	15–25
Obese	15
Carrying Twins	35–45

If you gain weight as you should while you're pregnant, your baby has a greater chance of gaining weight properly, too. You are not really "eating for two," though. The average woman needs to add only about 300 calories to her daily diet when she is pregnant. This is only an average, however, and you may need to eat more or less than this amount. For example, a teenager (who needs to fuel her own body's growth as well as her fetus's), an underweight woman, and a woman expecting twins should eat more than the average.

Although women who are overweight can have problems during pregnancy, it isn't a good idea to try to lose weight while you are pregnant. You may deprive your baby of needed nutrients. It is best to try to lose weight before you get pregnant and then again after birth.

Eating snacks during the day is a good way to get needed nutrition and extra calories. Pick snacks that have the right nutrients and are not high in sugar or fat. Fruit, cereal, and yogurt are healthier snacks than candy, soda, and potato chips.

You may feel more comfortable, especially during the later stages of pregnancy, eating small meals six times a day. To make these mini-meals, just divide the number of servings of the basic foods needed each day into smaller portions. Milk and half a sandwich made with meat, chicken, fish, peanut butter, or cheese with lettuce and tomato make an excellent mini-meal. Other ideas are low-fat milk and fresh fruits, cheese and crackers, and soup.

Iron

Iron is a mineral used by the body to make hemoglobin. Hemoglobin is the protein in the red blood cells that carries oxygen to the tissues and fetus. Just like other cells in the body, red blood cells die and are replaced by new cells in an ongoing process of renewal. The body is able to save the iron in blood cells when they die to use in making more hemoglobin.

Women lose iron when they bleed during their menstrual periods. This means few women have large enough stores of iron before they become pregnant. Most have trouble getting the extra iron they need each day during pregnancy. Women need more iron in their diet during pregnancy to support the growth of the fetus and to produce extra blood. Eating foods rich in iron can provide the iron you need. Many women find they cannot get all the iron they need from their diet, however. You may need to take an iron supplement to be sure you get enough of this important mineral.

Folic Acid

Like iron, folic acid is used to make the extra blood you must produce. It's hard to get all the extra folic acid you need just from your diet, so you will probably need to take pills or supplements of this vitamin, too. Folic acid can also help prevent neural tube defects when it is taken before conception and early pregnancy. It is recommended that all women of childbearing age should have 0.4 mg of folic acid daily. Women who have had a child with a neural tube defect are more likely to have another child with the problem. They are advised to take higher doses of folic acid—4 mg daily—preferably starting 1 month before they plan to become pregnant and continuing through the first 3 months of pregnancy. This amount should be taken alone, not in multivitamin preparations, to avoid taking harmful high levels of other vitamins.

Protein

Just as you need protein for the growth and repair of your muscles, so does your fetus. This extra need, plus your need to produce

Vitamins and Minerals

Nutrient	Functions in Body	Food Sources
Vitamins		
A	Needed for normal vision in dim light; prevents eye diseases; needed for growth of bones and teeth	Green, leafy vegetables; dark yellow vegetables (eg, carrots and sweet potatoes); whole milk; liver
Thiamine (B_1)	Helps body digest carbohydrates; needed for normal functioning of nervous system	Whole-grain or enriched breads and cereals; fish, pork, poultry, lean meat; milk
Riboflavin (B_2)	Helps body release energy to cells; promotes healthy skin and eyes	Milk; whole-grain or enriched breads and cereals; liver; green, leafy vegetables
B_6	Helps form red blood cells; helps body use protein, fat, and carbohydrates	Beef liver, pork, ham; whole-grain cereals; bananas
B_{12}	Maintains nervous system; needed to form red blood cells	Liver, meat, fish, poultry; milk (found only in animal foods—vegetarians should take a supplement)
C	Speeds healing of wounds and bones; increases resistance to infection; needed to form collagen (flexible tissue that helps support body)	Citrus fruits (eg, oranges, lemons, grapefruit); strawberries; broccoli; tomatoes
D	Helps body use calcium and phosphorus; needed for strong bones and teeth	Fortified milk; fish liver oils (you also get vitamin D when you're out in the sunshine)
E	Needed for use of vitamin A; helps body form and use red blood cells and muscles	Vegetable oils; whole-grain cereals; wheat germ; green, leafy vegetables
Folic acid	Needed to produce blood and protein; helps some enzymes function	Green, leafy vegetables; dark yellow fruits and vegetables; liver; legumes and nuts
Niacin	Promotes healthy skin, nerves, and digestion; helps the body use carbohydrates	Meat, liver, poultry, fish; whole-grain or enriched cereals
Minerals		
Calcium	Needed for strong bones and teeth; helps in blood clotting; needed for normal muscle and nerve function	Milk and milk products; sardines and salmon with bones; collard, kale, mustard, and turnip greens

Vitamins and Minerals *(continued)*

Nutrient	Functions in Body	Food Sources
Minerals *(continued)*		
Iodine	Needed to produce hormones that regulate body's energy use	Seafood; iodized salt
Iron	Needed to make hemoglobin; prevents anemia; increases resistance to infection	Red meat, liver; dried beans and peas; enriched cereals; prune juice
Magnesium	Needed for nerve and muscle function; helps body use carbo-hydrates	Legumes; whole-grain cereals; milk; meat; green vegetables
Phosphorus	Needed for strong bones and teeth	Milk and milk products; meat, poultry, fish; whole-grain cereals; legumes
Zinc	Needed to produce some enzymes and insulin	Meat; liver; oysters and other seafood; milk; whole-grain cereals

more blood, means that you should eat about 60 grams of protein each day. By choosing foods high in protein, you should be able to get the extra protein you and your fetus need.

Calcium and Phosphorus

Calcium and phosphorus are used to make the bones of the fetus. You need to get 1,200 mg of each every day—400 mg more than you needed before pregnancy if you're over 25. Drinking an extra quart of milk each day will give you the extra calcium you need. Milk and other dairy products are the best sources of calcium, but other sources include sardines, salmon with bones, and greens (such as collard, kale, mustard, or turnip greens). If you cannot or do not eat milk products, ask your doctor or nurse to suggest ways you can get the calcium you need.

Prenatal Vitamins

Except for iron, folic acid, and maybe calcium, you can usually get all the vitamins, minerals, and other nutrients you need during pregnancy by eating sensibly. In most cases, vitamin pills are not necessary. However, if your health care provider thinks your diet may not be supplying all the nutrients you and your fetus need, he or she may prescribe a prenatal multivitamin and mineral supplement.

If prenatal vitamins are prescribed, take them only as directed. Large doses of vitamins can be dangerous. Do not exceed the RDAs without the advice of your doctor or nurse. This is especially true of the fat-soluble vitamins A and D.

Nutrition During Breast-Feeding

During pregnancy, your body stores extra nutrients to prepare you for breast-feeding your baby. After the baby is born, you need food for your own body plus extra food to produce milk for the baby. You'll need about 200 calories more than you needed during pregnancy, or about 500 more than you needed before pregnancy. Your baby will drink about a pint of breast milk a day, increasing to a quart a day. That amounts to one extra serving of protein in your diet.

It's important that you keep eating enough protein and calcium while you are breast-feeding. Eat a variety of nourishing foods, as outlined in the Food Guide Pyramid.

Special Concerns

Most women will get all the nutrients they need during pregnancy if they eat a sensible diet and take vitamins as prescribed. However, some women need more nutrients than a normal diet provides. If you fit into any of the following categories, you may need a special diet.

Women with Poor Nutrient Stores

A pregnancy is a big adjustment for your body. If you have had three or more pregnancies within 2 years (including induced abortions and miscarriages), you probably have not had a chance to build up a store of nutrients between pregnancies. If you had a complicated pregnancy or a low-birth-weight infant, or if you are underweight, your nutrient stores may be poor. Talk to your health care provider about what extra nutrients you need and how to get them.

Special Diets

If you follow a special self-selected diet, you may not be getting all the nutrients you need. A vegetarian diet that includes milk, cheese, cereals, nuts, and seeds in addition to vegetables and fruits can suffice for a pregnant woman. But if you eat a vegetarian diet, it must be planned carefully. A vegetarian diet that has no milk in it or is otherwise very restricted does not supply all the nutrients a pregnant woman needs. If you are on a vegetarian diet, discuss food choices with your doctor or nurse, nutritionist, or dietitian. You may need to take supplements to get all the nutrients your body needs.

During pregnancy, some women feel strong urges to eat non-food items such as laundry starch, clay, or chalk. This is called *pica*, and it can be very common. Some women also get unusual food cravings. If you feel these urges, tell your health care provider.

If you have an eating disorder, you need special help. One disorder is anorexia nervosa—refusing to eat because you think you are too fat, even if you are far too thin. Another is bulimia, in which you eat large amounts of food and then make yourself vomit before your body can absorb the food. Both of these disorders can be life-threatening. They can starve your body of key nutrients and can harm your fetus. Your body will undergo a great deal of stress as it changes during your pregnancy, so it is important to tell your doctor or nurse if you have or have had an eating disorder. You should get counseling to help deal with the disorder.

Women Who Fail to Gain Weight

Women who suffer from eating disorders and women who are afraid of getting fat may have trouble putting on the extra pounds they need. During pregnancy your taste for certain foods may change. You may suddenly dislike foods you were fond of before. The extra room the baby takes up may mean your stomach feels full more quickly. If you have any problems that get in the way of eating balanced meals and gaining weight, ask your health care provider for advice.

Women with Certain Diseases

Some women have diseases that are long lasting and can cause problems with nutrition. The medicine used to treat the disorder may affect how the body absorbs food. Some diseases call for special diets that may make it hard for you to get all the nutrients you need. Examples include kidney disease, diabetes, and phenylketonuria, in which a person lacks a certain enzyme that processes foods. Your health care provider should be aware of any disease you have that could affect your nutrition. He or she may be able to change your medicine, recommend a different diet, or take other steps to help you get the nutrients you need.

Questions to Consider...

- Am I eating the right foods to give me the vitamins, nutrients, and calories I need during pregnancy?
- Am I eating too much fat?
- How much weight should I gain during pregnancy?
- Should I take a vitamin–mineral supplement?
- Do I need to change my diet?

Chapter 10

Changes During Pregnancy

Before pregnancy, the space inside your uterus is smaller than the round end of a teaspoon. As your fetus grows, your uterus expands to as much as 1,000 times its original size. This amount of growth, centered in one area, affects other parts of your body.

Many of the changes in your body that occur during pregnancy are triggered by hormones (substances made by the body to control the functions of various organs) that nurture the fetus and prepare for childbirth. These changes have a physical and emotional impact and may cause discomforts. Some may occur only in the early weeks of pregnancy. Others may happen only as you get closer to the end. Still others may appear early and then go away, only to come back later. This is normal and usually does not mean anything is wrong. Every woman's pregnancy is unique, as are her responses to it.

Talk with your doctor or other members of your health care team about your concerns, discomforts, and questions. They may be able to suggest things you can do to feel more comfortable.

Physical Changes

Backache

Backache is one of the most common complaints during pregnancy. It is usually caused by the strain put on the back muscles and by changes in your posture. Here are some tips to help lessen back pain:

- Wear low-heeled (but not flat) shoes.
- Avoid lifting heavy objects.
- Don't bend over from the waist to pick things up—squat down, bending your knees and keeping your back straight.
- Don't stay on your feet for long periods. If you must, place one foot on a stool or box.
- Sit in chairs with good back support, or use a small pillow behind the low part of your back.
- Arrange things at home and at work at a comfortable level, so that you don't have to bend or stretch too much.
- Check that your bed is firm enough. If it is too soft, have someone help you place a board between the mattress and box spring.
- Sleep on your side with a pillow between your legs for support.
- Apply heat or cold to the painful area or massage it.
- Special exercises may be helpful (see "A Healthy Back," Chapter 8).

Breast Changes

Starting early in pregnancy, your breasts undergo many changes to prepare for breast-feeding your baby. In fact, changes to your breasts may be one of the first signs that you are pregnant. By 6–8 weeks of pregnancy, your breasts may be noticeably larger. This is because the fat layer of your breasts is getting thicker and the number of milk glands is increasing.

Your breasts may continue to grow in size and weight throughout the first 3 months of pregnancy. Your breasts will feel firm and tender. As your breasts grow, wearing a bra that fits well will give you support. As breasts grow, their blood supply increases, and the veins close to the surface get larger and more noticeable. You may feel some tingling, or your breasts may be sensitive to touch.

Also early in pregnancy, your nipples and areolas (the darker skin around your nipples) will darken. Your nipples may stick out more now. Your areolas also grow larger. On the surface of the areolas are small glands called Montgomery tubercles. They pro-

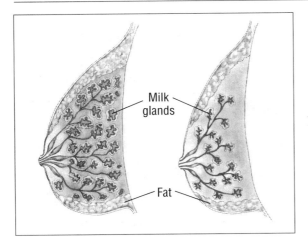

Milk glands

Fat

During pregnancy (*left*), the fat layer of your breasts thickens and the number of milk glands increases, making them larger than before pregnancy (*right*).

duce an oily substance that helps protect the nipple from cracking or drying out. The Montgomery tubercles now become raised and bumpy.

Some women's nipples do not stick out but instead are recessed (**retracted nipple**). If you have retracted nipples and you plan to breast-feed, your doctor or nurse may recommend that you try massaging the nipples so they protrude more. You can also gently press on either side of the areola with your forefingers. In time, this will cause the nipple to stick out.

By about 12–14 weeks of pregnancy, your breasts may start making **colostrum**, the fluid that will feed your baby for the first few days before your milk flows. This doesn't happen in every woman, so don't be concerned if you don't produce colostrum before delivery. Colostrum contains water, proteins, minerals, and antibodies that protect your baby from disease. Early in pregnancy, the colostrum will probably be thick and yellow, but toward the end of pregnancy, it will become pale and nearly colorless. Colostrum may leak from your breasts by itself or if you massage your breasts. It also tends to leak out during times of sexual excitement.

Breathing Problems

As the fetus grows inside your uterus, the uterus expands and takes up more room in your abdomen. By about 31–34 weeks of pregnancy, the uterus has grown so large that it presses the digestive organs and the diaphragm (a flat, strong muscle that aids in breathing) up toward the lungs. Because the lungs do not have as much

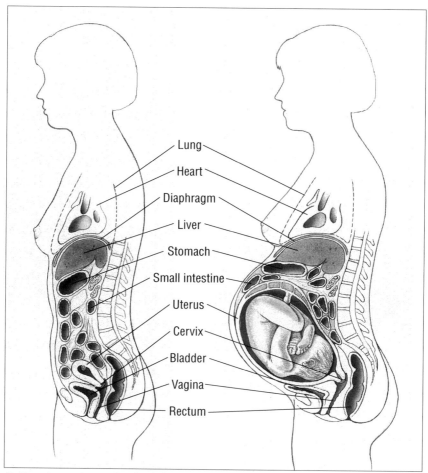

Lung
Heart
Diaphragm
Liver
Stomach
Small intestine
Uterus
Cervix
Bladder
Vagina
Rectum

As the uterus grows from the beginning (*left*) to the end (*right*) of pregnancy, it takes up more room in your abdomen, pressing the digestive organs and diaphragm up toward the lungs.

room to expand as before, you may find you are short of breath. Even if you feel you are not getting enough air, you need not worry about the fetus. It will get all the oxygen it needs.

A few weeks before you give birth, the fetus's head will move down in the uterus, or "drop," and press against the cervix. This usually happens between 36 and 38 weeks of pregnancy in women who have not been pregnant before, but in women who have already been pregnant, it may not happen until the beginning of labor. When the fetus drops, you will find it easier to breathe because the uterus will not be pressing as much on your other organs. This is called "lightening."

If being short of breath makes you uncomfortable, here are some ideas to try:

- Move a little more slowly, so your heart and lungs don't have to work so hard.
- Sit up straight.
- Sleep propped up.

Constipation

At least half of all pregnant women seem to have problems with constipation. One reason for this may be changes in hormones that slow the movement of food through the digestive tract. Sometimes iron supplements can cause constipation. During the last part of pregnancy, pressure on your rectum from your uterus may add to the problem. Here are some suggestions that may help:

- Drink plenty of liquids—at least 6–8 glasses of water each day, including 1–2 glasses of fruit juices such as prune juice.
- Eat food high in fiber, such as raw fruits and vegetables and bran cereals.
- Exercise daily—walking is a good form of exercise.

Headache

Headaches are common during pregnancy. Usually headaches do not signal a serious problem. How often they occur and how bad they are can vary. It is important to discuss with your health care team what medications you can use for the headache. You should contact your doctor if your headache does not go away, returns very often, is very severe, causes blurry vision or spots in front of your eyes, or is accompanied by nausea.

Fatigue

Many women feel very tired during pregnancy—especially in the beginning and at the end. If you get enough exercise and rest (including naps) and eat a healthy diet, you are likely to feel better.

Frequent Urination

You may feel the need to urinate often during pregnancy. This is mainly caused by pressure from the growing uterus on the bladder and increased urine production. Even though your bladder may be nearly empty, the pressure produces the same feeling as when the bladder is full of urine.

As your uterus grows and rises higher into your abdomen, the symptoms may go away. But in the last month or so you may need to urinate more often as the fetus drops into the pelvis and again presses against the bladder. Especially toward the end of pregnancy, you may find that the need to urinate wakes you up several times during the night. If the pressure of your uterus on your bladder causes you to leak some urine, you can do special exercises called Kegel exercises that help strengthen the muscles around the urethra (the tube that carries urine from the bladder out of the body). If you have pain when you urinate or if you often feel you must urinate right away, talk to your doctor. You could have an infection.

Kegel Exercises

Kegel exercises, or perineal exercises, are used to strengthen the muscles that surround the openings of the urethra, vagina, and anus. Your doctor or nurse can help you learn to perform these exercises. If you contract these muscles for about 10 seconds, 10–20 times in a row, at least three times a day, in time you will begin to notice some improvement in your ability to hold your urine.

Groin or Lower Abdominal Pain

As the uterus grows, the round ligaments (bands of fibrous tissue along both sides of the uterus) that support it are pulled and stretched. You may sometimes feel this stretching as either sharp pains in your abdomen, usually on one side or the other, or a dull ache. The pains are most common between 18 and 24 weeks of pregnancy. To help prevent these pains, avoid quick changes of position, especially when you are turning at the waist. When you do feel a pain, bend toward it to relieve it. Resting and changing your position also seem to help. If you have abdominal pain that persists or becomes more intense, call your doctor.

Hemorrhoids

Very often pregnant women who are constipated also have hemorrhoids. Hemorrhoids are varicose (or swollen) veins of the rectum. They are often painful. Straining during bowel movements and having very hard stools may make hemorrhoids worse and can sometimes cause them to protrude from the rectum.

Do not take drugstore cures while you are pregnant without first checking with your doctor or nurse. Hemorrhoids usually improve after the baby is born. Several things can help give relief or avoid the problem in the first place:

■ Avoid getting constipated.

■ Eat a high-fiber diet.

■ Drink plenty of liquids.

Indigestion

Indigestion is commonly called heartburn, but it does not mean that anything is wrong with your heart. It is a burning feeling that starts in the stomach and seems to rise into the throat. It occurs when digested food from your stomach, which contains acid, is pushed up into your esophagus (the tube leading from the throat to the stomach). Liquids that you drink also take up space in your stomach, so they can also add to the problem.

Changes that take place in your body during pregnancy may worsen indigestion. Changes in your hormone levels slow digestion and relax the muscle that normally prevents the digested food and acids in your stomach from entering the esophagus. In addition, your growing uterus presses up on your stomach.

To help relieve heartburn, try the following:

■ Eat five or six small meals a day instead of two or three large ones. (A glass of fluid may be equal in volume to a small meal, so avoid drinking large amounts of fluids with meals.)

■ Avoid foods that cause gas, such as spicy or greasy foods.

■ Do not eat or drink several hours before bedtime.

■ Wait 2 hours after eating before exercising.

■ Antacids may be helpful. Ask your doctor or nurse to suggest a type.

Insomnia

After the first few months, you may find it hard to sleep at night. As your abdomen grows larger, it may be hard to find a comfortable position. To get the rest you need:

- Take a shower or warm bath at bedtime (but be careful not to slip; the changes in your body can make it hard to keep your balance in a wet tub).
- Try the relaxation tips you learned in childbirth classes.
- Lie on your side with a pillow under your abdomen and another between your legs.
- Limit your daytime rest.

Leg Cramps

In the last 3 months of pregnancy, you may find that you have leg cramps. Although cramps were once thought to be caused by a problem with the amount of calcium in a pregnant woman's diet, this is no longer thought to be true. Stretching your legs before going to bed can help relieve cramps. Avoid pointing your toes when stretching or exercising.

Mouth and Tooth Changes

During pregnancy, the extra hormones in your body may cause your gums to swell and bleed. Floss and brush regularly to keep your teeth in good shape. Having a dental checkup early in pregnancy is a good idea to be sure your mouth is healthy. See your dentist right away if you have a dental problem during pregnancy. Putting off dental work can cause problems, especially if teeth or gums get infected. When you go for dental visits, be sure to let your dentist know you are pregnant. Local *anesthesia* and dental X-rays do not pose a risk during pregnancy.

You may notice an increase in saliva during pregnancy, causing your mouth to water more than you're used to. It is not known why this happens. You may also find that your taste in food changes. Foods you used to like may taste different. Foods you didn't care for may be appealing. You may crave certain foods. Try to keep eating a balanced diet. Tell your doctor or nurse about cravings for nonfood items (see "Special Diets," Chapter 9).

Nausea and Vomiting

Nausea and vomiting are most often caused by changes in hormones. They typically occur during the first 3 months of pregnancy, but sometimes happen later, too. Although they are called morning sickness, these symptoms can occur any time during the day, especially when the stomach is empty. Here are some tips to relieve nausea:

- Get up slowly in the morning and sit on the side of the bed for a few minutes.
- Eat dry toast or crackers first thing in the morning.
- Eat five or six small meals each day. Try not to let your stomach get completely empty.
- Avoid unpleasant smells.
- Avoid drinking citrus juice, milk, coffee, and tea.

If nausea or vomiting becomes severe, tell your doctor. Check with your doctor or nurse before taking any medication.

Nosebleeds

During pregnancy, the membranes inside your nose may swell, dry out, or bleed easily. Because of this, some women get stuffy noses or frequent nosebleeds. To deal with this problem, you can try drinking extra fluids and using a humidifier in your home. You can also use a gentle lubricant around the edges of your nostrils, such as petroleum jelly.

Numbness and Tingling

As the uterus grows, it rests on some of the nerves that go to your legs. Some nerves may also get pressed if your legs are swollen from retaining water. This pressure may cause numbness or tingling, usually in the legs or toes. These symptoms are rarely serious and go away after the baby is born. Sometimes the arms or hands are also affected.

A condition called carpal tunnel syndrome can cause a burning, tingling feeling in one or both hands and can make your fingers feel numb. Wearing a special splint can help relieve the discomfort. Some women also get numbness and tingling caused by hyperventilation, or overbreathing. Anxiety can make you feel short of breath, which causes you to breathe deeper and faster. If you hyperventilate, you may also feel sweaty and dizzy and your heart may pound. If you feel anxious and get these symptoms, breathe into a paper bag for a few minutes to restore the balance of oxygen and carbon dioxide in your body.

Skin and Hair Changes

Changes in hormones during pregnancy can cause skin problems that may be annoying but are not harmful. Some women get brownish, uneven marks around their eyes and over the nose and cheeks. This is called *chloasma*. Being in the sun tends to increase these marks. They usually disappear or fade after delivery, when hormone levels go back to normal.

In many women, a line running from the top to the bottom of the abdomen becomes dark. This is called the *linea nigra*. In others, reddish streaks or stretch marks may appear on the abdomen and breasts as they grow. They are caused by the skin stretching to support the growing fetus. There is no way to prevent stretch marks. They may slowly fade after pregnancy.

Two conditions that often appear together are redness of the palms and spider veins—usually small, red spots on the skin with lines branching outward. These also lessen soon after the baby is born. Some women find that their skin breaks out early in pregnancy, especially women who tend to get pimples before their periods. The best way to treat the mild acne of pregnancy is to wash your face often with a mild cleanser.

Changes in your hair may occur during pregnancy. Some women notice that their hair gets thicker. In others, it may become thinner. A few weeks after delivery, you may find that you lose large amounts of hair. This is not unusual. Your hair will soon return to its normal growth cycle.

Swelling and Varicose Veins

A certain amount of swelling (called *edema*) is normal during pregnancy. It occurs most often in the legs. Elevating the legs usually makes the swelling go away by the next morning. Swelling can begin during the last few months of pregnancy, and it may occur more often in the summer. Let your doctor or nurse know if you have swelling in your hands or face, because this may be a sign of another problem. A clue that your hands are swollen is that your rings are too tight. Never take medications (water pills) for swelling unless they have been prescribed for you.

Your veins can swell. This condition is called varicose veins. They appear most often in the legs but can also appear near the vulva and vagina. They are caused by the weight of your uterus pressing on your veins. The tendency to have varicose veins is inherited. They often occur if you must stand or sit for a long time. Varicose veins are usually not serious but can cause aching and soreness. Although varicose veins cannot be prevented, some of these suggestions may help relieve the swelling and discomfort that they cause:

- Elevate your legs when possible.
- Rest in bed on your side.
- Lie down with your legs raised on a small footstool or several pillows.
- Do not wear stockings or socks that have a tight band of elastic around the legs.
- If you must sit a lot on the job, stand up and move around from time to time.
- Try not to stand still for long periods of time.
- Exercise regularly, especially walking, swimming, or riding an exercise bike.
- Wear support pantyhose.
- Don't cross your legs when you sit.

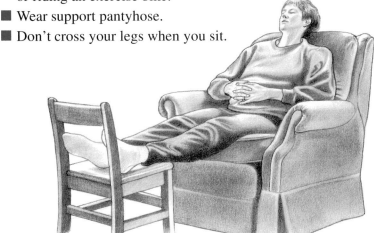

Vaginal Discharge

During pregnancy you may notice that the vaginal secretions you normally get increase in volume. This is because of increased blood flow to the skin and muscles around the vagina. Consult your doctor if the discharge is accompanied by pain, soreness, or itching in the vaginal area, or if the discharge has blood in it, is watery, or has a bad odor.

Emotional Changes

Pregnancy is a time of both physical and emotional changes. No matter how good you feel about being pregnant, you may have worries and questions. This is normal. Some women have mood swings during pregnancy. You may be fine one minute and feel like crying the next. A small problem that would normally not bother you may seem like a disaster. Although mood swings may ease after the first 12 weeks of pregnancy, you may have them throughout your pregnancy.

Physical factors also cause emotional changes. Extreme tiredness in early and late pregnancy may make you feel irritable or depressed. Fatigue is common in pregnancy and can cause or worsen feelings of sadness, especially toward the end. The extra weight you are carrying may make you feel heavy and slow. Resting and relaxing as often as you can will help improve your emotional and physical well-being.

Your moods can be hard on you, your partner, your family, and your friends. Don't blame yourself if you are often teary or short-tempered; the emotions you're feeling are hard to control. Ask loved ones to be patient and supportive.

Anxiety

Pregnant women and their partners often have fears about the pregnancy, labor and delivery, the effect of a child on their lives, and whether they will be good parents. It's quite common to have strange or scary dreams about the baby you are carrying. Usually there is nothing to worry about, but there are things you can do to ease your concerns.

Many parents-to-be worry that their child will not be normal. By far, most children are born healthy. You can ease your fears by taking steps to help ensure a healthy child: eating right; resting and exercising; avoiding drugs, alcohol, and unprotected sex with multiple partners; and getting early and regular prenatal care.

Women often feel anxious about labor and delivery, especially if they have not given birth before. Learning what to expect can be a big help. You may fear the pain and think you won't be able to stand it. You can prepare for childbirth by learning methods of breathing and relaxing, which help ease tension and pain. These methods are taught in childbirth preparation classes. Different kinds of pain medication also can help you during labor and birth. Even if you had not planned to use pain medication, don't think you have failed if you need it. You can't be a good participant in the birth of your baby if you are in a great deal of pain. Medication can help ease the pain enough so that you can do your part as you practiced.

Although the coaching and tips you get about giving birth may convince you otherwise, having a baby is a natural event. You don't get grades for how well you do when you have a baby. If you plan to use childbirth preparation techniques, don't worry about forgetting them. Instead, practice so they become second nature.

Every parent is new to parenthood at some time and must learn how to care for, feed, and bathe a baby. If this is your first child, usually a nurse or someone else at the hospital can help you learn the basics about caring for the baby before you go home. Once you're home, your family and friends will probably give you their own advice.

There are as many different ways of raising a baby as there are children. You will find the one that is right for you. Talking to other parents can help relieve some of your fears and provide practical tips you can use. Reading books or taking classes on child care can also be helpful. The baby's doctor may be able to recommend some for you.

Having a baby will mean big changes. Relationships with friends and family may be different. Your time will not be as flexible as before for doing things with other people, or your interests may shift. But, having a baby doesn't mean you will have to totally give up the life style you had before you became pregnant.

You and your partner can still enjoy many of the same activities you shared before and can now alter them to include your baby.

Stress

Stress is a part of everyone's life. Although we often think of stress as bad, it has a good side, too. Stress can create energy to meet a challenge. But too much stress—or stress that is poorly managed—can be harmful. Stress that builds up leads to distress.

Because pregnancy brings intense change, it involves a great deal of stress. It's important to recognize when the stress in your life reaches such a high level that you are having trouble coping. You can try these techniques to keep stress under control:

- Stay physically fit and exercise regularly to release tension.
- Eat a healthy diet.
- Get enough sleep.
- Stop smoking, drinking alcohol, and using drugs.
- Do muscle relaxation exercises, which involve tightening and releasing muscles throughout your body.
- Do stretching exercises.
- Listen to relaxing music.

Other techniques for coping with stress may require you to get training or visit a expert. The following have been found helpful and can be used during pregnancy:

- Guided visual imagery
- Self-hypnosis
- Meditation
- Yoga
- Biofeedback
- Mental health counseling

It is tempting to blame problems on stress, but stress can rarely be singled out as the main cause when things go wrong. You should seek help right way if your partner reacts violently to the stress of pregnancy with threats or physical abuse or if you have negative feelings toward your other children (see "The Battered Woman," Chapter 8).

Body Image

When you are pregnant, your body undergoes nearly a total remaking. It's all the more amazing because of how fast it happens. It can be hard for your mind to keep up with your body's changes. As your breasts enlarge, your waistline disappears, and your abdomen grows larger, you may have very mixed feelings. This change is an exciting, visible reminder of the new life growing inside you. There will probably be days, though, when you'll just feel fat and wonder if you'll ever return to normal. Most women have mixed feelings about the changes in their bodies. Exercise may help you feel better about how you look and, after delivery, can help you get back in shape.

Your Partner and Family

Both you and your partner share the joys, challenges, and worries of pregnancy. Together, you have many adjustments to make. Your old roles are changing, and you need to work to adapt to your new roles. Although you both may spend much of your time thinking about the baby, you need to remember to make time for each other. Try to understand and support each other. Talk openly about concerns and feelings. Pregnancy is a special time for a couple, but it can also cause stress and strains in your relationship.

Because the physical changes of pregnancy happen to the woman, it's easy to forget that the man is part of the pregnancy, too. He is making his own adjustments, getting ready to be a father. Make a special effort to include him in things. Don't shut him out. Let him be a part of your pregnancy plans. He should attend childbirth classes with you and join you in exercising, buying clothes for the baby, and getting the baby's space ready.

Some men get the same physical symptoms of pregnancy as the mother-to-be, such as weight gain, nausea, food cravings, or mood swings. Many theories try to explain why this happens, but no one knows for sure. You may find that your partner worries about the baby as much—or even more—than you do. On top of it all, he may worry about you. He may need reassurance that you are in no danger and that most babies are born healthy.

During pregnancy your sexual feelings about each other may change. Try to discuss them honestly. Talking can bring you closer and help avoid hurt and loneliness. Some couples find that they feel closer than ever during pregnancy.

Because your body may be more sensitive to touch, you may be more easily aroused. Many couples find a pregnant woman's larger breasts and rounded abdomen very sensuous. Other couples may not find sex as enjoyable now. Especially during the first and last weeks of pregnancy, when you are more likely to feel nauseated and tired, sex may seem like a big bother. Your thoughts may focus on the baby, and your sexual feelings may be pushed aside. You or your partner may worry about harming the baby if you have sex. In most cases, this will not happen, but for more guidelines, see "Sex," Chapter 8, and ask your doctor or nurse.

Your partner is not the only person affected by your pregnancy. Depending on who makes up your family and how close you are, many people may be involved. Your other children will probably want to help prepare for the baby's arrival. You can include them in shopping, sorting through hand-me-downs, and discussing possible names. Small children may have questions about where babies come from; teenagers may act embarrassed by your pregnancy.

Pregnancy can trigger sentimental feelings about your own childhood and may bring you closer to your parents. Or it can remind you of childhood conflicts, which can create emotional walls. You may find yourself thinking about your relationship with your mother more than usual. Remember that many people who love you are happy about your pregnancy and interested in its outcome. Try not to let them feel left out. However, think of your own needs first, and keep the level of privacy that is important to you.

Questions to Consider...

- How can I relieve morning sickness and other discomforts of pregnancy?
- What changes in my skin can I expect during pregnancy? Will they go away after the baby is born?
- How can I avoid constipation and hemorrhoids?
- What emotional reactions are common during pregnancy?
- What types of support do I need to deal with the changes of pregnancy?

Chapter 11

Special Care Pregnancies

Pregnancy puts new demands on a woman's body. It can alter the course of some health problems a woman had before pregnancy, and some conditions can affect the pregnancy itself. Women with medical problems can have healthy babies, but it takes extra effort. Their health and their pregnancies must be followed more closely.

If you have a problem that could complicate your pregnancy, you may need extra tests, more frequent prenatal visits, or treatment in a special clinic. You may need to stay in the hospital or may have to monitor your condition yourself at home. Your doctor may work with a team of experts to give you any special care you may need.

High Blood Pressure

The heart pumps blood rich in oxygen to all parts of the body through vessels called arteries. Blood returns to the heart through veins. Hypertension, or high blood pressure, occurs when the force of the blood in the arteries reaches greater-than-normal levels. This condition can occur before pregnancy and be chronic (long-term), or it can arise during pregnancy. High blood pressure that starts during pregnancy can be a sign of preeclampsia (also known as toxemia). These two conditions—chronic high blood pressure and preeclampsia—affect pregnancy and its outcome in different ways.

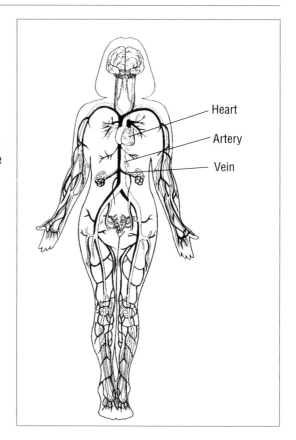

The heart pumps blood rich in oxygen through the arteries (light blood vessels) to all parts of the body. Blood returns to the heart through the veins (dark blood vessels).

Heart

Artery

Vein

Depending on how severe they are, both the mother and fetus can be affected.

Measuring Blood Pressure

Blood pressure is checked with a stethoscope and a device made of an inflatable cuff and a pressure gauge (sphygmomanometer). A blood pressure reading has two numbers separated by a slash: for example, 110/80. (You may hear this referred to as "110 over 80.") The first number is the pressure in the arteries when the heart contracts. This is called the systolic pressure. The second number is the pressure in the arteries when the heart relaxes between contractions. This is the diastolic pressure.

Blood pressure changes often during the day. It can rise if you are excited or if you exercise. It usually falls when you are resting.

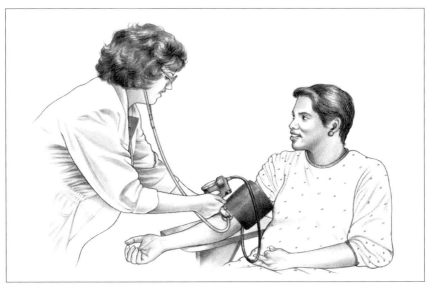

Checking a woman's blood pressure is a regular part of prenatal care.

These short-term changes in blood pressure due to an activity or event are normal. It is only when a person's blood pressure stays high for some time that it needs attention.

Because of the normal ups and downs in blood pressure, if you have one high reading, another reading may be taken to see whether it is your normal level. Your normal blood pressure can be an average of several readings taken at rest.

Blood pressure varies from person to person. In nonpregnant adults, readings less than 130/80 are usually normal. Blood pressure becomes abnormal when it reaches 140/90 or higher.

It is normal for blood pressure to drop a bit during the middle part of pregnancy and then go back to prepregnancy levels during the end of pregnancy. Because of these changes, it is important to have your blood pressure checked before pregnancy or in early pregnancy so your normal level can be determined. As a part of prenatal care, a woman's blood pressure is checked at each visit.

Chronic High Blood Pressure

Some women have long-term high blood pressure before they become pregnant. Diet, life style, and heredity play a role in chronic high blood pressure. Over the course of her life, a woman with untreated high blood pressure is more likely to have a heart attack or stroke. She is also at higher risk for problems during pregnancy. These include the baby being born too small or the placenta tearing loose from the wall of the uterus before the fetus is born. This is called premature separation of the placenta (abruptio placentae).

If you have chronic high blood pressure, you will need to bring it under control before you get pregnant by watching what you eat, losing weight, and perhaps taking medicine. During pregnancy, regular checkups are important to detect changes that may signal a problem.

Preeclampsia

High blood pressure that occurs for the first time in the second half of pregnancy along with protein in the urine and, usually, fluid retention is called preeclampsia. It affects about 7 of every 100 pregnant women. Although the cause of preeclampsia is unknown, it is more likely to develop in women who have chronic high blood pressure. Most women with preeclampsia, however, have never had high blood pressure. Preeclampsia usually occurs with first pregnancies and often does not come back in later pregnancies unless the woman has chronic hypertension or other problems with her blood vessels. With preeclampsia, blood pressure returns to normal after pregnancy, whereas chronic hypertension stays after delivery.

The blood vessels in the uterus supply blood to the placenta. When a woman has preeclampsia, the blood flow through these vessels may be cut by half or more. The degree of risk to the fetus depends on how severe the preeclampsia is and when it begins.

When blood pressure goes up during pregnancy, bed rest may be recommended. Resting will often lower your blood pressure or bring

---

Warning Signs and Symptoms of Preeclampsia

These signs and symptoms are sometimes linked to high blood pressure in pregnancy and should warn you to have your blood pressure checked:

- Severe or constant headaches
- Swelling (edema), especially of the face
- Pain in the upper right part of the abdomen
- Blurred vision or spots in front of the eyes
- Sudden weight gain of more than about 1 pound a day

Bed Rest

One of the most common treatments for certain problems of pregnancy is a simple one: bed rest. Staying in bed keeps you off your feet and lowers stress on your heart, kidneys, and other organs. Bed rest may be recommended if you have bleeding or show signs you could miscarry or deliver too early. It's rare to need total bed rest throughout pregnancy. More common is several days of bed rest or a few hours of bed rest each day. Some women, though, need longer periods of bed rest, and they may not be allowed to get up at all, even to use the bathroom.

Here are some tips to help you cope with bed rest:

- Find out exactly what is meant by "bed rest." Do you need to stay in a certain position, such as on your side or propped up? (You should not lie flat on your back, especially in the last half of pregnancy.) Can you spend any time on your feet each day, and if so, how much? Can you use the bathroom, or must you use a bed pan? What activities can you still do?
- Plan for bed rest according to the activities you can and cannot do. You may need to go on leave from your job, arrange for child care, get someone else to fix meals, and so on.
- Set up your room so things you need are in easy reach. These may include a telephone, television remote control, books or magazines, your prescription medications, paper and pen, toiletries, and hobbies such as crossword puzzles.
- Plan a daily routine. This can help you feel more in control. Wake up at a regular time each day, and set times for activities.
- Accept the fact that you need help. Allow your partner, family, or friends to take care of you. Don't feel guilty about it. Think of staying in bed as an act of love for the baby you are carrying.
- Keep eating right. Don't give in to gorging on junk food because you are bored. Be sure to eat fruits and vegetables and to drink lots of fluids. Although lack of activity can bring on constipation, proper eating helps prevent it.
- Do exercises while lying in bed if your doctor tells you it's okay. These may include deep breathing, pelvic tilts, leg lifts, neck circles, and Kegel exercises. Exercises can relax you and help avoid stiffness. Do not do any exercises unless your doctor tells you it's safe, and only do those he or she has prescribed.
- If you cannot exercise, at least take some deep breaths about every 20 minutes and wiggle your fingers and toes. This helps your blood circulate.
- Find out about support groups. There are groups that put people in touch with others who have been confined to bed. Ask your doctor or call local hospitals to see if they can refer you to a bed rest support group.

it back to normal. You may be advised to lie on your side, which improves blood flow to the uterus and kidneys. Some doctors recommend that women stay in a hospital as soon as their blood pressure goes up slightly; others wait until it's clear that bed rest at home has not helped to reduce blood pressure.

Preeclampsia occurs in degrees, from mild to severe, and can slowly worsen or improve. It can also get worse very suddenly. If preeclampsia is caught in mild stages and controlled by bed rest, the effects on the baby can be reduced. Women who are at risk for preeclampsia because they have kidney disease or chronic high blood pressure may be told to take a very low dose of aspirin every day. When a woman develops preeclampsia, attempts are made to let the pregnancy continue until the baby is old enough to be born without major complications.

If preeclampsia occurs early in pregnancy and is severe, the baby may need to be delivered. A premature baby is underweight and may have trouble breathing because the lungs are not fully formed. Preeclampsia can also be linked to poor fetal growth. Thus the decision to deliver depends on whether the risk to the fetus is greater in the mother's uterus or in a nursery and how dangerous the condition of the mother is. Severe preeclampsia can be fatal to the mother, although this is very rare. The disease affects almost all of the mother's organs, such as the blood system, liver, kidneys, and brain. Convulsions can occur without warning with preeclampsia. When convulsions occur, the disease is called eclampsia. Usually, the treatment for severe preeclampsia or eclampsia is to deliver the fetus.

Diabetes

Diabetes occurs when the body has a problem making or using *insulin.* Insulin is a hormone that helps the body use glucose, a sugar that is the body's main source of fuel. When the body doesn't make enough insulin, or when insulin or glucose does not have the effect it should, the level of glucose in the blood becomes too high. You can get diabetes before pregnancy, or it can develop during pregnancy. With either type, insulin may be needed to control glucose levels.

Gestational Diabetes

When a woman develops diabetes after she becomes pregnant, it is called gestational diabetes. It results from the effects of hormones made by the placenta during pregnancy. These hormones can alter the way in which insulin works. If abnormal glucose levels first appear in pregnancy, there may be no symptoms. Usually, the glucose level returns to normal after delivery. However, women who get gestational diabetes have a higher risk of developing diabetes again later in life.

Women over age 30 have a higher chance of developing diabetes during pregnancy. Those with a family history of diabetes and those who come from an ethnic background with higher-than-normal rates of the disease also have a higher risk. Nearly half of the women who develop gestational diabetes have no known risk factors, however.

You may be tested for diabetes during pregnancy. This safe and simple test is usually done at about 24–28 weeks of pregnancy. A sample of blood is taken 1 hour after you drink a special sugar mixture. If it shows your blood glucose level is high, a similar but longer test, usually taking 3 hours, will be done. This is called a glucose tolerance test.

Women who have uncomplicated gestational diabetes may not need insulin. Instead, they can control their blood glucose levels by eating a special diet and exercising. In that case, blood glucose levels usually are not tested daily. When insulin is used to control gestational diabetes, the diet and the insulin dose must be regulated to prevent the harmful effects of high and low blood glucose levels.

If diabetes is not controlled, the chance of having an overly large baby (***macrosomia***) increases. Macrosomic babies, which weigh close to 10 pounds or more, can be hard to deliver—especially their shoulders—and may have problems after birth. Special testing may be needed to check the baby before it is born. These tests might include ultrasound to estimate the baby's weight or amniocentesis to be sure the lungs are mature if the baby is being delivered before the due date. Very large babies are not necessarily healthier babies.

With gestational diabetes, blood glucose levels usually return to normal after birth, but diabetes can come back later. You may have another test months after delivery to make sure you are no longer diabetic. If you are overweight or obese, it is wise to follow a balanced program of diet and exercise after delivery. This may reduce the risk of problems in future pregnancies and may help lower the risk of developing diabetes later in life.

Preexisting Diabetes

About 1 woman of childbearing age in 100 has diabetes before pregnancy. At one time, diabetes posed a major health threat to the mother and fetus during pregnancy. Today, however, more is known about diabetes and how to control it, so pregnancy is safer for most women with diabetes. The outlook for pregnant women has improved to the point where the risks for a pregnancy complicated by diabetes are almost as low as those for a normal uncomplicated pregnancy. Ideally, the diabetes should be diagnosed and brought under control before pregnancy and then carefully monitored to keep blood glucose levels as normal as possible. With planning, control, and expert care, the chances for a successful pregnancy— a healthy baby and mother—are very good.

Risks

Although there is no cure for diabetes, it can be effectively treated. There is less risk to the fetus when diabetes is under control before and during pregnancy. Women who have diabetes when they become pregnant should get early care to help lower these risks:

- Preeclampsia, or high blood pressure during pregnancy, can require the baby to be delivered early or can slow its growth while in the uterus.
- *Hydramnios* (too much amniotic fluid in the sac surrounding the fetus) can make it hard for the mother to breathe and may also result in premature labor and delivery.
- Macrosomia (a larger-than-normal baby) occurs in less severe cases and can make delivery difficult.
- Birth defects are more common in babies of diabetic mothers, especially when the diabetes is not well controlled before pregnancy.
- Miscarriage occurs more often in diabetic women, especially when the condition is not under control.

- ■ *Respiratory distress syndrome* may affect the baby's ability to breathe after birth because the lungs are not fully developed.
- ■ Stillbirth, although uncommon, also occurs more often in babies of diabetic mothers.

Controlling Diabetes

Diet is an important way to control glucose levels. The number of calories in your diet will depend on your weight. You may need to follow a different diet during pregnancy than you did before you became pregnant, even if you have always kept your diabetes well under control. Your diet may be adjusted from time to time to improve blood glucose control or to meet the needs of the growing fetus. Usually the diet consists of special meals and snacks spread throughout the day. A bedtime snack helps keep blood glucose at the right level during the night.

Regular exercise also plays a key role in controlling diabetes. It lowers the amount of insulin needed to keep blood glucose at normal levels. How much exercise is right for each woman depends on the stage of pregnancy and other factors.

Some women with diabetes before pregnancy need to take insulin to keep their blood glucose at normal levels. Insulin cannot be swallowed. It must be injected. Insulin does not cross the placenta, so it does not affect the fetus directly. The amount of insulin needed to control blood glucose levels throughout the day varies from woman to woman. In many cases, insulin must be taken at least twice a day during pregnancy. Usually the need for insulin goes up throughout the pregnancy and levels off near the end. This means that the insulin dose needs to be adjusted at times for good control of blood glucose levels. Home monitoring of blood glucose levels plays a key role in finding out how much insulin is needed.

Women with diabetes that must be controlled with insulin will need to monitor their blood glucose each day to keep it normal as much as possible. There are many ways to do this, all of which are safe and simple to use. You will work with your health care team to determine the best method. Glucose control before pregnancy can help prevent problems while the fetal organs are developing.

Blood glucose meters or colored strips can be used to measure blood glucose levels at home. In either method, a simple device is used to get a small drop of blood, usually from the tip of the finger. The blood is placed on a strip of special paper and its color is compared with the colors on a chart, or the strip is placed in a meter to find out the blood glucose level. These methods give reliable results if used correctly.

Because blood glucose levels change throughout the day, the level usually must be checked many times a day. You will be advised how often you will need to check your blood glucose.

Glucose meter.

Special Care

A woman with diabetes usually needs to have certain tests done more often in her pregnancy. These tests can help find problems that may occur early, and steps can be taken to correct or lessen them. One test measures hemoglobin A_{1C}, a substance in the mother's blood. When levels are higher than normal, it means that the body's glucose has been poorly controlled for a number of weeks. Other tests such as ultrasound, amniocentesis, and fetal monitoring are used to check the status and growth of the fetus. These tests are especially important if the baby must be delivered early. Occasionally, you may need to stay in the hospital.

At one time, almost all women with diabetes had cesarean births because the problems that can occur with diabetes during pregnancy could be made worse by the added stress of labor and vaginal delivery. Today, however, with special tests and monitoring, most women with diabetes are able to give birth safely through the vagina.

Heart Disease

During their childbearing years, some women may have rheumatic heart disease or congenital heart disease. Rheumatic heart disease is caused by an infection called rheumatic fever. It can cause problems with the heart valves. Due to medical advances, both rheumatic fever and the heart problems linked with it have become rare in this country. Women with congenital heart disease are born with a defect in the heart. For example, their heart might have a hole between two of the four chambers. The type of defect and how severe it is determine the risk of having problems during pregnancy.

Ideally, heart disease should be diagnosed before a woman gets pregnant. Once it is diagnosed, all possible steps can be taken to correct the heart condition. Counselors can give information about the impact heart disease has on pregnancy and how pregnancy affects your heart. If you have serious heart disease, your doctor will team up with a cardiologist to manage your care throughout the pregnancy.

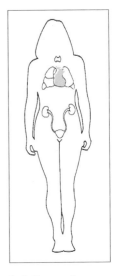

Pregnancy makes the heart work harder; labor and delivery cause added stress. The amount of blood the heart pumps increases by up to 40% during pregnancy. If you have heart problems, you may need to limit your activities to lower the demands on your heart. Rest and possibly medicine may be prescribed.

During labor, contractions increase the heart's work load, as do the pain and anxiety that go along with them. In spite of this, vaginal delivery is preferred over cesarean birth when possible because it causes less stress to the heart. Anesthesia may be given during labor to reduce pain and anxiety.

Women with heart disease are more likely to deliver early, and their babies are often smaller than they should be. The babies of mothers with congenital heart disease have a 4–5% chance of having the disease as well, although it may not be serious or life-threatening. In some cases this condition may be diagnosed prenatally with ultrasound, although it often is not detected until after birth.

Women with artificial heart valves who take blood-thinner medications by mouth usually will have their prescription changed to a medication taken by injection or shots during pregnancy. These women, as well as those with congenital heart defects, will be given antibiotics during delivery.

Lung Disorders

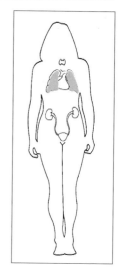

Pregnancy changes a woman's breathing patterns because the growing uterus alters the shape of her chest cavity. It is common for a pregnant woman to feel short of breath. (For hints on dealing with shortness of breath, see "Breathing Problems," Chapter 10.) Some lung disorders, however, can cause changes beyond shortness of breath.

Asthma, a lung disease that causes wheezing and breathing problems, is a common problem. It has not been shown to get worse during pregnancy, but it could pose problems if the fetus does not get enough oxygen. Most women with asthma can go through pregnancy safely by continuing to use inhalers or prescribed medications to help them breathe. Most medications for asthma are safe during pregnancy. However, you should tell your doctor or nurse about all the medications you take. If you have severe asthma, you'll probably continue to have attacks during pregnancy. You will need to keep control of your asthma and be watched closely.

Pneumonia is a lung infection that may be more serious in pregnancy than it is at other times. Because it can result in the

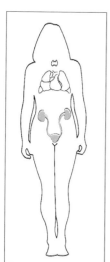

mother and fetus getting less oxygen, it should be diagnosed and treated promptly. A chest X-ray is usually a key step in finding pneumonia. The technician who takes the X-ray may place a lead apron on your abdomen to shield the fetus. This type of X-ray has not been shown to harm the fetus (see "Harmful Agents," Chapter 8). A pregnant woman with pneumonia is often hospitalized to receive antibiotics.

Kidney Disease

During pregnancy, more blood flows to the kidneys as they work hard to filter waste products faster for both you and your fetus. If your kidneys are scarred from a previous disease or do not function as they should, it could affect your pregnancy. With proper medical treatment, however, risks usually can be reduced. Some disorders that affect the kidney are linked with high blood pressure. Controlling blood pressure can lower the risk of problems during pregnancy.

Kidney disease can usually be diagnosed from your medical history, physical exam, and blood and urine tests. Protein in the urine may be a sign of kidney disease. It can be caused by diseases that interfere with kidney function. Patients whose kidneys don't function well or who receive dialysis are at risk for pregnancy losses and preterm deliveries.

Seizure Disorders

Women with epilepsy or seizures (convulsions) can have safe pregnancies. Seizures may be minor problems involving muscle twitches or major attacks involving blackouts and loss of bladder or bowel control. Usually women with seizures take medications prescribed to control or prevent repeated seizures.

A woman with epilepsy has a risk two to three times higher than normal of having a baby with a birth defect, especially cleft lip and palate or heart defects. The reason for the higher risk is not clear. It is known, however, that some medications to control seizures can cause birth defects. Because seizures could harm the mother or fetus, women with epilepsy should discuss continued use of medication with their doctors. Sometimes the medication can be changed before or during pregnancy to reduce the risks. Because medications that treat seizure disorders use up folic acid, an important nutrient, you may need to take folic acid supplements.

Autoimmune Disorders

The autoimmune disorders are a group of diseases in which the immune system, which is designed to protect the body, goes awry and attacks and harms the body's own tissues. Injury can happen to one organ, such as the thyroid, or to various parts of the body.

Most autoimmune diseases are chronic and have no cure. What causes them is not always known. Their symptoms can go away for a time and then flare up with little warning and no clear reason. The effects on pregnancy depend on the type of disorder.

Many autoimmune diseases have symptoms that overlap, making them hard to diagnose. Your doctor may work with a specialist to plan your care during pregnancy.

Systemic Lupus Erythematosus

Systemic lupus erythematosus (SLE) is a disease that can affect the whole body, including skin, joints, kidneys, and the nervous system. Its results can range from minor skin sores to a serious condition in which the kidneys fail and the nervous system, heart, and blood are affected.

Systemic lupus erythematosus tends to occur in young women during their childbearing years. It does not appear to affect fertility, but it increases the risks of miscarriage, premature birth, and stillbirth. Systemic lupus erythematosus may also slow the fetal heart rate.

In about 3 women in 10 with SLE, the disease gets worse during pregnancy, and symptoms can flare up after delivery. A woman with SLE whose kidneys are not affected and who goes 6 months without symptoms before getting pregnant has the best pregnancy outlook.

Systemic lupus erythematosus is treated with medications called *corticosteroids*. When these medications are taken during pregnancy, only about 10% of the medicine crosses the placenta. The fetus, thus, has little exposure to it. You may also be prescribed aspirin and drugs similar to aspirin to control joint pain. Usually the dosage is kept very low during pregnancy to avoid effects such as fetal bleeding.

Rheumatoid Arthritis

Rheumatoid arthritis is thought of as a disease of the joints because it most often causes pain, soreness, heat, and swelling of the small and medium-sized joints. Morning stiffness and a general feeling of fatigue and discomfort also occur. The disease can flare up and then lessen for a time, or it can become worse and damage joints. Rheumatoid arthritis can affect the blood—causing severe anemia—and occasionally involves the heart and lungs.

Many women find that their rheumatoid arthritis gets better during pregnancy, although some have a relapse between 6 weeks and 6 months after delivery. Rheumatoid arthritis can be treated with aspirinlike drugs and sometimes other drugs during pregnancy.

Antiphospholipid Antibody Syndrome

Women with this antiphospholipid antibody syndrome have high levels of a certain antibody in their blood. Antibodies are proteins the body makes to protect itself against foreign substances. Antiphospholipid antibody syndrome can involve blood clots and bleeding problems, such as bleeding longer than normal if you are injured. This disorder can cause miscarriage or other problems for the fetus, such as slow development or death.

Thyroid Disease

The thyroid gland can be affected by diseases that cause it to release too much or not enough thyroid hormone. Either can harm the fetus. Hypothyroidism, in which the thyroid is underactive, is treated with thyroid hormone pills. Blood tests are used to determine whether enough of the hormone is being taken.

Medications also are available to treat hyperthyroidism, or an overactive thyroid gland. Blood tests are done to figure out the proper dose of these medications. A patient with thyroid disease that is properly controlled during pregnancy can have a normal pregnancy.

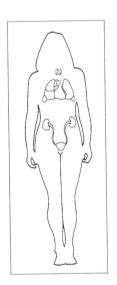

What You Can Do

If you have a chronic disease, you should receive care before you become pregnant. If this is not possible, see a doctor as soon as you know you are pregnant. You have probably already worked out a routine for control and treatment with your family doctor or a specialist. Now your routine may need to be changed. You may have to adjust how often you take your medication, as well as the type and the dose you take.

If you are just learning now that you have an illness, it can come as a shock. On top of learning about pregnancy and delivery, you must learn how to care for a medical condition. Your doctor or a specialist that your doctor recommends can help you adjust and work out a course of treatment. Pregnancy can affect medical conditions in many ways; the condition may get worse or it may temporarily get better after you deliver your baby.

The best actions you can take to increase the chances of having a healthy baby are to receive early and regular medical care and to follow your doctor's advice. Having a chronic health problem can complicate your pregnancy, but most women with these problems have healthy babies.

Questions to Consider...

■ Have I given my doctor complete information about my medical condition?

■ If I have preeclampsia, will my blood pressure return to normal after the baby is born?

■ If I have gestational diabetes, am I likely to develop diabetes later in life?

■ If I have a medical condition, how will its management change during pregnancy?

■ What effect will pregnancy have on my medical condition?

■ Have I told other doctors treating me that I'm pregnant?

Chapter 12

Complications of Pregnancy

Although pregnancy and childbirth are natural events, problems can arise. Some women have risk factors that increase their chances of complications. In even the most healthy and fit women, problems can happen with no warning. Some tend to occur over and over, whereas others are a one-time-only event. If you have a high-risk pregnancy, it is important for your doctor and health care team to watch your progress closely. They will adjust your prenatal care as needed and give you special care through labor and delivery. If you suspect or find any problems, such as the ones described here, contact your doctor.

Vaginal Bleeding

There are many causes of vaginal bleeding in pregnancy. When bleeding occurs, it's important to find out why. To do this, your doctor or nurse may ask you questions, examine you, or have special tests performed. Sometimes bleeding can become serious. You should report any bleeding to your doctor or nurse so he or she can decide the proper course of action based on the symptoms, signs, and stage of pregnancy. Your health and that of your fetus may depend on prompt treatment.

Early Pregnancy

At the beginning of pregnancy, some women may have slight bleeding (spotting or staining). This is called implantation bleeding. It

165

happens when the fertilized egg first attaches itself to the lining of the uterus. Some women may confuse this bleeding with a menstrual period. When there is doubt, lab tests can confirm early pregnancy.

During the first half of pregnancy, there is a possibility of miscarriage. Losing the fetus through miscarriage occurs in at least 20% of all pregnancies. It can occur at any time during the first half of the pregnancy, but it usually happens during the first 3 months. Sometimes when pregnancy is not progressing normally, the lining of the uterus may bleed. This is the most frequent sign that a miscarriage is coming. Another sign is cramping pain in the lower abdomen, which often comes and goes. The pain is usually stronger than menstrual cramps.

Many women who have bleeding have little or no cramping. In more than half of the women who bleed in early pregnancy, the bleeding stops and the pregnancy goes on to term. At other times, the bleeding and cramping become more heavy and strong, ending in miscarriage.

A woman may have repeated miscarriages. If she has three in a row, there's a chance she has an underlying problem. Repeated miscarriages call for more studies to see whether there is a problem and whether it can be corrected. The woman may be advised to see another doctor.

When bleeding occurs in early pregnancy, you will most likely be given a pelvic exam and maybe a pregnancy test. Ultrasound may be used to help see whether the pregnancy is located outside the uterus (ectopic pregnancy) or whether miscarriage has occurred or is about to occur.

Often when miscarriage occurs early in pregnancy, tissue is left in the uterus. If tissue remains inside the uterus after a miscarriage, the bleeding may not stop. In such cases, the tissue is removed by a surgical technique called ***dilation and curettage (D&C)***. The cervix is widened (dilation) and the tissue is gently scraped (curettage) or suctioned from the lining of the uterus.

In most cases, miscarriage cannot be prevented. It is the body's way of dealing with a pregnancy that was not developing normally. A miscarriage doesn't mean that a woman can't become pregnant again. Nor does it mean that anything is wrong with her health. There is no evidence that emotional stress or physical or sexual activity causes miscarriage.

Ectopic Pregnancy

Ectopic pregnancy is sometimes referred to as tubal pregnancy. It means that the fertilized egg (embryo) has started to grow someplace outside the uterus, usually in a fallopian tube. Ectopic pregnancy can be a serious threat to a woman's life, especially if it is not found until the embryo grows so large that it ruptures the tube. It is not possible to move the embryo to the uterus. Surgery is often needed to remove the embryo.

A procedure may be done called *laparoscopy,* which allows the doctor to look inside your pelvis using a thin device that transmits light. Surgery to remove the embryo can be done using this same device. In some cases a drug called methotrexate is used to treat an ectopic pregnancy. Although the same drug is sometimes used to treat cancer, ectopic pregnancy is not a form of cancer.

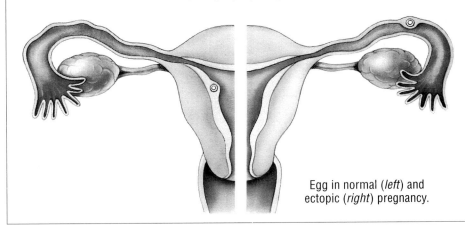

Egg in normal (*left*) and ectopic (*right*) pregnancy.

Late Pregnancy

During the second half of pregnancy, any bleeding requires medical attention. The cause may be something minor. If the cervix gets inflamed, for instance, the inflammation can cause bleeding that is not a big problem. Some bleeding can be serious, however, posing a threat to the woman or the fetus. Contact your doctor or nurse right away if you have bleeding in late pregnancy. You may need to go into the hospital for special care.

Heavy vaginal bleeding usually suggests a problem with the placenta. The most common problems are abruptio placentae and *placenta previa*. With abruptio placentae, the placenta comes loose from the uterine wall before or during birth. It usually brings vaginal bleeding and also constant, severe pain in the abdomen. The

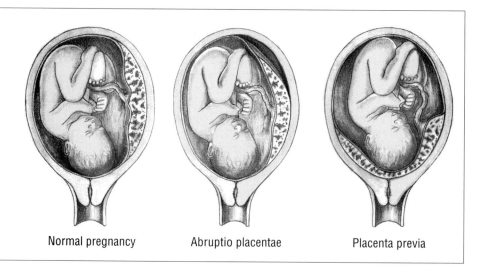

Normal pregnancy   Abruptio placentae   Placenta previa

fetus may get less oxygen, which could be dangerous. With placenta previa, the placenta lies low in the uterus, partly or completely covering the cervix, the baby's exit from the uterus. When the cervix starts to open in women who have placenta previa, they bleed and will require prompt care.

If you have bleeding in late pregnancy, you may need to be admitted to the hospital. Ultrasound may be recommended. Sometimes, a stay of several weeks in the hospital is required. Both abruptio placentae and placenta previa may be serious enough to require early delivery of the baby, usually by cesarean birth.

Blood Group Incompatibility

Everyone's blood is one of four major types: A, B, AB, or O. Blood types are determined by the types of *antigens* on the blood cells. Antigens are proteins on the surfaces of blood cells that can cause a response from the immune system. Type A blood has only A antigens, type B has only B antigens, type AB has both A and B antigens, and type O has neither A nor B antigens. There are other antigens that can make blood types even more specific: one of the most common is the Rh factor.

Rh Immune Globulin

If you are Rh negative and your partner is Rh positive, you can become sensitized. This means your body makes antibodies that can attack the red cells of the fetus if they are Rh positive. Sensitization can be prevented if you get injections of Rh immune globulin (RhIg), a product made from human blood. Rh immune globulin keeps the antibodies from forming, but it does not help if you are already sensitized—that is, if the antibodies have already formed in your blood.

Sensitization can occur any time fetal blood mixes with the mother's blood: during pregnancy or after an abortion, miscarriage, ectopic pregnancy, or amniocentesis. After any of these events, an Rh-negative woman is usually given RhIg to prevent sensitization. Its effects seem to last only about 12 weeks, so it is given again any time blood from the fetus and mother could mix.

A small number of Rh-negative women become sensitized during the last 3 months of pregnancy. To prevent this, they may be given RhIg near 28 weeks. When an Rh-negative woman gives birth to an Rh-positive baby, she will be given a dose of RhIg soon after, even if she received a dose at 28 weeks. This will remove the risk to the fetus during her next pregnancy. Repeat doses of RhIg are given every time the woman gives birth to an Rh-positive child.

It is safe for pregnant women to receive RhIg. The only known side effects are soreness from the injection or a slight fever. There is no risk of infection with human immunodeficiency virus (HIV) with RhIg.

How Rh Sensitization Occurs

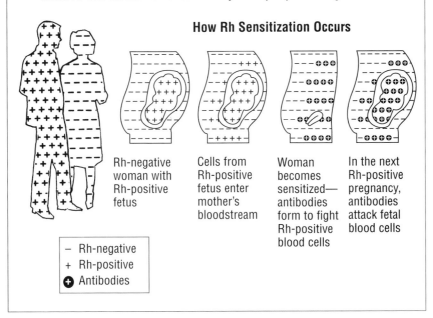

Rh-negative woman with Rh-positive fetus

Cells from Rh-positive fetus enter mother's bloodstream

Woman becomes sensitized— antibodies form to fight Rh-positive blood cells

In the next Rh-positive pregnancy, antibodies attack fetal blood cells

– Rh-negative
+ Rh-positive
⊕ Antibodies

As part of your prenatal care, you will have blood tests to find out your blood type. If your blood lacks the Rh antigen, it is called Rh negative. If it has the antigen, it is called Rh positive. More than 85% of people in the world are Rh positive. When the mother is Rh negative and the father is Rh positive, the fetus can inherit the Rh factor from the father, which makes the fetus Rh positive, too. Problems can arise when the fetus's blood has the Rh factor and the mother's does not.

If a small amount of the fetus's blood mixes with the mother's blood, which often happens, the mother's body may respond as if it were allergic to the fetus by making antibodies to the Rh antigens in the fetus's blood. This means the mother has become sensitized. Her antibodies can then cross the placenta and attack the fetus's blood, breaking down its red blood cells and causing anemia. This can lead to serious illness or even death in the fetus or newborn.

The first pregnancy poses little risk because it takes time for the mother's antibodies to build up after being exposed to the antigens. But once they are formed, antibodies do not go away. The best course is to keep the mother from being sensitized and forming antibodies in the first place. If you are Rh negative and blood tests show that you have not become sensitized, your doctor will prescribe Rh immune globulin (RhIg) injections. This blood product prevents the mother from forming antibodies. It is usually injected right after the birth of your first baby to prevent harm to your next one. It may also be given during pregnancy, usually at about 28 weeks.

If you have already become sensitized, your fetus is at risk. As your pregnancy progresses, your doctor will check the levels of antibodies in your blood. If they become high, special tests may be done to check your fetus's health.

If the fetus is anemic, it will need a blood transfusion. After 18 weeks of pregnancy, these transfusions can be given while the fetus is still in the uterus. If the fetus is old enough, early delivery may be an option. The baby can be treated in a special-care nursery. If you have become sensitized, other babies you have after your first may be at risk. They will need to be monitored carefully throughout pregnancy.

Breech

Most babies change position a few weeks before birth so their heads are down near the birth canal. If this doesn't happen, the baby's buttocks, or buttocks and feet, will be in place to come out first during birth. This is called ***breech presentation.*** It occurs in about 1 of 25 full-term births.

The causes of breech presentation are not completely clear. However, it is more common when:

- You have had more than one pregnancy.
- You have more than one fetus in the uterus.
- You have a premature delivery.
- Your uterus has too much or too little amniotic fluid.
- Your uterus is misshaped or has abnormal growths, such as ***fibroids.***
- You have placenta previa.

There are three main types of breech presentation:

1. *Frank breech.* The fetus's buttocks are aimed toward the birth canal and the legs stick straight up in front of the body, with the feet near the head.
2. *Complete breech.* The buttocks are down, with the legs folded at the knees and the feet near the buttocks.
3. *Footling breech.* One or both of the fetus's feet are pointing down and will come out first.

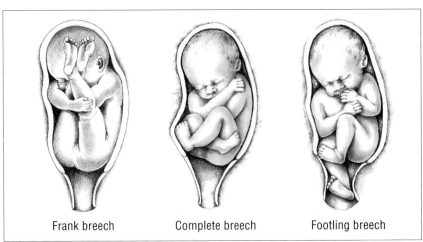

Frank breech   Complete breech   Footling breech

Although most breech babies are born healthy, they do have a higher risk for certain problems than babies in the normal position. Babies born early are more often born breech. Birth defects are also more common in breech babies and may account for why they have not moved into the right position before delivery. Your doctor may advise cesarean birth or that you try vaginal delivery after assessing a number of factors, such as the stage of your pregnancy, the size of the baby and your pelvis, and the type of breech position.

In some cases, the baby's position can be changed by a method called external version. It does not involve surgery; the baby is turned manually into the head-down position. The doctor places his or her hands at certain key points on your lower abdomen. He or she then gently pushes the baby, as if the baby were doing a slow-motion somersault. Often you are given medication first to relax your uterus. The turning is done while the doctor views the fetus with ultrasound.

An ultrasound exam done in advance allows the doctor to better check the status and placement of the baby, the location of the placenta, and the amount of amniotic fluid in the uterus. Before, during, and after external version, your baby's heartbeat will be checked closely. If any problems arise, efforts to turn the baby will be stopped right away. The best time for trying external version is at about 37–38 weeks.

Multiple Pregnancy

When a woman is carrying more than one fetus, it is called a *multiple pregnancy.* In the most common kind of multiple pregnancy, the uterus contains two fetuses (twins). Twins are born in about 1 of every 43 births in the United States. Twins occur in one of two ways; either two separate eggs are fertilized, causing fraternal twins, or a single egg divides into two fetuses, known as identical twins. Identical twins are somewhat rare, occurring less than once in every 100 births.

Even more rare is when three or more fetuses are produced in a single pregnancy. The risk in these pregnancies is greater than that in pregnancies with twins. Triplets, or three fetuses, occur

How Twins Are Formed

You may have wondered why sometimes twins look so much alike and other times don't seem to look alike at all. The answer has to do with how twins are formed.

Most twins are fraternal; each develops from a separate egg and sperm. The ovaries usually release one egg each month to be fertilized, but occasionally two or more eggs may be released. Fraternal twins each have their own placenta and amniotic sac. (Sometimes these twins will be described as dizygotic, meaning two zygotes, or two fertilized eggs.) Because each twin develops from the union of a different egg and a different sperm, these twins look no more alike than any brother and sister do. The twins can be both boys, both girls, or one of each.

Sometimes, for unknown reasons, one fertilized egg splits early in pregnancy and develops into two or more fetuses. Two fetuses formed this way are identical (or monozygotic) twins. They share a placenta, but each usually has its own amniotic sac. Because they share the same genetic material at the beginning, they are the same sex and have the same blood type, hair color, and eye color. These twins can look so much alike that even their mothers may have difficulty telling them apart. Some mothers find that painting the fingernails of one twin is helpful in telling one from the other.

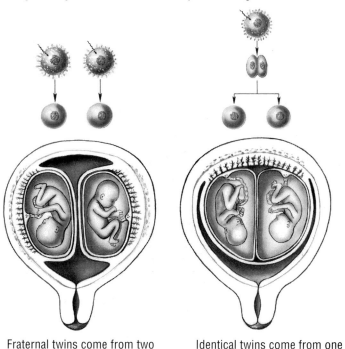

Fraternal twins come from two eggs and have separate placentas.

Identical twins come from one egg and may share the same placenta.

naturally in only 1 of 10,000 births. Three or more fetuses can be formed by more than one egg being fertilized, a single fertilized egg splitting, or a combination of both.

African–American women are more likely to have multiple pregnancies than white women, whereas Asian women are less likely. Some families are more likely than others to have fraternal twins.

With today's increased use of fertility drugs, multiple pregnancies are becoming more common. These drugs, taken under close medical supervision to help you ovulate, can cause more than one egg to be released from the ovaries at once.

Most multiple pregnancies are found before delivery. It may be suspected if:

- Fraternal twins tend to run in your family.
- Your uterus grows more quickly or is larger than expected.
- More than one heartbeat can be heard.
- You have been taking fertility drugs.
- You have extreme bouts of nausea and vomiting in the first trimester.
- You feel more fetal movement than you did in any pregnancies you had before.

If a multiple pregnancy is suspected, an ultrasound exam will be done to confirm it. Sometimes twins are discovered when an ultrasound exam is done for other reasons during pregnancy.

Multiple pregnancy can make pregnancy more uncomfortable than usual because the uterus becomes much larger. It also brings a higher risk of complications. For example, the mother is more likely to develop high blood pressure or anemia. She is also more likely to go into preterm labor.

In up to half of multiple pregnancies, the fetuses are small for the stage of pregnancy. There is also a tendency for the twins to be of unequal size. All of these factors may require more monitoring, bed rest, and early delivery.

You may need special care during labor and delivery. One or both of the twins may need to be delivered by cesarean birth. If both are head first, they are more likely to be delivered vaginally. The heart rates of both twins will be monitored throughout labor. A pediatrician or neonatologist—a doctor who specializes in the care of newborns—will examine the babies.

Preterm Labor

In most pregnancies, labor starts at about 40 weeks. Labor that starts before the end of the 37th week is considered preterm. Preterm labor can lead to preterm birth. About 1 of every 10 babies born in the United States is born preterm. Preterm birth accounts for three fourths of newborn deaths that are not related to birth defects.

Labor starts with regular contractions of the uterus. The cervix thins out (effaces) and opens up (dilates) so the baby can enter the birth canal. It is not known why some women go into labor early, but it is the single most important problem of pregnancy. Growth and development in the last part of pregnancy are critical to the baby's health. Preterm babies (also called premature babies or "preemies") are more likely to grow slower than normal. They often have learning and behavioral problems, as well as problems with their eyes and ears and with breathing. Difficulties in school are also more common in children who were preterm babies.

Preterm labor can happen in any woman, but those who did not get prenatal care seem to have a higher risk. A number of other factors have also been linked to preterm labor:

■ Past pregnancies with a history of preterm labor or birth
■ Current pregnancy
    —Multiple pregnancy
    —Defects in the uterus such as incompetent cervix or fibroids
    —Abdominal surgery during pregnancy
    —Infection in the mother
    —Bleeding in the second trimester of pregnancy
    —Underweight mother (weight less than 100 pounds)
    —Placenta previa
    —Premature rupture of membranes (your "water breaks")
    —High blood pressure
    —Chronic illness in the mother
    —Too much fluid in the amniotic sac
    —Birth defects in the fetus

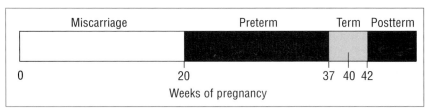

Most women give birth between 37 and 42 weeks of pregnancy (term). Babies born between 20 and 37 weeks are preterm; those born after 42 weeks are postterm.

Signs of Preterm Labor

If preterm labor is caught early enough, delivery can often be postponed. This gives your baby extra time to grow and mature. Even a few more days may mean a healthier baby.

Sometimes the signs that preterm labor may be starting are fairly easy to detect. For example, if the membranes rupture, you may feel a trickle or gush of fluid from the vagina. Other times, the signs are mild and may be harder to detect. Call your doctor or nurse right away if you notice any of these signs:

- Vaginal discharge
    - —Change in type (watery, mucous, or bloody)
    - —Increase in amount
- Pelvic or lower abdominal pressure
- Constant, low, dull backache
- Mild abdominal cramps, with or without diarrhea
- Regular contractions or uterine tightening, often painless
- Ruptured membranes (your water breaks)

You may need to be seen right away to check whether your cervix has begun to change. This is the only way to know whether you are really in preterm labor.

Fetal monitoring may be used to record the heart beat of the fetus and contractions of your uterus. Ultrasound may be used to estimate the size and age of the baby and to see where it is in the uterus. You may be watched for a time and then examined again to see whether your cervix changes.

If it appears that a preterm delivery will occur, your doctor will need to determine whether the baby's lungs are mature enough

---

Testing Lung Maturity

During the late stages of pregnancy, certain cells in the lungs of the fetus produce substances that coat the inner walls of the air sacs. This coating is called surfactant. It prevents the sacs from sticking together after the baby starts to breathe on its own after birth. A major problem with preterm babies, mainly those born before 32 weeks of pregnancy, is that these substances have not yet been produced. Without this coating, babies may develop a condition known as respiratory distress syndrome (RDS). It is the most common cause of death in preterm babies.

There are several tests that can be done on a sample of amniotic fluid to see if there is enough surfactant present to prevent RDS. Each laboratory that does this type of testing may use different combinations of tests. Based on the results, a test called an L/S ratio may be done. The ratio between two substances found in the amniotic fluid—lecithin (L) and sphingomyelin (S)—helps measure the lung maturity and, therefore, whether RDS is likely to occur.

---

to survive outside the uterus. If the lungs are not mature, the baby may develop respiratory distress syndrome, which is the most common cause of death in preterm babies.

If it looks as though labor is starting but you are not likely to deliver the baby for at least a day, you may be given medications called corticosteroids. These medications help the baby's lungs mature and help prevent certain problems, such as bleeding in the baby's brain. Studies suggest that corticosteroids are most likely to work when preterm labor begins between 24 and 34 weeks of pregnancy.

Preventing Preterm Birth

If labor is detected at its earliest stages and there is no sign that you and the fetus are in danger from infection, bleeding, or other problems, your doctor may try to stop labor to allow the fetus more time to grow and mature. Among ways to do this are the following:

- Bed rest
- Hydration—extra fluids given by mouth or through a tube inserted in a vein
- Drugs that can stop or suppress uterine contractions

Many different medications can be used to stop or slow preterm labor: they are called tocolytics. Which of these medications is the best to use is not always clear. They are usually injected. As with all medications, tocolytics can have side effects. Each woman responds differently. These side effects can include:

■ Fast pulse
■ Chest pressure or discomfort
■ Dizziness
■ Headache
■ Feeling of warmth
■ Shaky or nervous feeling

If you are not actually in preterm labor or if labor is stopped, you may be able to go home. To monitor yourself, lie down and gently feel the entire surface of your lower abdomen with your fingertips. Feel for a firm tightening over the surface of your uterus. Usually this tightening is not painful. If you feel these contractions, count them. Call your doctor or nurse for instructions on what to do next. You may be in preterm labor. Some women may need to stay in the hospital for a while. This depends on the findings of the exam and other factors.

Your Preterm Baby

Sometimes preterm labor may be too advanced to be stopped. In some cases, the baby is better off being born right away, even if it is early. Reasons can include infection, high blood pressure, bleeding, or signs that the fetus is having problems. Preterm babies are more likely to be delivered by cesarean birth. Preterm labor and delivery involve risks that require care in a hospital with special facilities. You or your baby may have to be moved to a different hospital that can provide this expert care. For information about babies born preterm, see "Babies Who Need Special Care," Chapter 16.

Premature Rupture of Membranes

The membranes that hold the amniotic fluid rupture at the beginning of labor. Some experts believe that when the fetus is at term, the membranes go through changes that cause them to weaken. Sometimes the membranes rupture before labor. This is called premature rupture of membranes. The reasons for it are unclear. Some causes may be infection or bleeding. One of every 10 women experience premature rupture of membranes.

When membranes rupture, the next likely event is labor. Generally, the closer you are to your due date, the sooner labor is likely to begin after the membranes rupture. If a woman does not go into labor, two problems can occur: the amniotic fluid and possibly the fetus could become infected, and the umbilical cord could be compressed because the fluid is not there to protect it. Premature rupture of membranes poses even more of a risk when it occurs preterm, before the baby is ready to be born. In general, if the fetus is not mature enough to survive outside the uterus, efforts are made to keep the pregnancy going. After that time, delivery is usually the best way to avoid the complications of infection.

If you are found to have rupture of membranes, you may need to enter the hospital. The correct diagnosis of rupture of membranes depends on a combination of history, physical exam, and lab tests. Rupture of membranes is confirmed by the presence of a pool of amniotic fluid in the vagina. Other tests, including ultrasound, can be done when the diagnosis is not clear. Although some of the fluid is lost when the membranes rupture, the fetus continues to produce more, which may continue leaking from the uterus. In the hospital you and your fetus can be watched carefully so care can be given promptly in response to any changes.

Postterm Pregnancy

Most women (80%) give birth between 37 and 42 weeks of pregnancy. These pregnancies are called term. Only 5% of babies actually arrive on the exact due date. Up to 10% of normal pregnancies are not delivered by 42 weeks. These are called ***postterm pregnancies***.

Knowing the gestational age of the fetus is key in diagnosing postterm pregnancy. It can be hard, though, to precisely pinpoint the age of the fetus. If you are unsure of your menstrual cycle history, for example, it is harder to predict your exact due date. For this reason, more than one method may be used to cross-check the age of the fetus (see "When Is the Baby Due?," Chapter 5). The due date should be set early in pregnancy, because it is less reliable when it is determined later.

If pregnancy extends beyond 42 weeks, the fetus's health could face some risks. These risks occur in only a small number of postterm pregnancies. More than 90% of babies born between 42 and 44 weeks have no problems resulting from the longer pregnancy.

As pregnancy moves past 42 weeks, a fetus has a higher risk of:

- Abnormal heart rate—a sign that the fetus may be having problems before delivery
- Macrosomia—the fetus grows larger than normal, which can pose problems for delivery
- *Meconium* aspiration—the fetus inhales meconium (greenish waste that is emptied from the fetus's bowels into the amniotic fluid). Usually, a baby delivered with meconium staining does just fine.

It is important to identify whether the baby is at risk so that action can be taken. As a fetus passes full term, the placenta may stop working properly. This means the baby may not get as much oxygen and nutrients and may not grow as fast. The baby may also make less urine, which reduces the volume of amniotic fluid in the sac. If the amount of amniotic fluid drops, fetal movements or uterine contractions can pinch the umbilical cord.

Several tests can be used to check on the well-being of the baby. Tests are usually started between 41 and 42 weeks of pregnancy. Some of the tests are done in the doctor's office, and others are done in the hospital. Tests that may be used include electronic fetal monitoring and ultrasound.

If the baby seems to be active and healthy and the amniotic fluid volume appears normal, the mother and baby may continue to be monitored at set intervals until labor starts on its own. Your baby may need to be delivered if it seems to be at risk. Your doctor may induce labor by giving the drug oxytocin. This drug causes uterine contractions.

Many women wonder why the doctor doesn't simply bring on labor at 42 weeks. First, it's possible the due date is off; estimates can be wrong. Often, neither the mother nor her doctor can be sure that the fetus is fully mature and ready to be born. Second, in some women, even at this point in pregnancy, the cervix is not ready for labor to start.

Women with postterm pregnancies are carefully monitored during labor. If problems arise, the baby may be delivered by cesarean birth. After birth, a postterm baby may need special care.

Questions to Consider...

- What does it mean if I have bleeding during pregnancy?
- Should I receive RhIg? If so, when?
- My baby is in a breech position. Will it turn?
- How do I know if I am in preterm labor?
- What can happen if my membranes rupture early?

Chapter 13

Infections During Pregnancy

Infections are caused by tiny organisms that invade the body and then multiply. The body draws on its immune system to fight back and try to kill the invaders. While this fight is going on, you get symptoms of the infection, such as a rash, pain, fever, and swelling. You also develop antibodies in your blood, which are special proteins that form in response to an organism to combat infection. Antibodies are a key part of the immune system. You are not aware of antibodies when they form, but you can be tested for them to see whether they are present. If antibodies are present, you have been exposed to a disease. In many cases, once antibodies to a disease are made, you are immune to getting the disease in the future.

Infections can range from a mild cold or flulike illness to a serious disease that is life-threatening. Certain infections can harm the fetus if the mother is exposed to them during pregnancy. Although a cold or flu is usually not serious to the mother or fetus, you should not treat it yourself with over-the-counter medications. Instead, call your doctor or nurse if you have symptoms.

You can be vaccinated against some infections. However, certain types of vaccines are not safe during pregnancy. A vaccine contains either a small amount of the same organism that causes the infection or a small amount of a similar organism. The amount is just enough to cause antibodies to form and make you immune, but not enough to make you ill.

The best way to protect yourself against infections to which you are not immune is to avoid being exposed to them before and during pregnancy. If you think you have been exposed to an infection, tell your doctor or nurse right away. Sometimes steps can be taken to avoid serious problems and lower the risk to your baby.

Sexually Transmitted Diseases

Sexually transmitted diseases (STDs) are infections that are passed through sex. All STDs can lead to serious problems, and some are especially harmful during pregnancy.

How Sexually Transmitted Diseases Can Affect You and Your Baby

Disease	Symptoms in Women	Effects On:	
		Mother	Fetus/Baby
AIDS*	Appetite or weight loss, fatigue, swollen lymph nodes, night sweats, fever or chills, persistent diarrhea or cough; may have no symptoms	Immune system damage, leading to infections (such as pneumonia) or cancers; death	Immune system damage leading to death in 3 years in most infants
Chlamydia	Vaginal discharge, painful or frequent urination, pelvic pain; may be no symptoms	Pelvic inflammatory disease, ectopic pregnancy	Eye infection, pneumonia
Genital herpes	Flulike symptoms (fever, chills, muscle aches, etc); small, painful, fluid-filled blisters on genitals or buttocks	Recurrent outbreaks	Severe skin infection, nervous system damage, blindness, mental retardation, death
Genital warts	Possible genital itching, irritation, or bleeding; warts may appear as small, cauliflower-shaped clusters	Warts grow in size and number; may have abnormal Pap test	Warts on the vocal cords in early adolescence
Gonorrhea	Vaginal discharge, minor genital irritation, pain and fever; most women have no symptoms	Pelvic inflammatory disease, arthritis	Eye infection if left untreated
Syphilis	A painless open sore called a chancre; later rash, sluggishness, or slight fever	Damage to heart, blood vessels, and nervous system; blindness, insanity, death	Miscarriage, stillbirth, syphilis in liveborn infant

*AIDS stands for acquired immunodeficiency syndrome.

If you think you may have an STD, get tested and treated right away. Your partner should also be treated, and neither of you should have sex until you have finished treatment.

Chlamydia, Gonorrhea, and Pelvic Inflammatory Disease

Chlamydia and gonorrhea are the most common STDs in the United States today. They are caused by bacteria that are passed from person to person during sex. They are alike in many ways, and often occur together. They also infect the same sites in a woman's reproductive tract. The most commonly infected sites are the cervix, rectum, and urethra (the opening through which urine is passed). The most common symptom in men with chlamydia or gonorrhea is a drip from the penis. Many women have no symptoms. They learn they have chlamydia or gonorrhea only when their sexual partners are found to have the disease. Sometimes a pelvic exam is not enough to make a diagnosis, and other tests need to be done. If you have these diseases, you can be treated with antibiotics, even during pregnancy.

Chlamydia and gonorrhea can cause pelvic inflammatory disease. This is a severe infection that spreads from the vagina and cervix through the pelvic area and may involve the uterus, fallopian tubes, and ovaries. Women who have repeated pelvic infections or whose infections last a long time may need surgery to remove damaged reproductive organs. Pelvic inflammatory disease does not always cause symptoms. When symptoms do appear, they range from mild to severe and may include pain in the pelvic area, vaginal discharge or bleeding, pain when urinating, and fever.

Chlamydia and gonorrhea can infect the fetus as it passes through the vagina during delivery, causing eye infection and other problems. A newborn's eyes are very sensitive to gonorrhea. To prevent damage, the eyes of all newborns are treated at birth whether or not the mother has a history of gonorrhea.

Herpes Simplex Virus

Genital herpes is an infection caused by herpes simplex virus. It causes sores and blisters on or around the sex organs. It is transmitted during sex, usually by direct contact with a person who has active sores. In some cases, the virus can be passed to others even when the sores have healed. Some people have only one outbreak of genital herpes. Others have repeated bouts throughout their lifetime. In rare cases, the baby can become infected with the herpes virus during birth. This can cause severe skin infection, damage to the nervous system, blindness, mental retardation, or death.

If you have ever had genital herpes or have had sex with someone who has, tell your doctor or nurse. He or she will want to see if you have open lesions. If there are signs of active infection when you are in labor, you may need to deliver by cesarean birth. Cesarean birth lessens the chance that the baby will come in contact with the virus in the vagina. When you have no herpes sores, the baby can be delivered vaginally.

Human Papillomavirus

Human papillomavirus (HPV) is a virus that causes genital warts (sometimes called condyloma). Warts in the genital area are easily passed from person to person during sex, including oral and anal sex. You can have HPV even without having genital warts, and you may not be found to have HPV until years after you've been exposed. Sometimes a Pap test will show signs of HPV infection. Some types of HPV infection are linked with higher rates of cervical cancer. There is a very slight risk that babies born to mothers with HPV can get an infection of the larynx, or voice box when they reach adolescence.

Although genital warts can go away on their own, usually they need to be removed by minor surgery or with a strong chemical painted on the skin. Many of these methods can be used during pregnancy. If warts are widespread, though, it may be best to wait until after the baby is born to begin treatment. In any case, your condition will be watched closely throughout your pregnancy.

Trichomoniasis

Trichomoniasis is an STD that affects the vagina. Women may have no symptoms, or they may have a vaginal discharge, burning, and irritation. Trichomoniasis is usually treated with metronidazole, an antibiotic. However, this medication should not be taken by women in early pregnancy.

Syphilis

Syphilis, a disease that has been known for hundreds of years, is a serious STD. It is caused by organisms called spirochetes. If untreated, syphilis often spreads through the body and can cause blindness, heart disease, nervous disorders, insanity, tumors, and death. Syphilis can be passed from a pregnant woman's bloodstream to her fetus, sometimes causing miscarriage or stillbirth. If the infant lives, it may be born with congenital syphilis. Infants with congenital syphilis may have problems of the nervous system, skin, bones, liver, lungs, or spleen.

Syphilis can be more difficult to detect in women. The sore that marks the site of infection—called a ***chancre***—may be in the vagina where it cannot be seen. For most heterosexual men, the chancre appears on the penis, but it may be anywhere around the genital area.

In its early stages, when a chancre is present, syphilis may be diagnosed by scraping tissue from the chancre. A blood test may or may not find the disease in the earliest stages. The chancre will go away even without treatment, but the disease remains. After the chancre goes away, the only sure way to diagnose syphilis is a blood test.

Treating an infected pregnant woman with antibiotics will halt further damage to her fetus, but it will not reverse any harm already done. If a woman is treated during the first 3–4 months of pregnancy, it is very unlikely that the infant will suffer any long-term damage. Treating an infected infant after birth will usually prevent more damage but will probably not correct any damage already done.

Human Immunodefiency Virus Infection and Acquired Immunodeficiency Syndrome

Infection with human immunodefiency virus (HIV) and acquired immunodeficiency syndrome (AIDS), the disease caused by HIV, are growing threats to women. Human immunodeficiency virus enters the bloodstream by way of body fluids—usually blood or semen—from an infected person. The main ways HIV is transmitted are sexual contact, intravenous drug use, and, in rare cases, blood transfusions—although the blood supply in the United States has been tested since 1985 to solve this problem. If a pregnant woman is infected, she can pass the virus to her fetus.

Once in the body, HIV invades and destroys cells of the immune system, the body's natural defense against disease. This leaves the body open to harmful infections that can cause death. When a person infected with HIV comes down with one of these serious infections, he or she is said to have AIDS. When a person is infected with HIV, he or she carries the infection for life. It may take more than 5 years for symptoms to appear. While HIV infection has no cure, treatment can prolong life.

About a third of pregnant women who are infected with HIV give the virus to their fetus. Most infected babies die within 3 years after birth. Because the virus can cross the placenta before birth, it may not matter whether the baby is born through the vagina or by cesarean delivery—infection may already have occurred. A mother who is breast-feeding may infect her infant after birth because the AIDS virus is found in breast milk. This can happen even if the mother didn't have the virus before pregnancy but got infected after the baby was born. Studies have shown that when HIV-infected pregnant women who have no symptoms of AIDS are treated with a drug called zidovudine (AZT), they are much less likely to pass the AIDS virus to the fetus. The woman must take the drug during pregnancy, labor, and delivery, and the infant must take the drug during the first 6 weeks of life.

If you think you may have been exposed to the AIDS virus, talk with your doctor or nurse about being tested. A test called the enzyme-linked immunosorbent assay (ELISA) is used to detect HIV. It will show whether your blood contains HIV antibodies—a sign that you have been infected. Positive results are then confirmed by Western blot, another test used as a double check. If both tests are positive, you are considered to be infected. A positive test does not mean that you have AIDS; it means that you have been infected with HIV and that you run a high risk of getting AIDS and passing it to others. About 1 time in 20,000, the tests will give a false-positive result. A false-positive result means the test shows you have been infected when you haven't been.

Other factors can cause test results that are not accurate. After you are exposed to the virus, weeks or months must pass before enough antibodies show up in your blood to produce a positive test result. This means that if you were exposed to the virus only a week before being tested, the test would show a negative result. A negative test can't tell you whether you are now infected; it only shows that you didn't have antibodies when the test was done. A negative test also doesn't mean that you are immune to AIDS. You still need to protect yourself from infection by using condoms and avoiding other risky behavior, such as intravenous drug use, sex with more than one partner, or sex with a partner who may use drugs or have other sexual partners.

Childhood Diseases

Although certain infections are thought of as childhood diseases, they can also strike adults. Some can cause serious problems in pregnant women. If you've had these diseases as a child, you probably won't get them again. You are immune because you have developed antibodies that protect you against them. There are vaccines for many of these diseases. If you haven't had these diseases yet, it's a good idea to be vaccinated against them before your next pregnancy.

Because many children do not get vaccinated, these diseases are becoming more widespread. If you are exposed to these diseases during this pregnancy, your doctor may be able to treat you or your fetus to prevent the fetus from getting ill.

Chickenpox

Chickenpox is caused by varicella–zoster virus. Adults who come down with chickenpox usually get sicker than children do. Pregnant women who get this infection are more likely than other adults to get other illnesses along with it, such as pneumonia. It takes about 14 days from the time you are exposed to chickenpox to get symptoms of the illness. Symptoms include fever and fluid-filled bumps that itch. Chickenpox can be passed on to others even before the rash appears.

If you get chickenpox a week or more before giving birth, the fetus can catch the infection in your uterus and be born with it. It is possible, however, that the antibodies you form while you're sick cross the placenta into the fetus's blood and help protect it from serious illness. The baby may be born with chickenpox, but

Vaccines

Vaccines help prevent diseases caused by infection. Like all medicines, vaccines should be used during pregnancy only when it is necessary and safe. Ideally, a woman should have had all her vaccinations before pregnancy; but if a vaccination is necessary during pregnancy, waiting until the fourth month is generally good advice.

Some vaccines are usually not given to pregnant women, but are safe to be used if you are likely to come in contact with the infections:

- Hepatitis B
- Pneumonia caused by *Pneumococcus*

Some vaccines are safe for pregnant women. They are not routinely given, however, unless you are likely to come in contact with the disease:

- Rabies
- Influenza
- Polio
- Diphtheria
- Tetanus

Certain vaccines should not be used during pregnancy because they contain a live virus, which might harm the baby you are carrying:

- Measles
- Rubella
- Mumps

Exposure to measles, rubella, and mumps should be avoided during pregnancy. Women should be vaccinated against these diseases at least 3 months before they become pregnant. If you are already pregnant but not vaccinated, you should get vaccinated right after you have your baby. Vaccination is safe for you and your baby while you are breast-feeding.

will likely recover fully. If you get chickenpox less than a week before delivery, however, there is not enough time for antibodies to develop and protect the baby. In such cases, babies are more likely to get very sick.

Because chickenpox is so easy to catch, pregnant women who are not immune to it should stay away from people who have the disease, especially near the time of their delivery.

If a pregnant woman does come in skin contact with an infected person, a drug called varicella–zoster immune globulin may keep her from getting seriously ill if it is given within 4 days of exposure. A vaccine for the virus that causes chickenpox is being developed.

Fifth Disease

Fifth disease got its name because it was the fifth to be discovered among a group of diseases that cause fever and skin rash in children. It is caused by a virus called parvovirus B19. This common childhood illness is usually mild but is very contagious. Its main symptom is a rash that usually starts on the cheeks and is later found on the backs of the arms and legs. In rare cases it causes joint pains and affects the nervous system. About half of all adults have antibodies to fifth disease, which means they have been exposed to it.

During pregnancy, infection with parvovirus B19 is cause for concern. Women who have long-term, close exposure to the disease, such as teachers in a school with an epidemic or mothers who have an infected child at home, are at higher risk of getting infected than are women whose contact is more casual. If you get fifth disease in the first trimester or early second trimester, you have a slightly higher risk of miscarriage (about 1–2% higher than normal). When infection occurs later in pregnancy, it can cause anemia in the fetus and may require treatment.

Rubella (German Measles)

There are different types of measles caused by various viruses. Most types do not cause problems during pregnancy. The type that has the most severe effects during pregnancy is caused by rubella virus and is known as German measles. Since 1969, when a vaccine for rubella was introduced, preschool and young school-age children have been vaccinated routinely. About 75–80 of every 100 women are protected against rubella by the time they reach childbearing age because they have been exposed to rubella, have had the disease, or have been vaccinated. You can be infected with the rubella virus without knowing. Once infected with rubella virus, you are immune for life.

It's a good thing that most people are immune to rubella, because the virus can cause birth defects and long-term problems in babies exposed to the virus while their mothers were pregnant. The risk depends on when during the fetus's growth the mother was infected. If she was infected during the first month, her baby has a one-in-two chance of being affected. By the third month, the risk is lowered to about 1 in 10. The most common problems include cataracts (an eye problem that can cause blindness), heart defects, and deafness—together called congenital rubella syndrome. Other disorders, such as diabetes, can develop later in life.

As a routine part of prenatal care, each pregnant woman is tested for antibodies to show whether she is immune to rubella. If there are signs that a woman is not immune but may have been exposed to rubella or if she develops symptoms (fever, rash, and swollen lymph glands), she will be tested again.

Because rubella can have such a severe impact on the fetus and because nothing can be done during pregnancy to protect the fetus, it is best to get the rubella vaccine before becoming pregnant. Women who have never had the disease or the vaccine can be vaccinated just after delivery, before they become pregnant again. Although the vaccine does not cause congenital rubella syndrome, the virus it contains may be passed to the fetus. Therefore, it is best to wait 3 months after getting the vaccine before you try to become pregnant. Should you get the vaccine early in your pregnancy, however, the risk that your baby will have a problem is very low.

Mumps

Mumps is a disease caused by a virus. Less than 1 case in 10 occurs in people older than 15 years. Mumps causes fever and swollen glands under the jaw, and it is less contagious than measles or chickenpox. This means that mumps is uncommon during pregnancy. If you do get mumps during pregnancy, your symptoms are likely to be no worse than if you were infected before pregnancy. When a woman gets mumps in the first 12 weeks of pregnancy, however, it doubles her chance of having a miscarriage. Mumps may also cause preterm labor. Because this infection is so rare during pregnancy, it is not clear whether it is linked to birth defects.

The vaccine against mumps that is given to children has greatly reduced the number of pregnant women who are exposed to the disease. Having mumps as a child also protects against getting mumps later. If you are pregnant and are one of the few women who are not immune to mumps, it would be a good idea to get vaccinated after you give birth. There is a very small chance that the vaccine could hurt the fetus if given during pregnancy, so it is not given to pregnant women.

Cytomegalovirus

Cytomegalovirus (CMV) infection is hard to detect because people who have it often do not have symptoms. People with symptoms experience fever, tiredness, swollen lymph glands, and sore throat. Rarely does CMV cause serious illness in an adult. Even though about 6–7 of every 10 people have been infected with CMV at one time or another, about 9 in 10 who have been infected never had symptoms.

Cytomegalovirus infection poses a problem during pregnancy and the period after birth because it can be passed to the baby through the placenta, the vagina, or breast milk. Unlike other viral infections, CMV can come back even if a person has been infected before and has developed antibodies. The risk of the fetus getting infected is greatest during the first bout of infection in the mother. Few women—only about 2 per 100—get their first CMV infection while they are pregnant. If they do, however, the chance of the fetus getting infected is fairly high. Studies have shown that among mothers with first-time CMV infections during pregnancy, about half of their fetuses are infected with CMV. Only 1 of these fetuses in 10 has signs of disease. Those who do have symptoms at birth have a higher risk of dying or having severe illness or handicaps. Some problems linked to CMV infection are *jaundice* (yellow skin and eyes caused when the liver doesn't work normally), microcephaly (having a very small head and often being mentally retarded), deafness, and eye problems.

Cytomegalovirus infection has no treatment. Because it rarely causes symptoms when a pregnant woman is infected, screening or general testing is not useful. It is not known exactly how CMV is spread, but it can be passed by close contact and through saliva, urine, or sex. The best way to keep from getting CMV is to avoid contact with infected people and to wash your hands often.

Hepatitis

Hepatitis is a viral infection that affects the liver. The four kinds of hepatitis are types A, B, C, and D. Hepatitis B (HBV) is the most serious type during pregnancy. It can be transmitted by blood, kissing, or sex.

People with HBV may not feel sick or show any signs of the disease. Some people who are infected can be chronic carriers, however. This means they keep the virus in their bodies all their lives and can pass it to other people. Some people who get infected with HBV develop serious liver problems, such as cirrhosis (hardening) of the liver and possibly liver cancer. About 1 in 250 Americans is a chronic carrier. Some people have a higher risk of HBV infection. You may be more likely to get the disease if you:

- Inject drugs and share needles
- Have multiple sexual partners
- Work in a health-related job with exposure to blood or blood products
- Live with someone infected with HBV
- Received blood products (for example, for a clotting disorder)

About 8 of every 10 infants born to women with chronic HBV get infected, usually during delivery. Most of these infants also become chronic HBV carriers and are at risk for the long-term problems of HBV infection.

Any teen or adult with a higher risk of getting the disease should be vaccinated. All infants should get the vaccine, too. The vaccine is usually given in three doses. The first two doses are given 1 month apart, and the third is given 6 months later. Hepatitis B may be avoided by using condoms during sex and by stopping any activity, such as sharing needles to inject drugs, that brings you in contact with another person's blood.

All pregnant women should be tested routinely for HBV. It can be hard to find without testing because its symptoms—nausea and vomiting—often occur in pregnancy. If you are infected, a drug called hepatitis B immune globulin can make the illness less severe. Bed rest, diet, and liquids may also be prescribed. Your baby will be given hepatitis B immune globulin and the first dose of HBV vaccine soon after birth. This approach is 95% effective in keeping babies from being HBV carriers.

Listeriosis

Listeriosis is an illness caused by bacteria found in certain foods. The foods most likely to be affected are milk, cheese, raw vegetables, and shellfish. Symptoms develop several weeks after you are exposed to the bacteria. They can include fever, chills, muscle aches, and back pain—or there may be no symptoms. When pregnant women are infected, the disease can cause serious problems for the fetus, including miscarriage. Babies born to mothers who were infected while pregnant can have trouble breathing, low body temperature, and other problems. Some who seem healthy at birth can get symptoms weeks later, such as fever or feeding problems. Some studies suggest that pregnant women are more likely to get the disease than most other people.

Because the symptoms of listeriosis are similar to those of the flu, it's not always detected. If you have a fever or flulike illness, samples from your vagina, cervix, and blood can be checked. If the bacteria are found, you can be treated with antibiotics. If there is a chance that a newborn is infected, he or she can also be tested and treated.

Group B Streptococcus

Group B streptococcus (GBS) bacteria are fairly common in pregnant women. They are usually found in the vagina and rectum. These bacteria are different from the streptococcus bacteria that cause strep throat. You can carry GBS in your body without symptoms. Group B streptococcus can infect your bladder, kidneys, or uterus, causing pain and inflammation. These infections are usually not serious and can be treated with antibiotics. When GBS is present but does not cause infection, the person is referred to as being colonized.

If GBS is passed from a woman to her baby, the baby may develop GBS infection. This happens to only a few babies. Babies who do become infected may have early or late infections.

Risk Factors for Group B Streptococcus Infection

Women with these risk factors are more likely to have babies with group B streptococcus (GBS) infection, and they may benefit from treatment during labor and delivery:

- Preterm labor (labor that begins before 37 weeks of pregnancy)
- Preterm premature rupture of membranes (breaking of the amniotic sac before 37 weeks of pregnancy)
- Prolonged rupture of membranes (more than 18 hours since the amniotic sac broke)
- Prior child with GBS infection
- Fever during labor

Early infections occur within the first 7 days after birth. Most occur within the first 6 hours. Most newborns with early infection got it from their mother during labor and delivery. Early infection can cause inflammation of the baby's blood, lungs, brain, or spinal cord. This can have serious results. Infections in some babies may result in death.

Late infections occur after the first 7 days of life. About half of late infections are passed from the mother to the baby during birth. The other half result from other sources of infection, such as contact with other people who are GBS carriers or with the mother after birth. Late infections can also cause some serious problems. The most common of these is meningitis, an inflammation of the membranes of the brain or spinal cord. Meningitis can have long-term effects on the baby's nervous system. Babies with late infections are less likely to die than those with early infections.

Testing

There are tests that can detect GBS, but they are not perfect. One way to test for GBS is through cultures. For cultures, samples are taken from the vagina and rectum and grown in a special substance. A urine sample may also be used for cultures. It may take up to 2 days to get the results.

The usefulness of cultures is limited because of the nature of GBS. A woman may be positive (colonized) at some times and not at others, so test results may be negative (not colonized) at the time the sample was taken, but positive at another time during pregnancy. Also, at any given time, one place in your body (for instance, the vagina) may be negative, while another (such as the rectum) may be positive. Thus, the test cannot always detect women who will be colonized at the time of delivery.

Treatment

The best way to try to prevent GBS infection in the baby is to treat the woman with antibiotics during labor. Treating the pregnant women before labor cannot be relied on to prevent infection in the baby. If she is treated during pregnancy, a woman can become positive again after treatment, before her baby is born. If she becomes positive, she can pass GBS to her baby.

A woman in labor may be treated even if she was not tested during pregnancy. Certain risk factors increase the chance that the baby of a mother with GBS will become infected. Treatment is most effective in these women.

Lyme Disease

Lyme disease is caused by a bite from an infected tick. When the tick bites, it injects a germ into the body that causes disease. The first sign of Lyme disease is a sore that often looks like a bull's-eye. This sore may go away, but the infection remains. It spreads to the joints, causing arthritis, and can cause muscle pain. Antibiotics will usually cure the infection. If untreated, it can attack the heart and nervous system.

Wood tick (*top*) and deer tick (*bottom*).

The germ the tick carries can pass from an infected mother to the fetus through the placenta. The result might be birth defects or miscarriage. However, it is too soon to tell for sure whether these problems are caused by Lyme disease or by something else. You can be treated with antibiotics if you have been bitten by a tick.

Ticks can carry diseases other than Lyme disease. It is wise for pregnant women to avoid heavily wooded areas and to wear long-sleeved shirts and long pants tucked into their socks in areas where ticks can be found.

Toxoplasmosis

The parasite that causes toxoplasmosis lives in some mammals, such as cats. Humans can get infected by eating raw or undercooked meat, especially lamb or mutton, or by coming into contact with cat feces. Toxoplasmosis causes only mild illness in adults, and often those exposed have no symptoms. About one third of the general public has been exposed to toxoplasmosis. Once you have been exposed, you develop antibodies and become immune to the disease.

Toxoplasmosis creates a problem in pregnancy only when the mother is first infected at that time. Of women infected with toxoplasmosis during pregnancy, about one third pass the infection to the fetus. Only one third of infected fetuses will show signs of the disease, however. The chances of the fetus getting infected are highest in the last 12 weeks of pregnancy, but the problems affecting the fetus are more severe when the infection occurs in the first 12 weeks.

If the mother gets infected, the lymph glands in her neck may swell and she may have fever, fatigue, sore throat, and rash—or she may not get symptoms at all. Her baby may be born prematurely or too small. It can also have fever, jaundice, eye problems, or other serious long-term problems. Both the mother and fetus can sometimes be treated with antibiotics. Infected babies are treated soon after birth to prevent long-term problems.

The best way to protect against toxoplasmosis is to avoid being exposed to it. Be sure meat is well cooked. Cats should be fed only store-bought cat food and be kept from eating mice, which could harbor the parasite. If your cat goes outside often, do not hold it close to your face. Keep the cat off your bed, blankets, pillows, and sheets. Because cat feces are not infectious during the first 24 hours, cat litter should be changed daily, and somebody else should do it. Once feces do become infectious, they stay that way for a long time. Pregnant women should wear rubber gloves or avoid gardening in areas where there are cat feces. Always wash your hands well, with soap and water, after touching soil, cats, or uncooked meat or vegetables.

Tuberculosis

Tuberculosis (TB) is a disease that affects the lungs and can spread to other parts of the body such as the brain, kidneys, or bones. It was becoming a rare disease in the United States, but the number of people with TB has started to rise again. It is caused by bacteria that are transmitted through the air, usually when an infected person coughs or sneezes. It develops slowly and may cause no symptoms at first, but over time TB can cause fever, weight loss, night sweats, a dry cough, and chest pain. Even before symptoms develop, TB can be found by a simple skin test. It can be treated with a combination of drugs that must be taken for several months.

Tuberculosis in pregnant women is relatively rare but it, too, is increasing. Women can be treated during pregnancy. When a mother has TB, the fetus can get infected through her blood or by breathing in the bacteria at birth. The baby can also get infected by contact with the mother after birth. For this reason, infants born to mothers with TB should be given a special vaccine or a drug that protects them from catching the disease. Women with TB should talk to their doctor to see if they can breast-feed.

Urinary Tract Infections

Urinary tract infections are common in pregnancy. Severe infections can cause problems for both mother and fetus. Some urinary tract infections can be found only by tests—there may be no symptoms to let you know that you are infected. Some symptoms linked with a urinary tract infection, such as pain when you urinate, can be caused by other problems such as infection of the vagina or vulva.

Cystitis is a lower-tract (bladder) infection. Its symptoms include an increased need to urinate, burning and pain when you urinate, pain in the lower abdomen, and sometimes signs of blood in the urine. This condition is treated with antibiotics.

Pyelonephritis is an upper-tract (kidney) infection. It can cause chills, fever, rapid heart rate, and nausea or vomiting and can lead to premature labor or septic shock, in which your blood pressure falls to dangerous levels. If you have pyelonephritis, you may be hospitalized and may need antibiotics. It may take a while before you recover.

Questions to Consider...

- ◼ Do I have all the vaccinations I need?
- ◼ If I'm pregnant and do not have all my vaccinations, which ones can I get during pregnancy?
- ◼ What can I do to avoid getting diseases if I'm not immune?
- ◼ If I own a cat, what precautions should I take?

Labor, Delivery, and Postpartum

For the past months, you have been getting prenatal care regularly and learning how you are changing and how your baby is growing. As you near the end of your pregnancy, you are probably eager for your baby to be born. Most women are a little nervous about what is to come. After the baby is born, your life will change. Your new baby will demand care and attention 24 hours a day. Attending to your own needs and getting support from others can make meeting this challenge a little easier. One of the best ways to relax and enjoy this special event is to know what to expect. Learning as much as you can will help make your baby's arrival a pleasant, exciting time.

Chapter 14

Labor and Delivery

Awaiting the birth of a child is an exciting and anxious time. Most women give birth between 37 and 42 weeks of pregnancy. However, there is no way to know exactly when you'll go into labor. Birth often occurs as much as 3 weeks before or 2 weeks after the due date, but not too often on the due date.

As you plan for the birth, you can take steps to help your labor go more smoothly. You should discuss them with your health care team before the time comes. These questions should be answered in advance:

- When should I call?
- How can I reach the doctor or nurse after office hours?
- Should I go directly to the hospital or call the office first?
- Are there any special instructions I should follow when I think I am in labor?

Before it's time to go to the hospital, there are many things to think about. You may not have time to think about them once labor begins, so they should be considered ahead of time:

- *Distance.* How far do you live from the hospital?
- *Transportation.* Is there someone who can take you at any hour of the day or night, or do you have to call and find someone? Do you have a reliable car?
- *Time of day.* Depending on where you live, it may take longer to get to the hospital during rush hours than at other times of the day or night.
- *Time of year.* Bad weather or other factors may make the trip longer.

■ *Home arrangements.* Do you have other children who must be taken to a baby-sitter's home? Do you need someone to feed and walk a pet? Do you need to make any other special arrangements?

It may be a good idea to rehearse going to the hospital to get a sense of how long it could take. Plan an alternate route you can follow to the hospital if you run into a delay on the preferred route.

Important Information: A Checklist

Be sure to think about the following and get answers to any important questions:

Before Labor and Delivery

- What phone number do I call if I have an emergency during my pregnancy?
- What phone number should I call when I go into labor?
- When my labor starts, where exactly do I go?
- Who will drive me to the hospital? How do I get in touch with him or her when I'm ready to go?
- Where can we park the car?
- Does my insurance plan require me to preregister at the hospital before I show up? If so, have I done this?
- Have I checked my maternity benefits at work so I know exactly what's permitted?
- Do I have the baby's car seat?
- Do I have film and batteries in my camera?
- Have I decided how I'm going to feed the baby, and have I bought the things I'll need for feeding?

At Discharge from the Hospital

- Have I made an appointment for my follow-up visit?
- How do I get in touch with my health care provider? With my baby's doctor?
- If I have stitches, how do I take care of them?
- Do I need any prescription medications? If so, how do I take them?
- Have I made plans for contraception?

Packing Your Suitcase

It is often a good idea to pack two suitcases: a small overnight case with a few personal items to take with you and a larger suitcase with all of your other things to be brought later. You may wish to find out in advance what items the hospital provides for you during labor and what you will need to bring yourself. Talking with hospital staff and other women who have delivered there can help you to plan. A childbirth educator is also a good source of information. Here are some items that you may wish to consider:

- Comfortable gown and robe
- Slippers
- Several pairs of socks
- Hair brush
- Toothbrush and toothpaste
- Glasses or contact lenses
- Pad and pencil
- Change for vending machine and telephone
- Telephone numbers of people whom you plan to call after the birth
- Clothes for both you and the baby when you go home
- Sanitary napkins
- Nursing bra

How Labor Begins

No one knows exactly what causes labor to start, although changes in hormones play a role. Most women can tell when they are in labor. Sometimes, however, it is hard to tell, even for an experienced doctor or nurse. Your condition may need to be watched for several hours.

Labor begins when the cervix begins to open, or dilate. The uterus, which is a muscle, contracts at regular intervals. When it contracts, the abdomen becomes hard. Between contractions, the uterus relaxes and the abdomen becomes soft. Certain changes may signal the approach of labor. Knowing what happens in labor makes it easier for you to relax and focus on the arrival of your baby when the time comes.

True Versus False Labor

You may have periods of "false" labor, or irregular contractions, that feel like your uterine muscles are knotting up. These cramps, called ***Braxton Hicks contractions,*** are normal, but they can be painful at times. They usually come more often in the afternoon or evening, after physical activity, or when you are tired.

It can be hard to tell false labor from true labor, especially because false labor can happen just at the time when you expect true labor. It's easy to be fooled and think that labor is starting. Sometimes the only way to tell the difference is by having a vaginal exam to find changes in your cervix that signal the onset of labor.

One good way to tell the difference between true and false labor is to time the contractions. Note how long it is from the start of one contraction to the start of the next one. Keep a record for an hour. During true labor:

- The contractions last about 30–70 seconds.
- They occur regularly (usually 5 minutes apart or closer).
- They don't go away when you move around.
- Walking makes the contractions feel stronger.

True Versus False Labor

Type of Change	False Labor	Labor
Timing of contractions	Often are irregular and do not consistently get closer together (called Braxton Hicks contractions)	Come at regular intervals and, as time goes on, get closer together
Change with movement	Contractions may stop when you walk or rest, or may even stop with a change of position	Contractions continue, despite movement
Location of contractions	Often felt in the abdomen	Usually felt in the back coming around to the front
Strength of contractions	Usually weak and do not get much stronger (may be strong and then weak)	Increase in strength steadily

While you are timing your contractions, feel free to walk around and finish household tasks. Be sure to make note of how the contractions feel. Other things you can do:

■ Pack your suitcase, if you haven't already.

■ Let your driver and the person who'll care for your other children know you'll be leaving for the hospital soon.

■ Review the relaxation techniques you learned in childbirth class.

■ Take a warm bath.

■ Try to rest—if it's nighttime, try to sleep.

Keep in mind that it's hard to time your labor pains precisely if the contractions are slight. It's best to be cautious. If you think you're in labor, don't call—go directly to the hospital.

Signs of Labor

Sign	What It Is	When It Happens
Feeling as if the baby has dropped lower	*Lightening.* This is commonly referred to as the baby's head dropping. The baby's head has settled deep into your pelvis.	From a few weeks to a few hours before labor begins (usually earlier with first babies)
Discharging a thick plug of mucus or an increase in vaginal discharge (clear, pink, or slightly bloody)	*Show.* A thick plug of mucus has accumulated at the cervix during pregnancy. When the cervix begins to open wider, the plug is pushed into the vagina.	Several days before labor begins or at the onset of labor
Discharging a trickle or a gush of watery fluid from your vagina	*Rupture of Membranes.* The fluid-filled sac that surrounded the baby during pregnancy breaks (your water breaks).	From several hours before labor begins to anytime during labor
Feeling a regular pattern of tightening or what may feel like a bad backache or menstrual cramps	*Contractions.* Your uterus is a muscle that tightens and re-laxes. The hardness you feel is from your uterus contracting. These contractions may cause pain as the cervix opens and the baby moves through the birth canal.	At the onset of labor

Labor Definitions

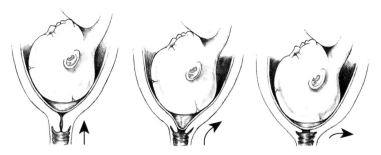

Effacement is the thinning out of the cervix. It is measured in percentages, from 0% (no effacement) to 100% (fully effaced).

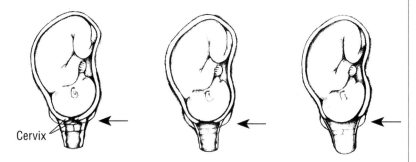

Cervix

Dilatation refers to the amount that the cervix has opened. It is measured in centimeters, from 0 centimeters (no dilatation) to 10 centimeters (full dilatation).

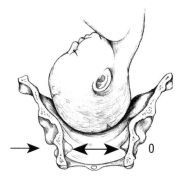

Station is the relationship of the baby's head to a bony landmark in the pelvis.

Other signs should prompt you to call or go to the hospital:

- Your membranes rupture (your "water breaks"), even if you are not having any contractions.
- You are bleeding from the vagina (but not if it is just "show"—the mucus plug expelled from your cervix before labor. This plug can be tinged with a little blood).
- You have constant, severe pain with no relief between contractions.

Although the word "pain" is used often to describe labor, how much discomfort is felt and where it is felt vary from woman to woman. If you have any questions about what you're feeling and what it may mean, call your doctor or nurse.

The Support Person's Role

Many fathers want to be active partners in the birth of their child. Often they choose to be in the delivery room when their baby is born. If a father does not want to get involved in the delivery itself, he can give support in other ways. The father can take childbirth preparation classes with you, be with you during labor, and take an active role in caring for you and the baby after delivery. Caring can take many forms. You can decide with the father what is best in this family-centered approach to childbirth.

The support person—sometimes called the coach—does not have to be the father. Any close relative or loved one can help you get ready for and go through birth. During delivery, the coach may want to stand near the head of the delivery bed, beside your shoulder. From this spot, he or she can give emotional and physical support while seeing your child being born just as you do. Or, the partner may prefer to stand at the end of the bed to see the birth up close or take pictures.

Here are some things the support person can do for you during labor:

- Do things with you to distract you—especially during the early part of labor—such as playing cards or games, talking, reading aloud, or walking
- Time your contractions
- Rub your back, if you wish
- Act as a focal point and breathe with you during contractions
- Offer comfort and encouragement

If a problem arises, your support person may be asked to leave the delivery room. There may not be time to explain why at that moment. In the best interest of the mother and baby, partners should leave right away if asked. The reason will be explained later, when time permits.

Easing Discomforts

In addition to the breathing and relaxation techniques you can learn in childbirth preparation classes, there are other ways of relieving discomfort you may feel during labor. Massages often feel good. You may want your partner to rub or firmly press on your lower back. You might also want to have an ice pack for your back or use tennis balls for massage. Frequent position changes can make you more comfortable. During contractions, you or your partner can try rhythmic stroking of your abdomen. Rubbing a little lotion on your skin first will reduce pulling on your skin. If you have leg cramps, massage or change of position can help relieve them.

You should not eat or drink during active labor. To keep your mouth moist, however, ask your doctor or nurse if you can suck on ice chips.

It is best to try to remain relaxed, especially between contractions. In early labor, when contractions are farther apart, watching television, playing games, or listening to music may be soothing. It may be helpful to try to rest or sleep during this time to prepare for the later, more active phases of labor, when more energy is required. When contractions are closer together and stronger, rest in between and take slow, deep breaths. If you become warm or perspire, cool, moist cloths can be soothing. Feeling warm is usually just a sign that you are working hard.

Admission

Once it appears that you are in labor, you will be admitted to the hospital obstetric unit. There your health care team will work together to care for you before, during, and after your delivery. If you haven't done so already, discuss your birth plan with your health care team.

The research you did and decisions you made earlier in your pregnancy will come into play now. Good preparation helps you take an active role and avoid surprises. If you've taken childbirth classes and have talked with your health care provider throughout your prenatal care, you'll already have the answers to many common questions. But never hesitate to ask questions of your doctor or other members of the health care team.

After you are admitted to the hospital, the steps to prepare you for delivery vary, but generally you can expect the following:

■ You may be asked to take off all your clothes and put on a special gown. (In a few hospitals you can wear a gown of your own.)

■ Your pulse, blood pressure, and temperature will be checked.

■ You'll be examined to find out how far labor has progressed.

When you're in active labor, an intravenous (IV) line may be placed into a vein in your arm or wrist. This is done by placing a needle in your vein over which a small, plastic tube is threaded and left in place and the needle removed. Medications and different types of fluid can be given as needed through your IV line.

Your doctor may not be with you the whole time you are in labor, but he or she will check on your progress. A team of nurses and other health care providers will care for you throughout labor. They will take your vital signs, such as heart rate and blood pressure, and time contractions to monitor the progress of labor. The baby's heartbeat will be checked regularly during labor. Labor and delivery nurses are trained to help you through the physical and emotional demands of labor. In teaching hospitals, resident doctors are often part of the team. Your labor may be in the same room used for delivery, or you may be moved to a delivery room for the actual birth.

Stages of Labor

The average labor lasts 12–14 hours for a first baby and is usually shorter for your other births. Labor happens in three stages. During each, changes take place in your body and how you feel. Every woman is different and every labor is different. What your mother or sister went through will not be exactly what you go through, and none of your labors, no matter how many children you have, will be just the same. Besides helping your cervix to efface (thin out) and dilate fully, the contractions during labor help the baby to come through the birth canal. Throughout labor, the baby moves deeper into the pelvis and farther down the birth canal. The baby's head and body move and turn for the easiest fit possible through the pelvis. The contractions continue to help the baby to be born, usually head first.

First Stage

This stage is usually the longest. It begins when your cervix starts to open and ends when it is completely open (fully dilated). Blood-tinged mucus (called show) is passed from your vagina at the onset of this stage. During the end of this stage, contractions become longer and stronger. The first stage of labor occurs in three phases: early, active, and transition.

Early (cervix dilated 0–5 centimeters)

What's Happening:

- Mild contractions begin at 15–20 minutes apart and last 60–90 seconds.
- Contractions gradually become more regular, until they are less than 5 minutes apart.
- You may see a small amount of show.
- You may feel relief that labor has finally started, and will likely feel excited.

What You Can Do:

- Take walks with your labor coach or support person.
- Take a warm bath or shower
- Relax with your partner
- Sleep if you can.
- Do relaxation techniques or meditation.

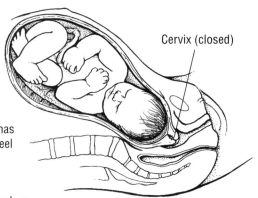

Cervix (closed)

Stage 1

Active (cervix dilated 5–8 centimeters)

What's Happening:
- Contractions get stronger and progress to 3 minutes apart, lasting about 45 seconds.
- Your membranes may rupture (your water breaks).
- You have increased bleeding from your vagina (bloody show).
- You may have a backache because the baby's head is pressing on your backbone.
- You may get leg cramps.
- You may feel anxious and more tired.

What You Can Do:
- Concentrate on your breathing.
- If your membranes rupture, expect the next contractions to be much stronger.
- Actively work with your labor coach.
- Urinate often; keeping your bladder empty gives the baby's head room to descend.
- Walk (if your doctor or nurse feels it is safe) and change positions, to help labor.
- Do relaxation techniques.
- Ask your coach or support person for a back rub. If you have leg cramps, ask to have your foot flexed.
- Stay off your back while you're in bed if you can. Being on your back may cause the baby to get less oxygen.
- Ask for pain relief if you wish to have it.

Transition (cervix is dilated 8–10 centimeters)

What's Happening:
- Contractions are 2–3 minutes apart and last about 1 minute.
- Your backache may get worse.
- You feel pressure on your rectum from the baby's head.
- Bloody show is quite heavy.
- You may have hiccups, nausea, vomiting, trembling legs, the urge to push, and a hard time relaxing.
- You may feel irritable, hot or cold, confused, angry, exhausted, and drowsy between contractions.
- If you push, it doesn't relieve the pain (the cervix is not fully dilated).

Stages of Labor *(continued)*

Transition (continued)

What You Can Do:
- Relax between contractions.
- Have a back rub at the spot where the baby's head is causing pain.
- Have someone fan you if you are hot.
- Keep your mouth moist by sucking ice chips or sipping water.
- Change positions often.
- Work closely with your labor coach.
- Take your contractions one at a time; don't think ahead to the next one.
- Wash your hands and face and ask for a clean gown.
- Ask for a cool cloth for your forehead.
- If you feel like pushing, tell your coach.
- Pant or blow instead of pushing.

Second Stage

When your cervix is fully dilated, the first stage ends and the second stage begins. This stage continues until the birth of the baby. It may last up to 2 hours or longer, especially during a first labor.

What's Happening:
- Contractions may slow to 2–5 minutes apart and last 60–90 seconds.
- It is time to start pushing with your contractions. The urge to push may become overwhelming.
- Your contractions feel different. They become more regular, with a well-defined rest period in between.
- Pushing feels good.
- Pressure on your rectum increases.
- You are alert and in control; the worst part of labor is over.
- The baby's head is usually born first.
- Your doctor or birth attendant actively helps with the birth.
- You may get local anesthesia and an episiotomy if needed.
- You feel great pressure and some stinging in the birth canal as the baby is born.

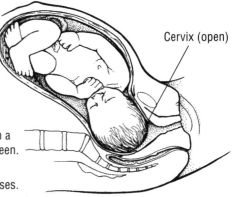

Cervix (open)

Stage 2 (early)

What You Can Do:

- Find a position for pushing that is comfortable for you. (Alternatives to lying down are squatting or kneeling.)
- Change position if you are not comfortable.
- Focus on your pushing. Work with your coach.
- Rest between contractions.
- Ask for a mirror if you want to see the baby coming out.
- Ask to have a warm cloth applied to your perineum to help focus your pushing efforts.
- Ask to touch the baby's head if you have lost your focus during pushing.
- Don't panic—everyone will help.
- Work closely with your birth attendant.
- Push only when asked, even if it is between contractions.
- Be prepared to change positions to aid the birth.
- Actively help with the birth by keeping your eyes open and pushing correctly.
- Hold your baby as soon as you can.

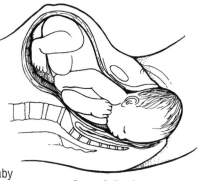

Stage 2 (late)

Third Stage

This last stage begins after the baby is born and ends when the placenta is expelled. It is the shortest stage and may last from just a few minutes to 15–20 minutes.

What's Happening:

- Contractions keep coming but are less painful.
- The placenta separates from the wall of the uterus and is delivered through the vagina.
- If you needed an episiotomy or had a small tear, it will be repaired.
- You may feel shaky or have chills.
- You may be very hungry.

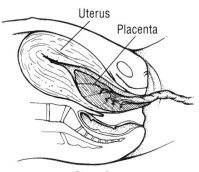

Uterus

Placenta

What You Can Do:

- Help expel the placenta by pushing when you are asked. Stage 3
- Ask for a warm blanket.
- Enjoy your baby and try breast-feeding, if that is your choice.

You probably will be asked to sign a consent form when you enter the hospital and possibly again if cesarean delivery is to be done. These papers can vary, but most spell out what will happen, who will be taking care of you during labor and delivery, why a procedure is being done, and the risks. Read this form carefully, and be sure to ask questions about anything you don't understand. Your signature on this consent means you understand your medical condition and give permission for the described care.

Monitoring

During labor, the heart rate of the baby will be monitored to check its well-being. Certain changes in the heart rate of the baby can signal a problem, so every woman gets some form of close monitoring while she is in labor. Fetal monitoring cannot prevent a problem from occurring, but it can alert your doctor or nurse to warning signs. No form of fetal monitoring is perfect, but techniques have improved over the years, and today more is known about what can happen to the baby during labor.

Fetal monitoring can be done by *auscultation* or with a machine called an electronic fetal monitor. The technique used depends on the hospital's policy, its equipment, and how many nurses are on hand.

Auscultation

Auscultation means listening to the baby's heartbeat at set times. The timing depends on how far along the mother is in labor and whether there are any risk factors.

A stethoscope can be used, which amplifies the heartbeat of the baby. The doctor or nurse presses one end of the stethoscope to your abdomen and listens to the heartbeat through ear pieces. Another way to listen is by ultrasound, which makes an audible signal of the baby's heartbeat. A small, hand-held device that sends out sound waves is placed against your abdomen. These waves are then reflected back from the baby. With ultrasound, anyone in close range can hear the noise of the baby's beating heart (see "Ultrasound," Chapter 6).

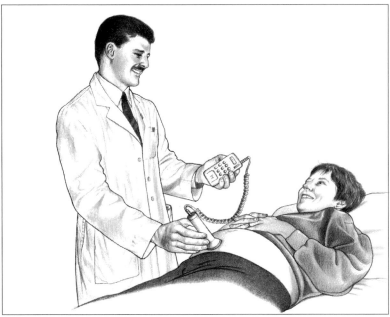

Ultrasound can be used to listen to the fetus's heartbeat.

When auscultation is used, the fetal heart rate is usually monitored and recorded after a contraction. The doctor or nurse will place his or her hands on your abdomen to feel your uterus contract. During times when the doctor or nurse is not listening to the heart, you can move about as you please, as long as there are no medical reasons for you to stay in bed. Auscultation has no known risks.

Electronic Fetal Monitoring

The second type of monitoring measures the baby's heart rate with electronic equipment. It provides an ongoing record that can be read by the doctor or nurse. Electronic fetal monitoring is either external or internal:

1. *External monitoring* requires that belts be placed around the mother's abdomen to hold two small devices in place. One device uses ultrasound to detect the fetal heart rate. The other is a pressure gauge to measure the length of uterine contractions and the time between them.

2. *Internal monitoring* can be used only after the fetal membranes (the amniotic sac in which the fetus grows) are broken. A small device called an electrode is inserted through your vagina and attached to the scalp of the baby to record the fetal heart rate. Sometimes a thin tube called a catheter may be placed in the uterus to measure the strength of uterine contractions. Most women who have had these devices put in during labor report feeling only minor discomfort, about the same as a routine exam of the cervix.

Sometimes both internal and external devices are used. The internal scalp electrode records the fetal heart patterns, and the external pressure gauge records uterine contractions.

With either internal or external monitoring, data about the mother and the baby are sent to a small machine. The information is recorded on a long strip of paper, or tracing, that is read by your doctor or nurse. The tracing shows patterns of the fetal heart rate in relation to uterine contractions.

Both methods of monitoring have benefits. With the external monitor, the cervix does not have to be dilated and the membranes around the fetus can be intact. Internal monitoring, however, may give more precise information about the baby's condition and the strength of

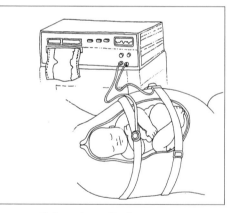

External monitoring uses two belts placed around the woman's abdomen.

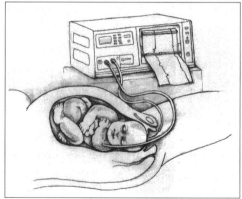

Internal monitoring uses two devices placed inside the uterus. One is attached to the fetus.

the mother's uterine contractions. Neither method affects the progress of labor. When monitoring equipment is in use, you will be asked to stay in bed because it helps keep the monitor in place.

Electronic fetal monitoring is more likely to be used in high-risk pregnancies. Although problems from electronic fetal monitoring are very rare, the spot where the electrode is placed on the baby's head can get injured or infected. Electronic fetal monitoring is just one way you may be helped with your delivery. Deciding to use it involves many factors. Talk over any questions you have about it with your health care team as you get ready for the delivery of your baby.

Pain Relief

Many women take childbirth classes to help them learn what to expect during labor and delivery. In these classes you also learn breathing methods, relaxation techniques, and other ways of coping with childbirth. From what they learn in these classes, some women are able to go through childbirth without pain medication. Other women find it helpful to use these techniques along with some pain medications. Throughout delivery, your nurse will be there to reassure you and help make you comfortable.

Your wishes will be taken into account in deciding what type of pain relief is best for you. Other factors, including your well-being and that of your baby, will also affect this choice. Often it is not possible to tell you exactly what kind of pain relief you will get until you are in labor or are ready to deliver. Many times these choices must be left open and flexible to see how your labor is going. Also, you may not always be able to have medicine just when you feel you need it.

Not all hospitals are able to offer all types of pain relief medications. An anesthesiologist—a doctor who is an expert in pain relief—may work with your health care team to pick the best method for you.

Pain-relieving drugs fall into two categories. *Analgesia* is the relief of pain without total loss of feeling. A person getting an analgesic stays conscious. Although analgesics don't always stop pain completely, they do lessen it.

What Affects Your Feelings of Pain?

People feel pain in different ways. Some have a worse time with pain than others. Things that can affect your feelings of pain are:

- Being alone. During labor and delivery it's important to have the support of people you care about or people experienced in childbirth.
- Being overly tired. Try to be well rested so you can cope with contractions.
- Feeling anxious and tense. Use relaxation techniques between contractions, and focus on your breathing during them.
- Expecting and fearing a lot of pain. Try to distract yourself. Don't focus on how much contractions hurt. Think about the final result—your new baby. If you're feeling afraid, go ahead and say so. Airing your fears gives others a chance to reassure you.
- Fearing the unknown and feeling helpless. Learn as much about childbirth as you can in advance by reading, asking questions, and taking childbirth preparation classes. This will make you feel more in control.

Anesthesia refers to the total loss of feeling. Some forms of anesthesia cause you to lose consciousness, whereas others remove the feeling of pain from parts of the body while you stay conscious.

Systemic Analgesia

Systemic analgesics are often given as injections into a muscle or vein. They lessen pain but will not cause you to lose consciousness. They act on the whole nervous system, rather than on one precise area. Sometimes other drugs are given with systemic analgesics to relieve tension or nausea.

Like other types of drugs, pain medicine can have side effects. Most are minor, such as feeling drowsy or having trouble concentrating. These medications are not given right before delivery to avoid slowing the baby's reflexes and breathing at birth.

Serious side effects are rare. Doctors and other health care professionals know how to give these drugs in ways that reduce the chances of side effects.

Local Anesthesia

Just as your dentist uses a drug to numb areas in your mouth, your doctor can use a local anesthetic to ease pain during delivery. Local anesthetics usually affect a small area. A procedure called *episiotomy* may be done before delivery to avoid tears in the mother's *perineum* during birth. Local anesthesia is helpful when an episiotomy is done or any tears that happened during birth are repaired.

Episiotomy

During delivery, when your baby's head crowns—appears at the opening of the vagina—the tissue of the vagina becomes very thinly and tightly stretched. Sometimes, even if the tissue is stretched as much as possible, it is difficult for the baby's head to fit through without tearing the mother's skin and perineal muscles.

To prevent your muscles from tearing and to relieve some of the pressure on your baby's head, a small cut may be made in the vagina and perineum while the area is numbed with a local anesthetic. This procedure is called an episiotomy.

Local anesthesia rarely affects the baby. After the anesthetic wears off, usually no effects linger.

Pudendal Block

Pudendal block is injected shortly before delivery to block pain in the perineum—the area between the vagina and rectum. It is especially helpful for numbing the perineum before birth. It relieves pain you may have around the vagina and rectum as the baby moves through the birth canal. Pudendal block is one of the safest forms of anesthesia, and serious side effects are rare.

Paracervical Block

With *paracervical block*, a local anesthetic is injected into the tissues around the cervix. It relieves the pain as the cervix dilates to allow the baby's head to descend into the birth canal. It also helps ease pain from the uterus contracting. Although a paracervical block gives good pain relief, it wears off quickly. Sometimes it slows the baby's heartbeat. Because of the effects on the baby, the heart rate of the baby is closely monitored. Because of concern about slowing of the heartbeat, this form of pain relief is not always offered.

Epidural Block

Epidural block, a regional anesthetic, affects a larger area than the other methods described. It causes some loss of feeling in the lower half of the body; the extent of the numbness depends on the drug and dose used. An epidural block is injected into the lower back. The drug is placed into a small space (the epidural space) outside the spinal cord, where the nerves that get signals from the lower body pass to reach the spinal cord. This kind of anesthesia helps ease the pain of uterine contractions and the pain in the vagina as the baby comes out. In larger doses, epidural blocks are used for pain control during cesarean birth.

You will be asked to sit or lie on your side with your back curved outward and to stay this way until the injection is over. You can move when it's done, but you may not be allowed to walk around.

The procedure itself should cause little discomfort. Your back will be washed with an antiseptic, and a tiny area of the skin will be numbed with a local anesthetic. After the epidural needle is in place, a small tube (catheter) is usually inserted through it, and the needle is withdrawn. That way, small doses can be given through the tube later, or the drug can be given continuously without your needing another injection. Low doses are used because they are less likely to cause side effects for you and the baby. It may take a short while for the medication to take effect. Although it will make you more comfortable, you may still be aware of your contractions. In some hospitals, a woman can get medications through the tube after delivery to help relieve her pain for as long as 24 hours.

Because modern techniques use low doses of pain medications, most women can deliver normally with an epidural. If the mother is very numb, however, it may be harder for her to bear down and help the baby move through the birth canal. This may slow labor. Epidural block can have some side effects. It may cause the mother's blood pressure to drop, which in turn may slow the baby's heartbeat. To prevent these problems, the mother is usually given fluids through an IV line in her arm before the drug is injected, and she may be asked to lie on her side to help her blood circulate.

Serious problems with epidurals are rare. If the covering of the spinal cord is pierced, you can get a bad headache, which can

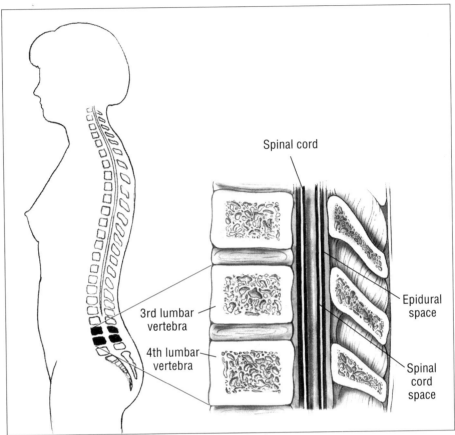

Insertion points for spinal and epidural anesthesia.

last a few days if it's not treated. If the drug enters the spinal fluid, the muscles in your chest can be temporarily affected, making it hard to breathe. If the drug enters a vein, you could get dizzy or, rarely, have a seizure. To reduce the likelihood that these unusual problems could occur, epidural anesthesia is given by highly qualified and experienced doctors.

Spinal Block

A *spinal block*, like an epidural block, is an injection in the lower back. While you sit or lie on your side in bed, a small amount of drug is injected into the spinal fluid to numb the lower half of the body. After the drug is given, you have to stay in bed. It brings good relief from pain and starts working fast, but it lasts only an hour or two. A spinal block is usually given only once during labor, so it is best suited for pain relief during delivery. A spinal block can be used for cesarean birth. It is also useful in a vaginal birth if the baby needs to be helped out of the birth canal with *forceps* or by **vacuum extraction**. Spinal block can sometimes cause the same side effects as epidural block, which are treated in a similar way. A saddle block is a form of a spinal block, but the medicine is allowed to drop to the lower part of the spine. The part of your body that loses feeling is the part that sits in a saddle—your buttocks, perineum, and vagina.

General Anesthesia

General anesthetics are drugs that put you to sleep, or make you lose consciousness. If you have general anesthesia, you are not awake during delivery and you feel no pain. General anesthesia is not used to relieve the pain of labor. It is used for cesarean birth and, at times, emergency vaginal delivery.

A rare but serious problem with general anesthesia occurs when food or acid from the stomach enters the windpipe and lungs and causes injury. Because of this, you should not eat solid food once labor has started. You may be given an antacid toward the end of labor to help prevent stomach acids from getting into your lungs.

Whether you should have general, spinal, or epidural anesthesia for a cesarean delivery will depend on your status and that of the baby, as well as why the cesarean delivery is being done. In emergencies or when bleeding occurs, general anesthesia is often preferred.

Helping Labor Along

Sometimes labor may need to be induced. A few of the conditions that may prompt induction of labor are:

- Your membranes ruptured but labor did not start.
- Your pregnancy is postterm (more than 42 weeks).
- You have high blood pressure caused by your pregnancy.

■ You have health problems such as diabetes or a lung disease.

■ You have ***chorioamnionitis*** (the membrane around the fetus is inflamed).

Labor may be induced when the risks of delivery for the mother or baby are lower than the risk of keeping the pregnancy going. The same methods used to induce labor can also speed up labor that is not going well. Inducing labor carries some risks; it should be done for a specific reason.

Labor can be induced in different ways. One is to break the membranes if they haven't broken already. This is done during a vaginal exam and usually causes no more pain than a regular exam. Most women go into labor within 12 hours after their membranes rupture.

Another way to induce labor is to use oxytocin. (Oxytocin is a natural hormone made by the body; what you are actually given is an artificial form of the hormone.) Oxytocin can help bring on contractions or make them stronger. The hormone, which is given by a pump, flows into your body through an IV tube in your arm. The pump controls the amount of oxytocin given.

If your cervix is not ready for labor, steps can be taken to make it soft and able to stretch for birth. The changes the cervix goes through before labor starts are called "ripening." One of the most common ways to make a cervix ripen is to place a gel into it with a syringe. The gel contains a special hormone called prostaglandin. Other methods include slender rods called laminaria, which are placed in the cervix and slowly swell.

Walking can help labor along and give you a feeling of control. Keep walking if you can and if your doctor or nurse feels it is safe. If your membranes have ruptured and the fetus is high in the birth canal, you should not walk.

Delivery

When your cervix has opened all the way, the baby starts moving down the birth canal. Usually it comes head first. You will feel an urge to push, or bear down. It can feel like the urge to move your bowels. Tell your doctor or nurse when you start to feel this way.

Generally, in early labor you should try not to bear down each time you have a contraction. You should try to relax between contractions. After the cervix dilates all the way, you will be told when to push and when not to push. To avoid pushing, you need to control your breathing. Even if you did not take a childbirth class or learn special breathing techniques, the nurse will help you. As the baby moves down the birth canal, your doctor or nurse keeps track of the progress and will tell you how to help it along. If necessary, an episiotomy may be done to prevent tears in the perineum. When the baby's head can be seen at the opening of the vagina, it is called crowning.

The baby's head will be born first. After the head comes out, the baby's body turns so that first one shoulder and then the other appears. After the shoulders come out, the rest of the baby's body follows quickly.

Just after birth, your doctor or nurse will hold the baby with his or her head lowered to help keep amniotic fluid, mucus, and blood from getting into the lungs. Sometimes the baby is placed on your abdomen or thigh while these fluids drain. The baby's mouth and nose may be suctioned with a small bulb syringe. You and your baby are still attached by the umbilical cord. The cord will then be cut and the placenta delivered. Your uterus will be massaged to keep it firm and hard. Your vagina, cervix, and perineum will be examined. If you had an episiotomy, it will be repaired now, along with any tears that may have occurred.

The baby will then be dried and wrapped in blankets; he or she may also be warmed with heat lamps or a heated bassinet. Drops or ointment to prevent infection will be put into the baby's eyes, and identification bands will be placed on you and the baby before you leave the delivery room. The baby's handprints and footprints may also be taken.

To check the health of your newborn, a method called the *Apgar score* is used. This method, described in Chapter 16, is used to assess the baby's health at birth and find out whether extra care is needed.

Unless you or your baby is having medical problems, you will probably be able to hold the baby. If you decided to breast-feed, you may be able to start at this time. Some babies want to nurse right away, although others do not. It is a very rewarding feeling for you and your partner to be close to your baby just after birth.

Forceps and Vacuum Extraction

Sometimes it is necessary to help delivery along by using forceps or a vacuum extractor. These devices are used when the fetal heartbeat slows or becomes erratic, when the baby's position makes delivery harder, or when the mother is too tired to push.

Forceps are a device that looks like two large spoons. The doctor inserts the forceps into the birth canal, places them around the baby's head, and gently delivers the baby.

Vacuum extraction is much like forceps delivery, but instead of spoons, a plastic cup is applied to the baby's head and held in place by suction. A handle on the cup allows the doctor to deliver the baby from the birth canal.

Cesarean Birth

If for some reason it is not safe for the baby to be delivered through the vagina, cesarean birth may be needed. A cesarean birth may be planned for reasons known in advance, or it may be needed because of problems that arise without warning. Having a cesarean de-

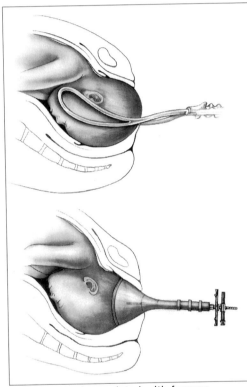

Delivery may be assisted with forceps (*top*) or a vacuum instrument (*bottom*).

livery does not mean that the mother or the health care team failed in any way. This method of birth should not make childbirth any less fulfilling. The way the baby is delivered is always less important than the overall goal: a healthy mother and baby.

There are many reasons why a cesarean birth might be chosen as the safest way to deliver your baby:

- ■ *Cephalopelvic disproportion* (the baby's head can't pass safely through the mother's pelvis because the fit is too snug)

■ Fetal stress, a warning that the baby is having trouble during labor and may need to be delivered right away (one reason is that the umbilical cord is pinched or compressed)

■ Placental problems

■ Abnormal presentation, in which a baby is born buttocks or feet first or in other uncommon positions

■ Failure to progress in labor

Another reason for cesarean birth is illness. For example, if you have diabetes or high blood pressure, your baby may need to be delivered at a time when vaginal delivery cannot be done safely. If you have an active herpes infection on your genitals, you may need a cesarean delivery.

In many hospitals, your partner or another support person may stay with you in the operating room for the cesarean birth. This depends on whether you're awake for the surgery, how urgent the surgery is, and the hospital's policy. If the support person is present at the birth, he or she will be given special hospital clothing to change into before entering the operating room.

Before you have a cesarean delivery, the nurse prepares you for the operation. You may be given medication to help dry secretions in your mouth and upper airway. Your abdomen is washed and may be shaved. To lower the chances of injuring the bladder—which is right near the surgical site—a catheter is placed in it to drain the urine. This catheter stays in the bladder during surgery to keep it empty. An IV line will be put in a vein in your hand or arm, which allows you to get fluids during the operation. Any medications you might need can also be given through the IV. After you are taken to the operating room, you'll be given anesthesia. If general anesthesia is used, you will not be awake during the delivery. If spinal or epidural anesthesia is used, you'll be awake but numb from just around your nipples down to your toes. The anesthesiologist will talk with you about the types of anesthesia (described earlier in this chapter) and will take your wishes into account.

A cesarean birth involves the following steps:

1. An incision is made through your skin and the wall of the abdomen. The skin incision can go vertically from the navel to the pubic bone, or it can go from side to side, just above

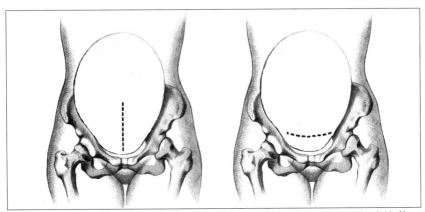

The incision made in the uterine wall for cesarean birth may be vertical (*left*) or transverse (*right*). The type of incision made in the skin may not be the same as the type of incision made in the uterus.

the pubic hairline. Your abdominal muscles are not cut but are spread apart. Your doctor will decide which incision is needed.

2. An incision is made in the wall of the uterus, making an opening through which the baby will be delivered. This incision can be transverse, vertical (classical), or low vertical. When possible, the transverse incision is preferred because it's done in the lower, thinner part of the uterus and it results in less bleeding. It also heals with a stronger scar. Sometimes, however, a vertical incision of the uterus is needed—for example, if you have placenta previa or if the baby is in certain unusual positions. After your delivery, be sure to ask about the type of incision that was used in the uterus.

3. After the baby and placenta are delivered, the incisions are closed with sutures that are absorbed in the body. Clips may be used to close the skin of the abdomen.

Because cesarean birth is a surgical procedure, it can involve risks:

■ The uterus or nearby pelvic organs can get infected.

■ You can lose blood, sometimes enough to require a blood transfusion.

- You can get blood clots in the legs, pelvic organs, and sometimes the lungs.
- Your bowel or bladder can be injured.
- You need to stay in the hospital longer and need more time to recover than if you had a vaginal delivery.

Many maternity centers have childbirth classes, programs, or support groups for couples who may need cesarean delivery. If you have questions or concerns about cesarean birth, ask your doctor or nurse so you can get answers before your baby is born. After a cesarean birth, it should not take long for you to function normally. You should be able to start breast-feeding right away if you wish.

Vaginal Birth After Cesarean Delivery

Once it was thought that if a woman had one cesarean birth, all babies she had afterward had to be born the same way. That thinking has changed. Today most women who have had cesarean births are encouraged to try giving birth through the vagina, as long as no risk factors are present. Most women who had a cesarean before can deliver through the vagina.

Reasons to consider a vaginal birth after a previous cesarean delivery, also known as VBAC, include:

- *Less Risk.* A vaginal delivery causes fewer complications than cesarean birth. A cesarean delivery is major surgery and calls for anesthesia. As with any operation, there is risk of infection, bleeding, and transfusion (getting blood), as well as the normal risks of surgery and anesthesia. If you have a vaginal birth, you don't need an incision in your abdomen, so these risks are much lower.
- *Shorter Recovery.* Your stay in the hospital is likely to be shorter after a vaginal delivery, and you'll have less pain than after a cesarean. Women who have a cesarean birth usually spend a few days longer in the hospital than women who have a vaginal birth. Recovery at home is usually faster

after vaginal birth, too. If you deliver by cesarean, you may need to limit your activity for a few weeks to let the incision heal. If you deliver vaginally, you can resume normal activities sooner.

■ *More Involvement.* Some women wish to be awake and fully involved in the birth process. Sometimes general anesthesia is used during a cesarean delivery, which means you are not awake and cannot experience the actual birth. There also may be more limits on who can be in the delivery room with you during a cesarean birth.

In deciding how your baby will be born, your own wishes and a number of medical factors will be weighed. A key factor is the type of uterine incision (not skin incision) used in your previous cesarean. Your doctor will need to consult your medical records to verify which type of uterine incision was used for that birth. Depending on the type of incision used, you may have a higher risk of the scar tearing or rupturing. This is the main risk to both you and your baby during an attempted vaginal birth after a cesarean. The risk varies with the type of uterine incision used for cesarean delivery:

■ The transverse incision is made across the lower, thinner part of the uterus. It heals with a stronger scar and is least likely to cause a problem in a future vaginal delivery.

■ The low vertical incision is an up-and-down cut made in the lower, thinner area of the uterus. The risks linked with vaginal birth after this type of uterine incision are not clear. If you have had this type of incision, discuss the options with your doctor.

■ The classical (high vertical) incision is an up-and-down cut made in the upper part of the uterus. This was once the most common type of incision used in cesarean births. Unfortunately, a complete break, or rupture, of the scar is more likely during labor if a classical incision was used in a previous cesarean delivery. This can cause serious bleeding that can pose a danger to both the baby and the mother.

In a cesarean delivery, the type of incision made in the skin may not be the same as the type made in the uterus. You cannot tell what kind of uterine incision you had just by looking at your scar. Even if it's not known which incision you had, you still may be able to have a vaginal birth. However, even if you plan for a vaginal delivery, keep in mind that something could arise that would require a cesarean birth.

Trying to deliver vaginally after a previous cesarean birth carries some risk, so certain safety measures will be taken during labor and delivery. During labor, electronic fetal monitoring detects the baby's heart rate. If a problem does occur during labor, you may need to have an emergency cesarean delivery. The facility in which you give birth should be equipped for this possibility.

For most women, the benefits of trying vaginal birth after a past cesarean delivery outweigh the risks. Even women who have had two or more cesarean births can safely try giving birth through the vagina. If all conditions are met, most women who have had a previous cesarean delivery can safely undergo vaginal birth.

After Delivery

You will be watched closely after delivery to be sure there are no problems. Your blood pressure, pulse, and temperature will be taken, your uterus will be massaged, and you will be checked for signs of heavy vaginal bleeding or infection. You will be urged to move about as soon as possible. A nurse or other adult should stay with you during your first several times out of bed.

If you have had a cesarean birth, you may not be able to get out of bed right away. Some hospitals encourage early contact between the parents and baby after a cesarean birth. In these hospitals, if the baby's condition at birth permits, the parents and child stay together in the operating room and recovery area.

Soon after surgery, the catheter is taken out of your bladder. You should then be able to start urinating on your own. You will get fluids by IV until you are able to eat and drink—usually for 1 or 2 days.

During the first few days or the first week after a cesarean birth, the incision usually hurts. Pain medication may be ordered to make it more comfortable to interact with your baby.

After delivery, most hospitals provide ways for the mother, father, and baby to be together. A perfect time to start learning about your baby is while you are still in the hospital. Examining your baby from head to toe and noticing special traits are joys for every mother. Sometimes, however, the baby does not look or act as you think a baby should. Most of the time, nothing is wrong— you are just noticing normal traits of a newborn. Many mothers form images of older babies while they are pregnant and are surprised at what a newborn really looks like. Take advantage of having your health care team at hand to answer your questions and reassure you. Nurses who work in maternity units are experts in teaching new parents infant-care skills.

Children who visit their mothers after the birth of a sibling respond better to their mothers and new brother or sister than children who do not. Most hospitals have policies for visits by brothers and sisters:

■ Children should not have been exposed recently to known infectious diseases such as chickenpox.

■ Children should not have a fever, a cough, or other symptoms that they are sick with a disease that can be passed on.

■ Children should be prepared in advance for their visit.

■ Parents should make sure children are watched by a responsible adult for the whole visit.

Be sure to find out about your hospital's visitation policy before your delivery. You may want to restrict visits so you have more time to rest and get to know your baby.

Discharge

If you have had a normal vaginal delivery, you will be discharged from the hospital soon after the baby is born. How long you stay depends on your health and your insurance policy. Often, mothers go home after 1 day because their insurance policy only permits a 1-day stay. If your baby had complications, he or she may need to stay longer.

How long you stay in the hospital after a cesarean birth depends on why the cesarean was done and how much time you need to resume normal functions. Most of the time, you can leave the hospital 2–5 days after a cesarean birth.

Other procedures may be done in the hospital before discharge, which could make your stay longer. For example, you may decide to have postpartum sterilization. If the baby is a boy, you and your partner may decide to have him circumcised (see Chapter 4).

Before you are discharged, you will be given instructions to follow in case of problems or an emergency. You should arrange a follow-up exam for you and your newborn. Your doctor or nurse will want to check you about 2–6 weeks after the birth (or sooner if you were discharged early). Your baby will probably be examined by a doctor once a month for the first 3 months. Be sure to have your infant safety seat ready for the trip home from the hospital. Use it every time your baby is in the car.

When you leave the hospital to care for the baby at home, keep in mind that you can take group classes or private lessons to learn some beginning skills of motherhood. These often include feeding, bathing, and diapering the baby, which will help you feel more at ease handling your newborn.

Questions to Consider...

■ When should I call the doctor or nurse once labor begins?

■ What should I do to get ready before I go to the hospital?

■ What type of fetal monitoring might I have?

■ What forms of pain relief will be available?

■ What options do I have in labor?

■ If I had a cesarean birth before, can I try a vaginal delivery?

Chapter 15

Dealing with Loss

It's natural to hope that your pregnancy will go smoothly and you'll have a baby that's perfect in every way. Most of the time, babies are born healthy. Once in a while things go wrong, and a baby dies. The chances of losing a baby are slim, but when it does happen there is shock, anguish, sorrow, and great pain. This chapter describes the normal grieving process and ways to work through it.

Causes of Loss

The loss of a baby can occur during pregnancy or after birth. Miscarriage is one of the most common causes of fetal loss. A miscarriage is the spontaneous loss of a pregnancy before the fetus is able to live on its own, outside the mother's uterus. It occurs in at least one fifth all pregnancies, usually in early pregnancy. A pregnancy can also be lost in later stages, and a baby can be delivered that shows no signs of life. This is called stillbirth.

A fetus may also be lost if there is an ectopic pregnancy. Ectopic pregnancy occurs when the fertilized egg grows outside the uterus, usually in the fallopian tube. About 1 pregnancy in 50 is ectopic. Often this problem is diagnosed in the first 8 weeks of pregnancy, even before a woman realizes she is pregnant. She may have pains, cramps, or vaginal bleeding that signals the problem, and must usually have treatment right away to remove it.

Sometimes newborns die after birth, either because they have a defect or were born too early. When babies die in their sleep for no clear reason, it is called sudden infant death syndrome (SIDS). About 3 of 1,000 babies die from SIDS between the ages of 1 and

4 months. Although no one knows what causes SIDS, it appears to be linked with long pauses in the baby's breathing known as apnea. It is believed that SIDS can be prevented if babies are laid on their backs or sides to sleep.

Although the loss of a baby can happen for several different reasons, expectant mothers feel the same grief. In many cases, the grief or feelings of remorse you have may also be shared by your health care team.

Grieving

Most women get emotionally attached to their babies long before the actual birth. This process is called bonding. The bond usually grows stronger throughout pregnancy. As the weeks and months of your pregnancy go by, you begin to think of your fetus as a person. You imagine how the baby will look and what he or she will be like. Around 16–20 weeks of pregnancy, when you first feel your baby move, the bond may become much more intense. The father also develops a strong tie to his unborn child. He may have many of the same feelings you do.

Losing your baby can bring intense sadness and shock. It is almost always unexpected. The loss of a baby at any stage—during pregnancy or after birth—is a tragedy. Your feelings can be the same as when anyone you love dies, such as a parent, partner, sibling, or lifelong friend.

Grief is a normal, natural response to the loss of your baby. Working through grief and mourning your loss are healing processes that help you adapt and move ahead with your life.

The Stages of Grief

Grieving includes a wide range of feelings. Just as each pregnancy is unique, ways to react to losses of pregnancy are unique, too. How intense your feelings are does not always correspond to the time in pregnancy when the loss occurs. For example, a miscarriage can bring the same sorrow as a stillbirth.

There is no correct way to grieve for the loss of a baby or death of a loved one. Each family member mourns in his or her own way. The process you follow may be affected by your past experiences with death, the culture you were raised in, your role in the family, and what you think others expect of you. Grieving is a difficult and tiring process. It can take up to 2 years or more. Often, the feelings of loss never disappear completely.

Grieving happens in stages that overlap and repeat day to day and week to week. These stages have a common pattern in many people, but do not always follow the same course.

- *Shock, Numbness, and Disbelief.* When faced with news of their baby's death, parents often think, "This is not really happening" or "This can't be true." You may deny to yourself that the loss has occurred. You may have trouble grasping the news, or you may feel nothing at all. Even though you and your partner may be together physically, you may each feel a very private sense of being alone or empty.

- *Searching and Yearning.* These feelings tend to overlap with your initial shock and get stronger over time. You may start looking for a reason for your baby's death—who or what killed it? It is common during this stage to feel very guilty. You may imagine that somehow you brought about your baby's death and blame yourself for things you did or did not do. You may have dreams about the baby and yearn for what might have been. You may even think you are going crazy.

- *Anger or Rage.* "What did I do to deserve this?" and "How could this happen to me?" are common feelings after losing a baby. You may direct your anger at anyone: your partner, the doctor or nurse, the hospital staff, even other women whose babies were born healthy. If you feel angry toward your partner—or if he feels angry toward you—it may be hard for you to comfort each other. In this stage of grief you may find yourself questioning your religious beliefs. It's good to accept your anger, express it, and try to get it out of your system. Anger becomes unhealthy when you try to deny it.

- *Depression and Loneliness.* In this stage, the reality that you have lost your baby hits you hard. You may feel tired and run down, sad, disoriented, and helpless. You may have trouble getting back into your normal routine. The support from friends and family that you received during the early weeks of your loss may be gone, even though you still need comfort and kindness. Your relationships with people may be strained because others do not understand your feelings and emotions. Slowly, however, you start to get back on your feet and work through your loss.

■ *Acceptance.* In this final stage of grieving, you come to terms with what has happened. You start to have renewed energy, and your baby's death no longer rules your thoughts. Although you will never forget your baby, you begin to think of him or her less often and with less pain. You pick up your normal daily activities and social life. You laugh with friends and make plans for the future. You now can start planning your next pregnancy as a separate event, rather than confusing it with the pregnancy you lost.

Other Signs of Grieving

As you grieve, you may have other feelings or symptoms that are natural and normal. These are more likely to occur in the first months after your loss and may include:

■ Aches and pains in the breasts and arms
■ A tight feeling in the chest and throat
■ Heart flutters
■ Headaches
■ Trouble sleeping or nightmares
■ Loss of appetite
■ Tiredness and easy fatigue
■ Loss of memory and trouble concentrating
■ Fantasies about the baby and images of the baby in your mind

Grieving mothers often feel as if their bodies have failed them. At first you may want to ignore your health or appearance. These feelings may be worse if your body is sore or slow to heal from the baby's birth. Though you may feel indifferent about your own health, you need to take special care of yourself. If at any time you have concerns about what's going on in your body or mind, find someone who you are comfortable with to talk to.

You and Your Partner

A relationship may suffer from the stress of the loss of a child. You may have trouble getting your thoughts and feelings across to each other. One or both of you may feel hostile toward the other. You may find it hard to start having sex again or doing other things together that you used to enjoy. These reactions are normal. Try to be patient with one another. Let each other know what your needs are and what you are feeling. Take time to be tender, caring, and close. Make an extra effort to talk openly and honestly.

Throughout the grieving process, your partner may not respond in the same way as you do. Your partner may feel different things at different times, or may not be ready to talk about the loss when you are. Each person should be allowed to grieve in his or her own way. Try to understand and respond to your partner's needs as well as your own.

Making Decisions

When you lose a baby, you must face certain decisions—even if you don't feel like facing anything. You also may choose to take certain actions, such as naming the baby or holding a memorial service, that help you through the healing process.

Saying Goodbye

One of the most important decisions you will make is whether to see your baby when it is born. Although this may sound scary or morbid at first, the experience of other bereaved parents is that seeing your baby will be very helpful to you. It can help you realize your loss more fully and make it easier to let go of him or her. It also creates a very personal memory of your baby that you can carry with you.

Even if your baby has features that are not normal, you should consider seeing him or her. A nurse can wrap your baby in a blanket so that you can see as much or as little as you want. Most parents find that the truth is far kinder and gentler than what they had imagined.

Choosing a Name

Naming the baby helps give him or her an identity. A name allows you, your friends, and your family to refer to a specific child, not just "the baby you lost." You may want to use the name you first chose, or use another one.

Mementos

Parents usually treasure mementos of their baby. Consider asking the nurse to give you a lock of hair, a handprint or footprint, an identification bracelet, or a crib card from your baby.

Photos can also help establish the reality of your baby. Even if you don't think you will want pictures of your baby, have them taken anyway so that you will have them if you change you mind later.

Autopsy

Your doctor may ask to do an autopsy—an examination of your baby's organs—to help find the cause of death. Although it may not be possible to tell exactly why your baby died, an autopsy can help answer questions about what happened. The information provided by the autopsy may be useful for your family in planning future pregnancies. Many parents express relief at knowing the cause of death. Others are relieved to know that no special problems were found. An autopsy does not delay burial and does not prevent having an open casket.

Funeral or Memorial Service

You may choose to have a religious or memorial service. For many parents, it is a great comfort to have family and friends acknowledge the life and death of their baby and to show their sorrow at a special ceremony.

You will need to decide what to do with your baby's body. You may wish to contact a funeral home for burial or cremation. Some parents find solace in having a grave site they can visit. Some hospitals can take care of your baby's remains, if this is what you prefer. Usually they will have the body cremated.

Going Home

It's hard to leave the hospital with empty arms and face an empty nursery. Once you arrive home, it may also be hard to deal with the reactions of family and friends. Most people will not be aware of the impact your loss has on you or how best to support you as you mourn. Although they do not mean to hurt you, people often fail to understand the pain involved in losing a baby, especially if the baby was not born alive or did not live long.

In an effort to make you feel better, they may say things that cause you pain, such as "You're young, you can try again," "Be grateful for your other children," "Some things happen for the best," "Be brave," or "You'll get over it." Some people may avoid you or may avoid talking about the baby because they feel awkward.

At this difficult time you must put your own needs first. Let people know what you want from them and how you are feeling. There is no need to force yourself to be polite or brave just to please others. To ease the discomfort of telling other people what has happened, you can send out announcements of the baby's birth and death. People you know casually who see that you are no longer pregnant may be unaware of your loss and may ask questions. Prepare a simple sentence you can use in response.

If you have other children at home, tell them in a direct way that the baby has died. Trying to shield children from death doesn't work. They can sense your sadness, anger, and fear, and they will feel left out. When telling young children about what happened to the baby, it is very important to avoid placing blame. Make sure they understand that the baby's death is not their fault. Children often feel anger and jealousy toward a new baby, and the news of the baby's death may make them wonder if their thoughts and feelings somehow caused it.

It is not unusual for children to fear that they or their parents may also be in danger of dying. You need to reassure them that nothing they did caused the baby's death and that there is no risk to them. Children's response to death varies depending on their ages and personalities. Let them know you recognize and understand their pain over the baby's death and that you feel the same way. Be sure to include your children in any funeral or memorial service.

Once you've returned home, don't pretend that nothing has happened. Sometimes you have no choice but to go back to your job or resume a full life right away. If you can, take off the time you had planned after the baby's birth. Returning to the pressures of work and seeing co-workers can be hard if you are not up for it physically and emotionally.

Don't be surprised if feelings of grief come back on your due date or on anniversaries of your baby's birth or death. This is called an "anniversary reaction" or "shadow grief." You may dread these days and suffer through them, while family and friends seem to have forgotten. It helps to be aware of these anniversary feelings and to let others know how you feel. Often parents find that doing something special to mark the date—such as visiting the grave site, or donating money in the baby's name—is helpful.

Seeking Support

As you go through grieving, you will feel very defenseless at times. The pain of your baby's death can remind you of hurts from the past, such as other losses and deaths, infertility, or family problems. Often these old hurts can return and get in the way of the healing process.

Find a network of people who can support you right after the baby's death and in the months that follow. It is important to know you are not alone. A number of people have the understanding and skills to help you. Your doctor or nurse may be able to direct you to support systems in your community. These can include childbirth educators, self-help groups, social workers, and clergy. Some of these resources may be more helpful than others. You will need to find the one that fits your needs.

Many grieving parents find it helpful to get involved with groups of parents who have gone through the same tragedy. Members of such support groups respect your feelings, understand your stresses and fears, and have a good sense of the compassion you need.

Professional counseling can also help to relieve your pain, guilt, and depression. Talking with a trained counselor can help you understand and accept what has happened. You may wish get counseling for yourself only, for you and your partner, or for your entire family. Some reasons for seeking help may be:

- Getting "stuck" in one phase of the grief process so that you cannot work through certain problems.
- Having severe physical or emotional problems that keep you from functioning. These include feeling unable to return to work, losing interest in your health and looks, having trouble sleeping, or staying in bed all day.

Another Pregnancy?

Before thinking about becoming pregnant again, allow time for you and your partner to work through your feelings about this baby. After losing a baby, some couples feel a need to have another baby right away. They think it will fill the emptiness or take away the pain. A new baby cannot replace the baby that was lost, however. If you have another baby too soon after your loss, you may find it hard to appreciate the new child as a separate and special person.

Should you choose to have another pregnancy, keep in mind that the chances of losing another baby are usually very small. Even so, you may be very anxious and worried during your next pregnancy. Talk with your doctor or nurse about the reason for the first baby's death. Find out the chances of it happening again and what you can do to reduce these chances. Certain tests may be suggested before or during your pregnancy to find problems as early as possible.

The Future

The hurt will never vanish completely, but it will not always be the main focus in your life and thoughts. At some point you will be able to talk and think about the baby more easily and with less pain. One day you'll find yourself doing more of the things you used to do—enjoying favorite activities, renewing friendships, and looking forward to the future.

Questions to Consider...

- Should I ask for mementos of my baby?
- When I go home, how will I respond to everyone's questions?
- Whom can I turn to for support during the next few months?

Chapter 16

The Newborn Baby

Birth is a point in a gradual process of growth that starts with conception and goes into adulthood. While hidden away in the uterus, the fetus changes physically and gains the ability to start functioning on its own. At birth you can start watching your baby develop and witness many changes as they occur.

You'll never forget the first time you see or hear your baby. Although that moment may feel like a beginning, it's not so much a beginning as a transition. You must adjust to caring for this new being in a different way than you cared for the fetus inside you, and your baby must adapt to a new environment.

The heart and lungs in particular go through major changes while the baby is being born and adjusting to life outside the uterus. Although some risk goes along with these changes, in most births they occur without problems. Doctors and nurses are trained to care for the baby. Often all they need to do is follow some basic steps to ensure that everything is going well.

Physical and functional changes you will see in your baby around birth and in the early days afterward involve the baby's looks, size, and responses. Knowing what changes to expect will help you to relax and enjoy watching your baby grow.

Appearance

At birth, babies can look quite different than they do a few days or weeks later. Television and magazines often use infants who are 1–3 months old to depict newborns. As a result, many parents are surprised when their baby does not look the way they expected.

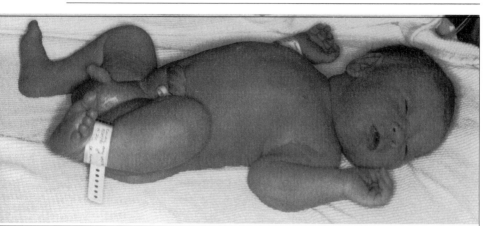

A newborn baby.   *Photo courtesy of Dartmouth Hitchcock Medical Center.*

When given their baby after birth, parents often look at the face first and then at details such as the hands and feet. Doctors and nurses do this as well, but they also listen to the heart and lungs with a stethoscope to check the baby's health.

The baby may tend to keep his or her arms and legs drawn up close, the way they were inside the uterus. The baby's face and head may change quite a bit in the early days. The face may be a bit swollen and the eyes puffy for a few days. Babies have two soft spots on the top of the head where the skull bones have not joined. These soft spots make the head somewhat flexible, and it may take on a long or pointy shape during birth. Babies born by cesarean birth can look the same way if their mothers went through labor before delivery. If labor did not occur, their faces and heads may look more like those of babies several days old.

The genitals of newborns may look swollen or very large for such small bodies. In boys, the scrotum may be red. Girls may have a slight bloody, clear, or white discharge from the vagina. Both sexes may have enlarged breasts, which may even leak a few drops of milk. These signs are the result of the infants' exposure to high levels of the mother's hormones in the uterus. They will go away soon after birth.

Skin

A baby who has just been born is often covered with a greasy, whitish coating called **vernix**. There may also be traces of blood and other material. This is normal. The baby's skin may look very delicate. Being exposed to air after the vernix is washed away may cause the baby's skin to peel slightly. The baby may also have fine hair along the back and shoulders, which is called **lanugo.** This hair is shed before birth or soon after; it may take 1 or 2 weeks to go away.

After birth, the baby's skin color may not be uniform. Besides having the whitish vernix covering the skin, some newborns may look bluish or gray, especially their hands and feet. This is related to early changes in the baby's circulation, and it usually goes away. The skin color of babies of different ethnic and racial backgrounds may change somewhat as they grow older. Hair and eye color may also change.

After a few days some babies' skin becomes tinted yellow. This is called jaundice. Jaundice is caused by a buildup of bilirubin, a greenish yellow substance formed during the normal breakdown of old red blood cells in the body. All people have some bilirubin in their blood, which is removed by the liver. During pregnancy, the placenta and the mother's liver remove bilirubin from the fetus. The baby's liver doesn't start removing bilirubin until a few days after birth.

Parents should not worry too much if jaundice appears a few days after birth. Although high levels of bilirubin can be toxic to the baby's nervous system, the levels in most babies are not likely to cause problems. Before the baby's liver begins to function naturally, the level of bilirubin in the blood can be checked. If it's high, the baby can be treated.

Weight and Age

Everyone wants to know how much a baby weighs at birth. The hospital will give you that figure, usually in pounds and ounces. (Doctors and

---

Heel-Stick Tests

Before your baby is discharged from the hospital, a blood sample will be taken from his or her heel to check for certain diseases. One of these is phenylketonuria, a defect that leaves the baby's body unable to break down a substance called phenylalanine. Phenylketonuria causes mental retardation, which can be avoided if the disease is caught early and treated with a special diet. Other diseases the heel-stick test may check for are hypothyroidism (low thyroid hormone), which can lead to mental retardation, and sickle-cell anemia. The test can also be used to check the baby's glucose and bilirubin levels.

nurses express weight in grams: 2.2 pounds = 1,000 grams = 1 kilogram.) There is no such thing as a proper or "good" weight, but there is a range that is considered normal for the age at which the baby is born.

The normal age of a baby at birth is between 37 and 42 weeks from the first day of the mother's last menstrual period. Together, the baby's age and weight can show whether a fetus has grown normally before birth.

Response to Birth

The baby's responses will be checked at 1 minute and 5 minutes after birth with a procedure that produces something called an Apgar score. This score helps assess your baby's condition and well-being at birth. It is named after Dr. Virginia Apgar, who had a strong interest in babies' response to birth and life on their own. The Apgar score checks five areas: heart rate, breathing, muscle tone, reflexes, and skin color. Each area is assigned a number from 0 to 2. The Apgar score is the total of those numbers. Most babies score above 7. Although the Apgar score is a good tool that helps in understanding the baby's progress at a given time, it does not by itself show how well the baby did before birth or what the future will hold. Other signs will also be checked to get more information on the baby's general health.

Another test that may be used to check the baby's health is umbilical cord blood analysis. In this test, a sample of blood is taken from the umbilical cord right after birth, and the pH level is

The Apgar Score

Component	Score		
	0	1	2
Heart rate	Absent	Slow (<100 bpm)*	>100 bpm
Respirations	Absent	Weak	Good, strong cry
Muscle tone	Limp	Some bending	Active motion
Reflex irritability	No response	Grimace	Cough or sneeze
Color	Blue or pale	Body pink; extremities blue	Complete pink

* bpm stands for beats per minute.

checked. The pH is used to measure the balance of chemicals in the blood. It can show whether the baby needs special attention.

The First Cry

The baby's first cry is often related to his or her first breath. It's an instinct for babies to take breaths at the time of birth. Why this occurs is not clear. It seems to relate to the birth process and to changes that take place in the makeup of the baby's blood.

The lungs replace the placenta at birth as the organ that carries oxygen to the blood. Not only must the lungs be able to fill with air when the baby is born, but all related structures—such as muscles and the airways leading from the mouth and nose—must be ready to function.

After birth, the change in pressure between the lungs and the air outside causes the lungs to fill and expand with air. This air movement lets the baby breathe and cry.

Many babies will cry loudly and often at birth. Others don't cry when they are born—they start breathing without crying. (Later they may respond to being handled with cries, however.) Members of the health care team will watch the baby's breathing closely and will take steps to help if the baby's breathing is not adequate.

Circulatory Changes

While the fetus is in your uterus, blood moves to and from the placenta through vessels (two arteries and a vein) in the umbilical cord. At birth, the placenta separates from the inside of the uterus and is expelled.

Just after birth, when the baby's lungs are filling with air, doctors and nurses often listen to the chest carefully with a stethoscope. They can hear air entering the lungs and may detect sounds or murmurs linked with changes in blood flow that are a normal part of the baby's adjustment. They may also feel the baby's pulse in areas such as the arm or groin. These examinations are part of the normal routine to check the baby's well-being.

Temperature Control

The healthy fetus gives off heat through the placenta to its mother and is protected from heat loss by the mother's warmth that surrounds it. At birth, babies enter a world that is much cooler than the mother's uterus. Because babies are wet, they can lose a great deal of heat as the moisture evaporates. The temperature of most babies drops during birth. Heat can be retained by drying and wrapping the baby just after birth.

Newborns have controls to maintain their body temperature, but these systems are not as efficient as those in older children and adults. The newborn can easily become too hot or too cool. Normal infants need some clothing in the first week after birth, such as a cotton shirt or gown, in addition to a diaper and perhaps a light blanket. The room should be free of drafts and not too warm or too cool (70–75°F) or dry (35–60% humidity).

Nervous System

A baby's basic reflexes, such as those that control breathing, work well. Newborns can interact with people and respond to sound and light. Parents may notice a complex reflex action, such as the startle or Moro reaction, in which a newborn extends the arms, legs, and head

One of the newborn's basic reflexes is the startle reflex.

and then draws the arms back to the chest in response to a strong stimulus such as a sound. Sight, hearing, and the ability to feel pain are present from birth, but are easier to notice as the baby matures.

At birth the baby also will have the rooting and sucking reflexes. The rooting reflex is a natural instinct to search for the breast. If the baby is stroked on one cheek or the side of the mouth, he or she will turn in that direction with lips pursed, ready to suck. This helps the baby find the nipple at feeding time. Newborn babies suck when they feel pressure on the roof of their mouth, behind their upper gums. They also have a grasp reflex, which is why their fingers close so readily around yours.

Gastrointestinal System

The placenta was the main source of food for the fetus before birth. After birth, the baby is able to feed by sucking and swallowing milk through the mouth and moving it into and through the digestive tract. Although unable to handle an adult diet, a baby can digest carbohydrates, proteins, and fats soon after birth. Feeding can take place early the first day. The fetal intestine contains a green-black, sticky substance called meconium, which you usually see within 24 hours when the baby's first bowel movement occurs.

Behavior

As newborns adjust to life outside the uterus, their basic needs and responses are similar. Beyond this, however, each baby has a unique personality. Wide variations in how each baby behaves and interacts with people can be seen from birth. Some are quiet and calm and may have seemed quiet in the womb. Others cry and kick with vigor.

After going through the stress and adjustments of birth, the baby often has a brief period (an hour or so) of being alert and may suckle if put to the mother's breast. The baby may then fall asleep or be drowsy for the next few hours or even a few days.

At first, babies spend most of their time sleeping (in short stretches that total 14–18 hours per day) and are alert briefly in between. Some babies spend more time awake from the start and are fussy rather than quiet and alert. Others may spend long periods sleeping and will be quiet when they wake up.

Bonding with your baby usually starts during pregnancy and gets more intense at birth. But, not all mothers feel a tight bond right away. Some new mothers have some hesitation at first, and it may take longer to feel a bond with their newborn. The baby may not look as the mother expected, or she may have had a difficult birth, such as a preterm delivery, that makes it harder to bond. In a short time, a few days at most, mother and baby will interact more closely as they adapt to each other. Attachment is the gradual process of developing a loving connection between a baby and the parents over time. The difference between bonding and attachment can be compared with love at first sight versus the building of a loving relationship.

Care of the Baby

Newborn babies are well equipped to function from the start, but they are not independent. They need help in many ways.

Safety Steps for Newborns

The following guidelines can help ensure the safety of your baby:

- If your baby is healthy, lay the baby on his or her back or side to nap or sleep. This reduces the risk of sudden infant death syndrome (SIDS), a mysterious ailment that kills nearly 6,000 babies under age 1 in the United States each year. A few years ago parents were advised to put babies on their stomach to sleep, but this thinking has changed. If your baby has health problems, talk to his or her doctor about the best sleeping position.
- Make sure your baby sleeps on a firm mattress or other hard surface. Do not let him or her sleep on pillows, comforters, waterbeds, sheepskins, or other soft surfaces.
- Always use an infant car safety seat whenever your baby will be riding in a car, van, or truck. These are specially designed to protect babies and small children if a crash occurs. They can be bought or rented. For more information, see Chapter 4.
- Do not leave your baby unattended—even for a second—in bathtubs, on changing tables, or anywhere that the baby could fall or drown. Keep everything you need within arm's reach. If you have to answer the phone or doorbell, take the baby with you.
- Don't put pillows or soft stuffed toys in the crib while your baby is very young; they can smother the baby.
- Check your baby's toys and clothing for ribbons, buttons, or other parts that can be pulled off easily and swallowed. These can lodge in the baby's throat and block his or her airway.
- Use the harnesses that come with infant seats, strollers, and high chairs.
- Don't allow anyone to smoke around the baby. Babies and young children exposed to smoke have more colds and respiratory infections, as well as a higher risk of SIDS.

Feeding

Breast milk, including the colostrum of the first 2–4 days, is designed just for infants. Breast-fed infants have fewer feeding problems, tend to be less constipated, and have fewer infections and allergies than babies who are bottle-fed. Breast milk is the best source of food for your newborn. However, if you choose not to breast-feed, there are formulas that come close to human milk.

If you are nursing, you can try the first feeding as soon after birth as possible, when the baby is alert, awake, and ready to suck. Although you may produce only a small amount of fluid at the time, you'll probably feel rewarded by making the attempt. The colostrum of the first few days does not need to be supplemented with bottle-feeding. The baby has little need for food in the first days because he or she is born with extra fat stores and water. These fat stores and water are lost in the first days, which explains why babies tend to lose weight after birth.

If your baby is to be fed formula, the first feeding should take place within 6 hours of birth. Bottle-fed babies usually need to be fed less often than breast-fed babies because formula takes longer to digest.

It may take a while for you and your baby to get used to the technique of nursing. When the nipple is placed in the baby's mouth, the baby starts sucking, causing milk to flow. For about the first 24 hours, newborns should nurse for only 3–5 minutes on each breast at each feeding. This time should be gradually increased until the baby nurses for 15 minutes or longer on each breast. Although most of the milk is taken in the first 5–10 minutes, the infant may want to suck longer at times. Each baby is different and will set his or her own pattern. Some babies want to nurse only every 4 hours. Others nurse as often as every 1 to 1 1/2 hours, especially in the first few weeks after birth. Keep in mind that babies are not programmed from the start to eat at regular times. Don't be surprised if your baby nurses for 15 minutes, falls asleep for 2 hours, and then nurses from each breast for 15 minutes. You don't have to nurse the baby at both breasts at one feeding. Just try to remember which breast was used and offer the other at the next feeding. Placing a safety pin on your bra may help you to remember.

If you are worried that your baby is not getting enough milk, check with the baby's doctor. He or she will be keeping track of the baby's growth and weight gain. If your baby wets at least six diapers and has one bowel movement every 24 hours, he or she usually is getting enough milk. The stool of breast-fed infants looks different from that of infants who are bottle-fed. It is yellowish and loose, with less odor.

Feeding provides contact between mother and baby that strengthens their bond. Adjust your routine to make enough time for this important activity and to make it as comfortable as possible.

Bathing

Keeping the baby clean promotes good health and hygiene. It's a good idea to give the baby a full bath in the first few days after birth. The baby's skin and scalp can be cared for without a total body bath, however. Sponge baths with a mild soap, especially around the diaper area and in skin creases, will do fine.

The baby's first bath should not be given until he or she has adjusted after birth and has a stable temperature. The hospital staff will likely show you the right way to bathe your infant. If you have any questions or feel unsure about how to do it properly, don't hesitate to ask for special instructions before you leave the hospital.

Bathing Your Baby

- Use a special basin made for bathing babies, not a regular bathtub.
- Fill the basin with 2 inches of water that feels warm to the inside of your elbow or wrist. Make sure the water isn't too hot.
- Never leave the baby alone in the bath, not even for a second. If the phone or doorbell rings, take the baby with you. Keep a dry towel nearby in case you have to take the baby from the bath quickly.
- If your baby seems to enjoy the bath, don't rush it. Let him or her relax, splash, and explore the water. Infants don't need bath toys, the water itself is fun enough.

Eye Care

Shortly after birth, hospital staff place a medicated ointment or liquid in a newborn's eyes. This is done to guard against possible infection from germs that could enter the eye during birth. More treatment is not needed unless the eyes show signs of infection, such as redness or discharge. If such signs appear, talk with a doctor or nurse. Otherwise, all you need to do is wipe each closed eye gently with moist cotton or cloth to keep the area clean.

Cord Care

The stump of the umbilical cord usually shrivels and falls off in 7–10 days. When the stump falls off, the spot underneath becomes the baby's navel. (The way the stump looks has nothing to do with whether the navel sticks out or goes in.) It's important to take care of the cord area because it can get infected. Keep it clean and dry, but do not cover it with gauze, bandages, or diapers. Some health care professionals suggest using ointment or other substances during the first week or so. If redness spreads to skin around the stump, call your doctor or nurse.

Diapering

Newborns usually pass stool and urinate in the first 24 hours. Some will begin in the delivery room, and others will wait more than 24 hours. If passing these wastes is delayed, the doctor may want to explore the reason. Most newborns urinate 6–18 times and pass stool as much as 7–8 times daily. You can use either cloth or disposable diapers. These need to be changed each time the baby wets or soils the diaper, so have a good supply of clean ones on hand.

Dressing

In general, babies need about the same number of layers of clothing as their parents. One-piece baby suits made with soft material that doesn't irritate the skin and with easy access to the diaper area are practical. In warm weather only a diaper may be needed. In air-conditioned rooms, outside, or on cold days, infants may need more layers than adults because they don't move as much. The climate and season can guide your choice of clothes to bring to the hospital for the baby to wear home.

How to Diaper Your Baby

Have everything you need within easy reach before you start to change your baby's diaper. Never leave the baby alone on a changing table or raised surface. He or she could roll or slide off.

Things you'll need:

- A clean diaper and fasteners
- Ointment or petroleum jelly if the baby has a rash
- Diaper wipes (without alcohol) or a basin with lukewarm water and a washcloth
- Cornstarch for hot weather or if the baby has a moist rash

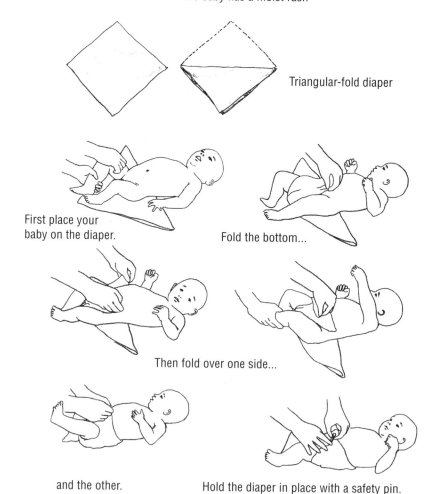

Triangular-fold diaper

First place your baby on the diaper.

Fold the bottom...

Then fold over one side...

and the other.

Hold the diaper in place with a safety pin.

What to do:

- Take off the dirty diaper and gently wipe the baby's bottom with the baby wipes or damp washcloth. (Some babies are sensitive to baby wipes, so don't use them if your baby's skin gets irritated.)
- Apply a light dusting of cornstarch if the weather is very hot or the baby has a moist rash.
- Put on the new diaper as shown.

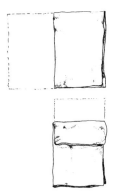

Rectangular-fold diaper

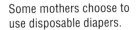

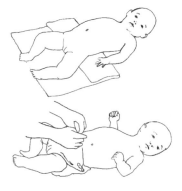

You may wish to fold about one third of a cloth diaper down to increase the absorbency. If you have a baby boy, place the extra padding in front. For girls, place padding in back.

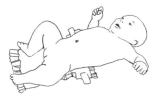

Some mothers choose to use disposable diapers.

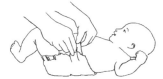

Circumcision

If you chose to have your baby boy circumcised, a light dressing such as gauze with petroleum jelly will be placed over the head of the penis after the surgery. Keep the area as clean as possible. Wash the penis with soap and water daily and change diapers often so that urine and stool do not cause infection. If a plastic ring has been used for the circumcision, it will be left on. The ring will slip off when the edge of the circumcision is fully healed, which takes about 7–10 days.

Babies Who Need Special Care

Few babies have serious problems at birth. When they do, however, there is help. All parts of the United States are included in a regional system of intensive care units that take care of babies who have special needs. If it is suspected before birth that your baby could have a problem, you may need to deliver in a hospital with an intensive care nursery. This may be a different hospital from the one in your community. If you deliver in a hospital without an intensive care nursery and a problem comes up without warning, your baby may be moved by an expert team to a facility that offers special care.

Pediatricians are specialists who have been trained to find and treat problems in babies and children. Neonatologists are pediatricians with extra training in the care of babies. Other experts such as pediatric surgeons may be called on depending on your baby's needs.

Babies with problems are usually cared for in an intensive care nursery or a neonatal intensive care unit. They may be placed in special beds to keep warm, called incubators or isolettes. They may be fed through a tube or connected to a respirator to help them breathe. Babies in these units are monitored by specially trained nurses and complex equipment.

Neonatal intensive care units are often busy and may seem strange at first. You may feel that everyone else is taking care of your baby and there is no place for you. Be assured that the highly skilled personnel cannot take your place as a parent. They will

Some preterm infants are kept in an incubator, which maintains proper levels of temperature and humidity.

urge you to be with your baby. Contact is important for both baby and parents. As soon as possible, talk to your baby and stroke him or her in the incubator. The baby needs to hear your voice and feel your touch. Soon you may be able to hold and cuddle your baby for longer periods and help with care.

There are a variety of reasons why a baby may need special care. Some of the most common are described here.

Preterm

The single largest problem for newborns is preterm birth and its complications. Preterm, or premature, babies are born before 37 weeks. The younger and smaller the baby is, the greater the risk of problems and the need for intensive care. Preterm babies look different from term babies: they may be red and skinny because they have little fat under their skin and their blood vessels are close to the surface. The earlier a baby is born, the less developed it is. This lack of development can lead to breathing problems called respiratory distress syndrome, feeding problems, or increased risk of infection.

Levels of Perinatal Care in U.S. Hospitals

In the United States, a regional perinatal care system has been organized to make sure all babies get the best care possible. As part of this system, each hospital is assigned a category, or level, of care. If a baby is born in one type of hospital and needs special care that the hospital doesn't have, the baby will be moved right away. A team of experts will travel with the baby to be sure it is well cared for during the trip to the new hospital. Depending on where you live, the baby may stay nearby or may need to go to another city.

- *Level I.* These hospitals can perform routine and cesarean deliveries. They offer anesthesia, ultrasound, transfusions, electronic fetal monitoring, lab services, and other services. They can prepare small or sick babies to be transferred to a level II or III facility.
- *Level II.* These hospitals can do everything that is done in a level I hospital, as well as manage high-risk mothers and fetuses and small, sick newborns who are moderately ill.
- *Level III.* These hospitals provide specialized perinatal care services for mothers, fetuses, and newborns—from those who are healthy to those who are seriously ill. These facilities also do research, try out new technology for high-risk mothers and babies, and compile data.

Growth Restriction

When a baby is smaller than expected for the amount of time spent in the uterus, he or she is said to have intrauterine growth restriction (IUGR). This condition is fairly common and can have a number of causes. Many times, IUGR can be detected, or at least suspected, before birth. If IUGR is discovered in advance, treatment can be started before the baby is born.

Postterm

Postterm (overdue) babies, those born after 42 weeks, sometimes have problems that term babies do not. They may develop a condition known as postmaturity syndrome and need special care. When the baby stays in the uterus too long, the placenta may be less able to take care of the baby's nutrition and other needs. Most babies who are born at 42 weeks do fine, however.

Infection

An infection can be passed from the mother to the fetus during pregnancy or to the baby as it is born. Both the mother and the baby have natural resistances to many infections and can fight them when they occur, but some agents can cross the placenta and infect the fetus in the uterus (see Chapter 13).

Only a small number of babies get infected during or after birth. Hospitals have policies aimed at reducing the spread of infection. The hospital staff will check your baby for signs of infection. They can give you advice on ways to decrease the risk of infection, such as washing your hands often, using good hygiene when you feed the baby, caring for the umbilical cord properly, and avoiding people with obvious infections.

Going Home

If no special problems come up, many babies and mothers go home as early as 24 hours after birth. At this early stage, you are both still recovering and adjusting. The first days at home should be quiet. Try to get extra help from your partner, relatives, or friends. Unfortunately, parental leave from work is not given to all parents of newborns. Some communities have agencies that may be able to give you help and support.

It's best if you arrange pediatric care for your baby before birth. Talk to friends and health professionals about the choices in your community and choose a provider that meets the needs of your family. Pediatricians often like to meet mothers and fathers before the first child is born.

Babies are very sensitive. They need time to adjust without being exposed to too many sounds, intense light, or handling by many people. Give yourself and your baby a week to adjust. Keep trips and visits from friends and relatives short. Use this time to begin to develop a routine for you and your baby.

Try to set up the first follow-up visit for your baby before you leave the hospital. The timing depends on how long you were in the hospital, whether any special problems (like jaundice) need monitoring, and when these visits are typically done in your local

When to Call the Doctor

You should call your baby's doctor right away if you notice any of these signs in your baby:

- Has trouble breathing—baby has to work hard to get air in and out
- Cries more or differently from usual, moans as if in pain, or acts very fussy
- Has a fever of more than 100°F
- Vomits or has diarrhea more than two to three times in a day
- Has even one large, very watery bowel movement if the baby is less than 3 months old
- Passes blood or blood clots with urine or bowel movement
- Has a seizure (shaking arms and legs)

You should also call if your baby:

- Seems weak and has no energy to cry as loudly as usual
- Refuses to feed, nurses poorly, or doesn't want more than half of the usual bottle
- Doesn't wake up as alert as usual, or for older babies, is not playful, even for a short time
- Just doesn't "seem right" and you are worried

area. The first visit may be between the first week and first month. If your baby had an early discharge, you may want to schedule an exam early.

In any family where a new baby has been added, the focus tends to be on the mother and infant. The social network can also include the father, siblings, relatives, and friends. All add to the life and growth of the infant and are affected by the birth.

Some babies adapt easily to their new environment, but others do not. Much of the challenge of parenting in the first days and weeks centers on learning how to read the signals of this special and unique child. Parents must respond when the baby gives signs of hunger and a need for sleep or attention. They must also start to build feelings of trust that give the baby the security to grow into a healthy child.

Questions to Consider...

- When can I start breast-feeding the baby?
- How should I care for my baby's umbilical cord stump?
- What does it mean if the baby's skin turns yellow a few days after birth?
- When should I see the pediatrician?
- When should I return for postpartum care?

Chapter 17

Postpartum Care

Being a new parent is exciting and demanding. It brings major changes to your life. There are changes in your body, your emotions, your relationships with friends and relatives, and in how you live. Every family adjusts in a different way.

The adjustment from being pregnant to being a mother starts soon after delivery. It is often hard to believe that childbirth is over and that this new baby is really yours! Very often your focus is not completely on the baby, but on what took place during labor and delivery. You want to talk about it, share it, and relive it in your mind.

As you leave the hospital and start a new routine at home, you will develop the skills that you need to care for your infant. This is often an anxious time as you wonder whether you will be able to do all it takes to be a good mother. Tasks that you once did with ease may seem harder. Relax and remember that you are not born with these skills. They are learned, and it takes time.

Being aware of what is happening to your body and your emotions can prepare you to better face the ups and downs of the first few months of being a new mother. Bringing a baby into the world is hard work. It will take a while to regain your strength after the strain of labor. Taking care of your physical and mental well-being is a key factor. A proper diet and daily exercise will increase your energy level and help you get back in shape.

As you resume your daily life, you will be faced with returning to work, perhaps using child care, and family planning. Your partner and others who are important to you can help with certain decisions and ease your adjustment to your new role. You can also attend support groups for new parents to share concerns and get useful tips.

265

Your Changing Body

While you were pregnant, the fetus's growth and changes in your body took place little by little over a 9-month period. Now that your baby has been born, it will take some time to adjust. Remember that it took your body 9 months to get in this shape, and it may take about as long, with your effort, to return.

Uterus

After delivery, your uterus is hard and round and can be felt at the level of your navel. It weighs about 2½ pounds. Six weeks later, it weighs only 2 ounces and can no longer be felt by pressing on your abdomen. The opening of the uterus—the cervix—shrinks to the size of a nickel within 1 week of delivery.

Lochia

The vaginal discharge that occurs after delivery is called *lochia*. It consists mostly of blood and tissue that was lining the uterus. For the first few days after delivery, the discharge is bright red, perhaps with a few small clots. The flow becomes lighter, turning more to pink and decreases, although the bright red flow may re-

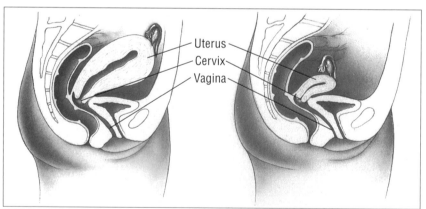

Just after birth, the uterus measures about 7 inches long and weighs about 2½ pounds (*left*). It can be felt just below the navel. In 6 weeks it has returned to normal size (*right*). The normal size of the uterus is about 3 inches long, weighing about 2 ounces.

sume at times, such as after breast-feeding. In about 10–14 days, the discharge turns white or yellow and gradually stops. How long the discharge lasts differs for each woman.

Return of Menstrual Periods

Your menstrual period will return in about 4–9 weeks after delivery if you are not breast-feeding, although it could start even sooner. Your periods may be shorter or longer than they were before your pregnancy, but they will gradually return to what is normal for you. If you are breast-feeding, your periods may not start again for months, perhaps not until you stop breast-feeding. Your ovaries may begin to function before you have your period, however. This means that you can ovulate and become pregnant even before your menstrual period returns. You should start using birth control 2–3 weeks after delivery if you do not want to get pregnant again right away.

Perineum

The area between your vagina and rectum, called the perineum, will have stretched during delivery. You may also have had an episiotomy, an incision or cut to widen the vagina to keep your skin from tearing during delivery. The stretching and episiotomy may cause this area to feel numb or have less sensation. It may also feel swollen, bruised, and sore. This area needs time to heal. Over the weeks after the birth, the muscles in the perineum will start to regain some of their tone. You can help this process along by doing Kegel exercises. Do these simple exercises (described in Chapter 10) as often as you can, anytime and anywhere. Start them as soon as you feel comfortable enough after birth.

Abdomen

Many women are surprised and disappointed that their abdomens are flabby after delivery, making them look like they're still pregnant. During pregnancy the abdominal muscles stretch. It takes time for good muscle tone to return. You can do some simple exercises to help tighten the muscles (see "Exercise" in this chapter). Until these muscles tighten and start working with your back muscles to help your posture, you may have a tendency to get backaches.

Discomforts

After delivery, you may feel soreness or pain at times. Most of these discomforts don't last and can be relieved.

Afterbirth Pains

Afterbirth pains are caused by the uterus contracting and relaxing as it goes back to its normal state. The contractions tend to be mild with first babies. They are usually stronger if you have had babies before or if you are nursing, but they last only a few days. Try changing your position, lying on your stomach with a pillow under your abdomen, and keeping your bladder empty. If nursing your baby brings on these afterbirth pains, it may be helpful to take over-the-counter pain medication 30–60 minutes before you plan to nurse. After a few days, this should no longer be necessary.

Painful Episiotomy

Cold packs applied to the perineum right after delivery often lessen the soreness or stinging of an episiotomy. Later on, cold packs or a warm sitz bath (sitting for a short time in warm water) can also make you more comfortable and help the healing process. In the hospital, you will be taught how to clean the area to prevent infection. Always wipe yourself from front to back to avoid infecting the perineum with germs from the rectum.

Hemorrhoids

Hemorrhoids can develop or get worse during pregnancy, labor, and delivery. These swollen veins in the rectal area can bulge out and get sore. Sprays, ointments, dry heat, or sitz baths can provide some relief. Cold witch hazel compresses are also very soothing. The hemorrhoids will gradually get smaller and may even disappear. Eating a diet rich in fiber and drinking plenty of fluids can also help avoid constipation, which may cause pain during bowel movements.

Problems with Urination

You may have trouble passing urine in the first days after delivery. You may feel the urge but can't urinate, or you may feel pain and burning when you urinate. This is caused by the pressure of the baby's head on your bladder during delivery, the stretching of your muscles, and swelling near your urethra—the opening where urine comes out. To ease soreness and lessen swelling, try a warm sitz bath. Pouring warm water over your perineum while you urinate may be soothing and help stimulate the urine flow. Your doctor can also give you medicine to relieve the pain. Doing relaxation and breathing exercises may help as well.

Another problem that can happen is incontinence: you may have trouble controlling the flow of your urine. You may not be able to tell exactly when you need to pass urine and may find the flow starts on its own. Usually, with time, the bladder's muscle tone will return to normal. It may help to do Kegel exercises to tighten bladder muscles. If you continue to have problems with incontinence, pain, or difficult urination, tell your doctor.

Warning Signs

After delivery, you should continue to watch for any abnormal changes in your health. Call your doctor or nurse if you notice any of the following symptoms:

- Fever over 100.4°F (38°C)
- Nausea and vomiting
- Painful urination, burning, and urgency (sudden, strong desire to urinate)
- Bleeding heavier than your normal period
- Pain, swelling, and tenderness in legs
- Chest pain and cough
- Hot, tender breast
- Persistent perineal pain with increasing tenderness

Bowel Problems

After delivery, your bowels may be sluggish for many reasons: stretched abdominal muscles, aftereffects of childbirth, and emptiness because you haven't eaten. Certain types of anesthesia and pain medication can cause constipation. Adding to the problem, you may be afraid to have a bowel movement because of pain from your episiotomy or hemorrhoids. Eating foods high in fiber and drinking plenty of fluids can ease constipation. Take short walks as soon as you can to get your bowels moving.

You may also have the opposite problem: trouble controlling your bowel movements. This is caused by stretching of the nerves and tissues in the perineum. The urge to have a bowel movement may feel different than it used to, or you may pass stool and gas between bowel movements. If this happens, call your doctor.

Swollen Breasts

About 2–4 days after delivery, when your milk comes in, your breasts may become very full, hard, and sore. This discomfort is caused by engorgement of the breasts with milk and will subside as you get into a regular pattern of breast-feeding. If you are not nursing your baby, severe engorgement shouldn't last more than about 36 hours. To relieve discomfort, wear a well-fitting support bra and apply ice packs to your breasts. If you are not nursing, do not empty or pump your breasts; this will only cause more milk to be produced. You can take medication to ease the pain until your milk supply dries up.

Breast-Feeding

Almost every woman can produce milk after her baby is born and breast-feed with success. Still, breast-feeding may not be for all women. Many factors are involved in each woman's decision: life style, desire, attitude, and time. If you choose to bottle-feed, your baby will still be well nourished. If you use only bottle-feeding, you will lose your milk supply after a few days and will no longer have the option of breast-feeding. You can also use a combination of methods:

- Breast-feeding with no bottles for the first 6 months
- Breast-feeding for a short time, such as 6 weeks or 3 months, and then bottle-feeding
- Breast-feeding supplemented by bottle-feeding now and then

Breast-feeding alone for at least the first 3–4 weeks will help establish your milk supply and avoid confusing the baby about which nipple is being used. (Bottle-feeding and nursing require different techniques on the part of the baby.)

Breast-feeding is a natural way to nourish your baby, but it takes learning and practice. Not all mothers and babies get the hang of it right away. If you have any concerns, such as worries about whether the baby is getting enough to eat, talk to your doctor or nurse. He or she can also refer you to a lactation specialist for expert help. Before you leave the hospital, ask for the phone number of a lactation specialist in your area. La Leche Leagues, a support network for nursing mothers, can also help with questions and concerns.

Here are some common questions and answers about breast-feeding:

- *Are my breasts too small?* Breast size doesn't matter. The amount of milk a woman's breasts make does not depend on their size or shape.
- *Do I have to prepare my nipples?* The size and shape of your nipples do not affect your ability to breast-feed. If your nipples are flat or inverted (turned in), you can still breast-feed. You can try wearing plastic breast shells in the last month of pregnancy to make your nipples stick out. It may also be helpful to expose your nipples to air or dry heat. If your nipples are erect, there is no need to prepare the breasts.
- *Will my breasts sag or be uncomfortable?* Breast-feeding itself will not make your breasts sag. Your breasts may look a little different after pregnancy or nursing, but most changes in breast shape are caused by aging. Each pregnancy, how-

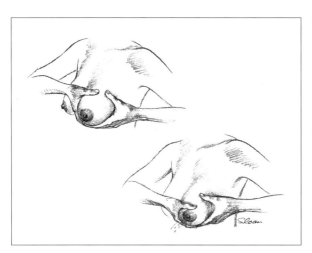

To manually express milk, massage the breast, working evenly around each one toward the nipple. With thumb and forefinger about an inch from the nipple, press in and up to release the milk. Do not squeeze the nipple itself—this will close the ducts.

ever, does cause some change as the breasts enlarge and get ready to make milk. Breasts are heavier while you are pregnant or nursing, and the increased weight can stretch the ligaments that support them. Wear a good support bra to help avoid this.

■ *What if I couldn't breast-feed the last time?* If you have given birth before but did not breast-feed, that does not mean you can't breast-feed now. If you tried breast-feeding but felt it was not a success, you may have better luck this time. Discuss your experience with your doctor or nurse, a childbirth educator, a lactation specialist, or other nursing mothers. Sometimes a change in technique will solve the problem.

■ *Can I breast-feed if I plan to return to school or work after the birth?* Yes. Some mothers just breast-feed a few times a day and use formula for the baby's other feedings. Other women may collect milk from their breasts before going to school or work. They leave the milk with the baby's caretaker while they are away. Women often can pump breast milk at work or while they are away from home.

■ *How should I store milk that I pump from my breasts?* You can put your milk in sterile glass or plastic containers and store it in the refrigerator for up to 48 hours. If you need to store it longer, you can keep it in a regular freezer for 2–3 weeks or in a deep freeze for several months. Thaw frozen milk quickly under running water or gradually in the refrigerator. Do not leave it at room temperature for a long time. Do not expose it to very hot water or put it in the microwave. After milk has been thawed, it can be kept in the refrigerator for up to 24 hours.

■ *Will I be able to make enough milk for my baby?* The amount of breast milk made by your body is based on demand—in other words, on how often and how much your baby nurses. Drinking 8–12 glasses of fluid a day, eating a balanced diet, and getting enough rest help establish and maintain your milk supply.

■ *How will I know if my baby is getting enough to eat?* Most newborn babies nurse from 10–12 times a day depending on their growth needs. The larger your baby is at birth, the more the baby will be able to hold in his or her stomach and the less often he or she will need to eat (from every 2 hours to every 4 hours, for example). Six wet diapers and one bowel movement every day usually show that your baby is getting enough to eat. Babies' sleep schedules vary, however, and some babies may need to be woken up to eat if they have been sleeping for more than 4 hours. If you have any doubts or concerns, ask your pediatrician or lactation specialist.

■ *Can I breast-feed if I have breast implants?* You may be able to breast-feed with implants, depending on where the implants are in your breast. Talk with your doctor if you have implants and want to nurse your baby.

Breast-feeding is not for every woman. Women who have infections that could be passed to the baby—such as human immunodeficiency virus (HIV), the virus that causes acquired immunodeficiency syndrome (AIDS)—and women who are taking certain medications should not breast-feed. If you are taking medication,

Breast Pumps

Most nursing mothers find it easier to use a pump to express milk than doing it by hand. A good design has two cylinders, one inside the other, attached to a rigid section that fits over your breast. You slide the outer cylinder up and down, which creates suction and draws milk into the inner cylinder. Other models work well, too. Avoid pumps with a rubber bulb at one end that look like a bicycle horn: the milk can flow back into the bulb, which is hard to clean and can invite germs. Your doctor, nurse, or lactation specialist can advise you what to buy.

If you are going back to work and plan to use a breast pump regularly, an electric model may be easier and faster for your needs. Electric pumps can usually be rented or purchased through a lactation specialist or hospital supply company. Many experts believe that electric pumps more closely mimic a nursing baby, are less likely to cause injury, and work better at emptying the breast. Though they are more costly, the added benefits of speed, efficiency, and not having to buy any or as much formula may help offset the expense.

check with your doctor to see whether it could affect the baby if you breast-feed. The levels of most medications in breast milk are so low that they have no effect on the baby. Some women may experience atrophic vaginitis—an irritation of the vagina caused by a shortage of estrogen—during the time they breast-feed. Over-the-counter lubricant can help.

Bottle-feeding takes more preparation than breast-feeding. Everything you use to feed your baby must be well cleaned and sterilized before each feeding. These items include the bottles, the nipples, and the scrub brushes. The formula must be prepared exactly as the directions say. Formula that is too weak or too strong is not good for the baby. Bottle-feeding also costs more than breast-feeding. You must buy all the formula, bottles, nipples, and bottle brushes. A government program called the Special Supplemental Food Program for Women, Infants, and Children (WIC) provides formula for mothers who cannot afford it. The program also provides food vouchers for nursing mothers to help make sure they get the extra nutrients needed to maintain their milk supply.

Postpartum Depression

It is very common for new mothers to feel sad, afraid, angry, or anxious after childbirth. Most new mothers have these feelings in a mild form called postpartum blues, baby blues, or maternity blues. When the feelings are more extreme and last longer, however, they signal a more serious condition called postpartum depression, which may call for counseling and treatment.

Blues or Depression?

Many new mothers are surprised at how fragile, alone, and drained they feel after the birth of a child. Their feelings don't seem to match their expectations. They wonder, "What have I got to be depressed about?" They fear that these feelings somehow mean that they are bad mothers.

In fact, about 7 of every 10 new mothers have the baby blues after childbirth. About 3 days after birth new mothers may find themselves feeling sad and weepy, anxious, and moody. For no clear reason, they may feel angry at the new baby, their partner, or at their other children. They may cry without warning, and at times they may have trouble sleeping, eating, and making decisions. They almost always question whether they are able to handle the important new job of caring for a baby.

As baffling and scary as these thoughts and feelings seem at the time, the baby blues usually last only a few hours to a week or so and go away without treatment. Periods of sadness and anxiety after childbirth do not mean that you are a failure as a woman or as a mother, or that you are mentally ill. They mean that your body is adjusting to other changes that follow the birth of a child.

A much smaller group of new mothers gets postpartum depression, which is marked by intense feelings of sadness, anxiety, or hopelessness that disrupt their ability to function normally. If not recognized and treated, postpartum depression can get worse or last longer than it needs to. Among the signs and symptoms of postpartum depression are the following:

- Having baby blues that don't go away after 2 weeks, or having strong feelings of depression and anger that begin to surface a month or two after childbirth
- Feeling sadness, doubt, guilt, helplessness, or hopelessness that seems to increase with each week and gets in the way of your normal activities
- Not being able to sleep even when tired, or sleeping most of the time, even when your baby is awake
- Having marked changes in appetite
- Worrying about the baby too much or having little interest in or feelings for the baby or your family
- Having nervous or panic attacks
- Fearing that you'll harm the baby or having thoughts of harming yourself

If you have any of these signs, discuss them with your doctor or nurse and get help right away.

Return to Daily Living

Bringing home a new baby is a special time for both you and your partner. But sometimes you may feel insecure. If you try to keep in mind that your relationship with each other will be changed, that your patterns of daily living will be new, and that old routines may no longer work, you will be able to start your new family life at home feeling more relaxed.

A new baby touches the lives of the entire family. Each member has a role and should be urged to get involved in the baby's care. One of the best things to do is talk to your partner, your parents, your friends, and other mothers. Share your concerns and listen to those who are important in your life.

The stress of parenting can cause a new mother or father to lose control and possibly hurt the baby. Be careful not to take your emotions out on your baby. Babies can get injured easily. Even shaking a baby can hurt him or her. Get help from your doctor or nurse or a social worker if you feel you might hurt your baby.

Mother and Baby

First-time mothers often believe that knowing how to care for a newborn should be automatic. In fact, new mothers must learn mothering skills just as they learn any other important life skill. It takes time and patience.

Some mothers are burdened by thoughts of having a perfect baby and being a perfect mother. Babies have distinct characters from birth—some are simply easier to care for than others. If a mother thinks she is not living up to the "perfect mother" ideal, whether the ideal is her own or that of her friends or parents, she may feel inadequate and depressed. Most women find it very demanding to juggle the work a new baby makes, household duties, other children, and a job, even if they have a good income and emotional support. In reality, there is no such thing as a perfect mother.

Fatigue is common during the first weeks after birth. Rest, or lack of it, will be a critical factor in your new life. It can be hard to get enough rest because of the baby's erratic schedule. Try to sleep when the baby sleeps. Do not use this time to catch up on chores. If you have an older child, try to arrange for quiet play while you and the baby rest. Although everyone will want to see the new baby, try to limit visitors. There will be plenty of time to show off the baby when you feel comfortable and well rested.

Don't hesitate to accept offers of help from your family, partner, and friends. Often people who offer don't know what they can do for you or what will help you most. Be specific. Ask a friend to bring a casserole for dinner, to stop at the grocery store, to drop off laundry, or to watch the baby or older child for 2 hours so you can rest.

Include labor savers in your budget if you can. Use a diaper service or disposable diapers. Use prepared formula if you are not breast-feeding. Get someone to help clean the house. You may need to resign yourself to the fact that some things will be left undone. It is more important for you to get the rest you need than for the housework to meet your usual standards.

Partner

A new father's needs and concerns often are not given enough attention. Much of the advice fathers get is related to how to help the mother, but adjusting to a new baby in the home can be just as hard for him. The father may also have mixed feelings about parenthood. He may throw himself into work or start spending time away from home, or he may find himself fully engrossed in being a father.

A father's bonding with his new child is enhanced if he helps take care of the baby. A new mother may find it hard to let someone else attend to the baby at first, more because of her own concerns about doing everything right than because she doubts the father's ability. It is very important that the father hold and care for the baby and get to know his son or daughter.

When possible, encourage your partner and your baby to get to know each other when both are not cranky or stressed. Pressing the care of a fussy baby on a tired, work-weary partner as soon as he steps in the door can make it more difficult for either one to relate to the other. Your baby's mood will not always mesh with your partner's. However, if at least one of them is not irritable, there is a better chance that the effect will be calming instead of creating tension and frustration.

Sometimes the father is not involved in the baby's life. Today, there are many forms of "family." Many women raise children on their own as single parents. They may turn to family and friends for support.

Siblings

Your older children may react to your new baby in many ways. They may be disappointed: the baby may not be the playmate they pictured and may even be the "wrong" sex. No matter how well you prepared the older children, they may be annoyed that all the baby does is eat, sleep, and cry. They may be jealous and insecure about the new baby and may express these feelings in ways to get attention. They may throw temper tantrums, ask to be fed from a bottle or your breast, wet their pants, change their sleeping or eating patterns, or get angry with you for paying so much attention to the baby. They may display anger toward the baby by hitting, biting, or throwing things.

When a new brother or sister comes home from the hospital, it's a perfect time for the father to strengthen his relationship with the older child. Sending the older child to stay with someone else for a while is not a good idea. Instead, ask a relative or friend to stay with you and pay extra attention to the needs of the older child.

The relationship between siblings is one of the longest and most important relationships there is. Try to promote the bond early in your pregnancy. Explain to the older sibling the role he or she can play in guiding and teaching the new baby. Read books together about pregnancy, childbirth, babies, and being a big brother or sister. If sibling preparation classes are available in your area, take your child to one. Here are some other things you can do:

- Before the baby is born, let your older child feel the fetus move and hear its heartbeat.
- Take your child on a tour of the hospital before you give birth.
- Show your child pictures and videos from when he or she was a newborn, especially if they show you or your partner taking care of the child.
- Set up the new baby's sleeping area well in advance. This way the older child will get used to it and won't feel displaced abruptly.

■ Give the older child a new doll so he or she has a "baby," too.

■ Plan for time alone with the older child to do what he or she wants. Spend time with your older child while the baby is sleeping or otherwise occupied. As little as 15 minutes spent alone with the older child talking, reading, or having a special play time helps remind the child of how important and special he or she is.

■ Try not to ignore the older child even though you're busy. Listen to him or her and respond to questions.

■ Include the child in baby-care activities such as diapering, dressing, bathing, feeding, and burping. Let the child amuse the baby with singing, talk, and smiles. If the older child wants nothing to do with the baby, that's okay, too.

Grandparents

When a grandchild is born, some grandparents hold back, not wanting to interfere. Others may give lots of advice, which you may welcome or see as a nuisance. Every situation is different.

If grandparents are coming to stay and help, set a date for their return home. If there are problems or conflicts, it is important that the new parents make the decisions and that they back up each other in these decisions.

Exercise

Daily exercise can help restore muscle strength and return your body to the shape it was in before pregnancy. Although exercise may seem like an effort, it can actually make you less tired because it raises your energy level and helps your general sense of well-being.

If you had a cesarean delivery, a difficult birth, or complications, check with your doctor before starting an exercise program. Otherwise, start when you feel up to it. Follow the same general guidelines as you did when you were pregnant (see Chapter 8).

If you didn't exercise during pregnancy, start slowly with easy exercises and gradually build up to harder ones. If you exercised regularly throughout the pregnancy, you have a head start on getting back in shape. However, you should not try to return to the same level and intensity right away.

Walking is a good way to get back into exercising. Brisk walks several times a week will prepare you for more strenuous exercise when you feel up to it. Walking in and of itself is an excellent activity, even if you don't plan on adding other exercises later. Walking is easier to do than most other exercises because you need no special equipment other than comfortable shoes, it's free, and you can do it almost anywhere or anytime. Walking has the added advantage of getting both you and the baby out of the house for exercise and fresh air without the added problem of finding child care. Interacting with others and your environment not only has physical benefits but also can help relieve stress and tension.

You will want to design your own exercise program to meet your own needs. This program can include making your heart and lungs stronger, toning your muscles, or both. Swimming is an excellent example of an exercise that can do both. Your doctor or nurse can recommend other types of exercises for you. There are also specially designed postpartum exercise classes that you can join. Resources that may be helpful are health and fitness clubs, women's spas, the YWCA or YMCA, and local community colleges, hospitals, and adult education programs. Whatever program you get involved in, make sure it's one you can stick with. Continuing to exercise over the long haul is more important than starting right away after birth.

Postpartum Exercises

Leg Slides

This simple exercise tones abdominal and leg muscles. It does not put much strain on your incision if you have had a cesarean birth. You should try to repeat this exercise several times a day.

- Lie flat on your back and bend your knees slightly.
- Inhale, slide your right leg from a bent to a straight position, exhale, and bend it back again.
- Be sure that you keep both feet on the floor and keep them relaxed.
- Repeat with your left leg.

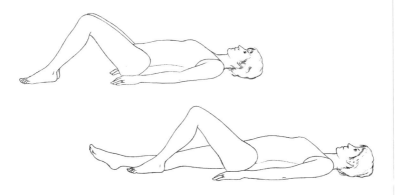

Postpartum Exercises *(continued)*

Head Lifts

Head lifts can progress to shoulder lifts and curl-ups, all of which strengthen the abdominal muscles. When you feel comfortable doing 10 head lifts at a time, proceed to shoulder lifts.

- Lie on your back with your arms along your sides. Bend your knees so that your feet are flat on the floor.
- Inhale and relax your abdomen.
- Exhale slowly as you lift your head off the floor.
- Inhale as you lower your head again.

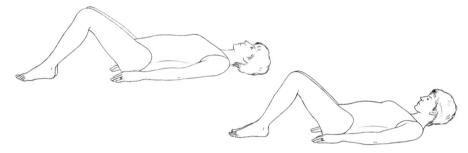

Curl-ups

Begin the same way as you would for head lifts, lying on your back with your knees bent and your arms at your sides. Keep your lower back flat on the floor.

- Inhale, relaxing your abdomen.
- Exhale. Reach with your arms, and slowly raise your torso to the point halfway between your knees and the floor (about a 45° angle).
- Inhale as you lower yourself to the floor.

Shoulder Lifts

Begin the same way as you would for head lifts. When you feel comfortable doing 10 shoulder lifts at a time, proceed with curl-ups.

- Inhale and relax your abdomen.
- Exhale slowly and lift your head and shoulders off the floor. Reach with your arms so that you don't use them for support.
- Inhale as you lower your shoulders to the floor.

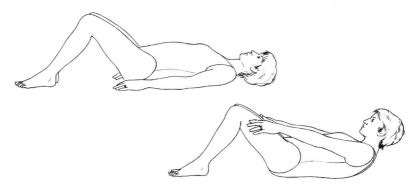

Kneeling Pelvic Tilt

Tilting your pelvis back toward your spine helps strengthen your abdominal muscles.

- Begin on your hands and knees. Your back should be relaxed, not curved or arched.
- Inhale.
- Exhale and pull your buttocks forward, rotating the pubic bone upward.
- Hold for a count of three, then inhale and relax.
- Repeat five times and add one or two repetitions a day if you can.

Nutrition and Diet

You will lose up to 20 pounds in the first 4 weeks after delivery. It is tempting to try to lose more so that you can wear your regular clothes again. Be patient. If you keep eating the well-balanced diet that you began in pregnancy, in an amount that's right for your body weight, you'll be close to your normal weight within several months. Combining this diet with exercise will keep your muscles toned.

If you are breast-feeding, you need extra fluid, calories, calcium, and protein. A nursing mother needs the foods normally required for her own body plus extra food to produce milk for her baby—about 500 more calories a day than she needed before pregnancy. It is easy to add the extra food needed for nursing if you are already eating a well-balanced diet of foods in the Food Guide Pyramid (see Chapter 9).

Calcium, which is particularly important for nursing mothers, is supplied by milk, yogurt, cheese, cottage cheese, ice cream, and ice milk. If you cannot tolerate milk products, your doctor or nurse can suggest other sources of calcium. You should avoid nicotine, alcohol, and other drugs that can harm your baby because they can be passed to the baby through the breast milk.

Work

You will need to stay at home for a certain period after delivery to regain your strength before returning to work. Certain factors should be taken into account when deciding whether or when to resume working after the birth of your baby. You have to consider money, of course, and the cost and options for child care. If you are breast-feeding, you may want to look into breast pumps and begin practicing the technique. This will also get your baby used to accepting a bottle. Breast milk can be saved to be given to the baby later if you can't be there for every feeding.

Employers are becoming more flexible and offering more options to working mothers. Many women work part-time or even share one full-time job. Some employers offer child care at the work site for newborns and toddlers, so you can visit your child during breaks and at lunch. Options such as flexible hours and job

Child Care Options

A baby may be cared for in the parents' home or at another location. For care in the home, contact employment agencies specializing in child care professionals. This private care is very expensive, however. You may wish to place your child in a day care center or in the home of a licensed provider or a relative. Your pediatrician can be a good source of information on child care. Here are some points to consider in selecting child care:

- Gather information about the available centers. Find out where they are located, what the hours of operation are, and the cost of care.
- Visit the center. Be sure to go more than once. Make an appointment the first time, and then drop in unannounced. See what the physical setting is like. Observe the children who are there. Find out what a typical daily schedule is and what is typically served to the children at meal and snack times. Be sure that the facilities are well equipped and large enough to handle the number of children and that enough care providers are present (one adult per three to four infants, four to five toddlers, or six to nine preschoolers).
- Check credentials. When you leave your child in the hands of a professional, you should know something about that person's background and priorities. If the person is licensed or registered with the local government, ask to see the document. If there are any written policies concerning philosophy, procedures, or discipline, be sure to get copies. Find out if the care provider has had training in first aid, if he or she is willing to give your child prescribed medications, and what plans are in place in case of a medical emergency. If possible, get recommendations from others who have used the center or care provider.

sharing also are helpful, and many women find that they can work at home.

Sexuality

Sometimes you may not be as interested in sex as you were before you gave birth. Sheer fatigue can be a big reason why you—and your partner—may lose interest in sex. Your changing roles as new parents may cause emotional turmoil that decreases your interest in sex. The baby's demands may affect your desire as well.

Before you have sex, you should wait until the healing process is complete to avoid hurting delicate tissues. Sexual intercourse can usually be resumed as soon as you feel comfortable—

usually in about 3–4 weeks. It is important for you and your partner to discuss this beforehand with your doctor or nurse and with each other so you will not misunderstand each other or feel frustrated later.

When you think you are ready to resume sexual relations, proceed slowly and gently. You may be afraid of the pain. Try to choose a time when you are not rushed and try different positions. Many women find that sitting or kneeling on top of their partner allows them more control and freedom of movement, which helps aid relaxation and arousal. You may notice that your vagina is dry. This decreased lubrication is a normal response of your body. It may last as long as you breast-feed or until your first menstrual period. Use a water-soluble cream or jelly or saliva to lubricate your vagina during this time.

If you have problems, you and your partner should talk about them. Spend time together without the baby at least once or twice a week. Try to avoid talking about the baby and the household at these special times. Talk about yourselves and each other. Rediscover what brought you together in the first place. There are other ways of sharing your sexual feelings—stroking, touching, or cuddling—that can be very satisfying.

Family Planning

Once you and your partner decide to start having sex again, you should consider how you wish to space your children. For most women, an interval of about $1\frac{1}{2}$ to 2 years between births is best. Because you can be fertile after giving birth, you should choose some form of birth control before you have intercourse for the first time.

Today there are many methods of birth control for women and men. Each has advantages. It is best to discuss these methods in detail with your doctor or nurse and with your partner to select the one that best meets your needs. Here are some things to consider:

- How well the method works as a contraceptive
- How safe it is for your whole body
- How much it costs
- How easy it is to use

Birth Control Methods

Hormones
- Birth control pills
- Implants
- Injections

Intrauterine device (IUD)

Barrier methods

- Diaphragm
- Cervical cap
- Condom (male and female)
- Spermicidal cream, jelly, foam (chemicals that kill sperm)

Natural family planning

Sterilization

- Tubal sterilization for women
- Vasectomy for men

Any method of birth control can do a good job of preventing unwanted pregnancy if it is used the right way and used all the time. At any given time, a couple will that find one form of birth control suits their needs better than others.

Birth control pills, hormone implants in your arm, hormone injections every 3 months, and the intrauterine device (IUD) are the most effective methods of preventing pregnancy, especially if you want the option of having more children later. These methods act continuously—you do not have to insert them or follow special instructions each time you decide to have sex. Others, such as diaphragms and condoms, must be used each time you have intercourse. Still others are surgical procedures that are meant to be permanent once they are performed.

Breast-Feeding and Family Planning

While you are breast-feeding, you may not ovulate or have menstrual periods. This lowers your chances of getting pregnant compared with women who do not breast-feed. Breast-feeding is not a form of birth control, however. You can ovulate before you start to menstruate again after pregnancy. If you don't use birth control, you can become pregnant, even if you are breast-feeding.

If you plan to use birth control pills while you are breast-feeding, do so after you have been breastfeeding for several weeks. Birth control pills that contain estrogen may cause a slight decrease in the amount of milk you produce, but this shouldn't pose a problem. You may want to consider using the minipill, which does not contain estrogen, while you breast-feed. The minipill has only one hormone, progesterone. It does not interfere with milk production. It also is a better choice for women with certain health problems.

Hormones

With hormonal birth control, a woman takes hormones like those her body makes naturally. Hormones work by preventing ovulation. When there is no egg to be fertilized, pregnancy cannot occur. You still have monthly periods, however.

The most-used method of hormonal birth control is the birth control pill, or oral contraceptive. It is also one of the most effective and widely used forms of birth control. A woman needs to take the pill exactly as prescribed.

Implants are another form of hormonal birth control. Six soft plastic tubes the size of a match stick are placed just under the skin of your upper arm. This is done through a small cut after you get local anesthesia. After the tubes are inserted, you don't need to do anything else to prevent pregnancy. Implants provide birth control for up to 5 years. They can be removed when you want to stop using them, or they can be replaced with new implants after 5 years. To remove them, the doctor makes another small cut at or near the original site.

Injections of hormones are a third option. Each injection provides birth control for 3 months, so you only need four injections a year. While using this method you don't need to do anything else to prevent pregnancy.

Intrauterine Device

The intrauterine device is a small plastic device containing copper or hormones. It is inserted in and left inside the uterus. The presence of the IUD prevents the egg from being fertilized. The risk of pelvic infection is higher with an IUD if a woman or her partner has more than one sexual partner. The IUD usually is not recommended for women who have not had any children.

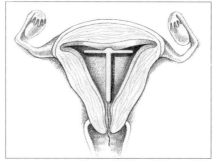

Intrauterine device (IUD).

Barrier Methods

Barrier methods include spermicides, the diaphragm, cervical cap, and condom (male and female).

- Spermicides are chemicals that kill sperm. They are placed in the vagina close to the cervix. They include creams, jellies, foams, and vaginal inserts and suppositories.
- The diaphragm is a round rubber dome that fits inside the woman's vagina and covers her cervix.
- The cervical cap is a small rubber cup that fits over the cervix and stays in place by suction.
- The male condom is a thin sheath made of latex (rubber), or animal membrane worn by the man over his penis.
- The female condom is a plastic pouch that lines the vagina. It is held in place by a closed inner ring at the cervix and an open outer ring at the opening of the vagina.

The diaphragm, cervical cap, and male and female condoms act as barriers. They keep the sperm from getting to the egg. These methods are used with spermicides to further lower the risk of pregnancy. Some couples combine barrier methods rather than relying on only one. They may use different ones at different times, or they may use two methods together for better effectiveness. Barrier methods must be used each time you have sex.

Natural Family Planning

Natural family planning is also called periodic abstinence or the rhythm method. It involves avoiding sex during those times in your menstrual cycle when your chances of becoming pregnant are greatest. By knowing when you expect to ovulate, you and your partner know when to abstain from sex. Ways to predict ovulation are watching for changes in your body temperature, watching for changes in your cervical mucus, and counting the days during your menstrual cycle.

These methods are often combined to prevent pregnancy. For natural family planning to work, the couple must understand how the method works and pay close attention to the woman's cycle. Until the woman's cycles are regular after having a baby, this method does not work well. If you are interested in this method, your doctor or nurse may be able to suggest counselors who can teach you about it.

Sterilization

If you and your partner are certain that you don't want to have any more children, sterilization is a means of permanent birth control. It is done by surgery under general or local anesthesia. Although sterilization cannot guarantee that you will never become pregnant, more than 99 of every 100 women who are sterilized do not become pregnant. Sterilization is popular because it frees a couple from the need to use birth control methods.

As is true of any operation, sterilization has some risks. Serious problems happen in about 1 in every 1,000 women who have the operation. Most of the time they can be treated and corrected.

When the woman is sterilized, it is called *tubal sterilization*. The surgery involves cutting, banding, or clipping the fallopian tubes, which blocks sperm from reaching and fertilizing the egg. The operation does not affect the menstrual cycle or the woman's ability to enjoy sex.

A man is sterilized by *vasectomy*, in which the vas deferens (tubes through which sperm travel) are tied off so sperm cannot be released. The operation does not affect the man's ability to have erections or to ejaculate. Vasectomy is more than 99% effective in preventing pregnancy.

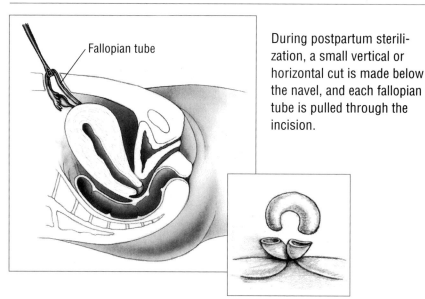

During postpartum sterilization, a small vertical or horizontal cut is made below the navel, and each fallopian tube is pulled through the incision.

A section of the tube is closed off with surgical thread, and the section between the ties is removed.

Both procedures can be done at any time, usually on an outpatient basis, which means you can go home the same day. Women often choose to be sterilized right after the birth of a baby, while they are still in the hospital. It can be done more easily at this time because the uterus is still enlarged and pushes the fallopian tubes up so they can be sealed through a small cut in your navel.

When thinking about sterilization, remember that it is supposed to be permanent. You and your partner must be sure you do

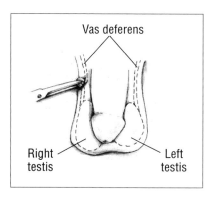

During a vasectomy, one or two small cuts are made in the skin of the scrotum. Each vas is pulled through the opening until it forms a loop. A small section is cut out of the loop and removed.

not want any more children—now or in the future. If there is any chance that you would want children again, perhaps through re-marriage, think about other forms of birth control. Surgery to re-verse sterilization can be tried but does not always work.

Follow-up Visit

You should make an ap-pointment to visit your doctor or nurse 2–6 weeks after the birth of your baby. Your weight, blood pressure, breasts, and ab-domen will be checked, and you will be given a pelvic exam. Your doctor or nurse will determine how well your body has

Your doctor or nurse can answer any questions you might have and can help you plan your routine postpartum care.

recovered from the changes you have gone through and will be able to tell if there are any problems.

You should discuss any questions or concerns you have about birth control, sex, or your emotions. This is the best time to re-solve any problems you may be having and to prepare for an on-going program of health care for the future.

Questions to Consider...

- What can I do to relieve the pain of breast engorgement?
- How can I help my older children adjust to the new baby?
- What does it mean if I feel sad and anxious? If I think these feelings are lasting too long, what should I do?
- What form of exercise is best to start with after I've recov-ered from delivery?

■ When can my partner and I start having sex again?
■ Can I keep nursing after I go back to work?
■ What birth control method is best for me?

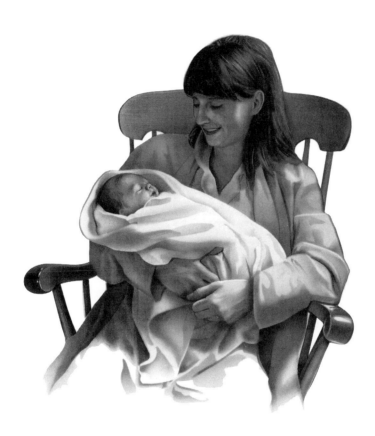

Personal Pregnancy Diary

My Health Care Team

Doctors' names:

_____

_____

_____

Pediatricians' names:

_____

_____

_____

Doctors' addresses:

_____

_____

_____

Pediatricians' addresses:

_____

_____

_____

Telephone/answering service:

Day _____

Night _____

Hospital _____

Telephone/answering service:

Day _____

Night _____

Hospital _____

Nursing staff:

_____

_____

Nursing staff:

_____

_____

Receptionist:

_____

Receptionist:

_____

My Childbirth Education

Educator:

_____

Beginning date: _____

Ending date: _____

Telephone: _____

Educator's address:

_____

_____

_____

First Signs

I first heard my baby's heartbeat: _____

I first felt my baby move: _____

Medications

Medications Taken	Dose	Date Started	Date Ended

Vital Statistics

My prepregnant weight: _____ lbs. Last menstrual period _____

My blood type: _____ Rh factor: _____

Rubella status: _____

Special Tests

Date	Procedure	Findings

Prenatal Visits

Visit	Date	Weeks	Weight	Blood Pressure	Uterus Height (cm)	Questions/Comments
1st						
2nd						
3rd						
4th						
5th						
6th						
7th						
8th						
9th						
10th						
11th						
12th						
13th						

Labor and Delivery

My due date: _____   My labor began: _____

My baby was born: _____   Time of delivery: _____

Delivered by: _____

My baby's weight: _____   Length: _____

Hospital where my baby was born:

_____

_____

_____

Medical Record

Mother: _____   Baby: _____
                 (no.)   (no.)

Postpartum Visits

Mother

Date: _____   Weight: _____   Blood pressure: _____

Family planning: _____

Comments: _____

_____

_____

Baby

Date: _____   Weight: _____   Length: _____

Special Care: _____

_____

Baby's feeding: _____

Comments: _____

_____

_____

My Baby's Growth Charts

When you take your baby for a checkup, he or she will be weighed and measured. Your baby's steady growth in height and weight is one of the best signs that he or she is healthy. Track your baby's growth by filling in the length and weight at each age.

Length for Age—Boys

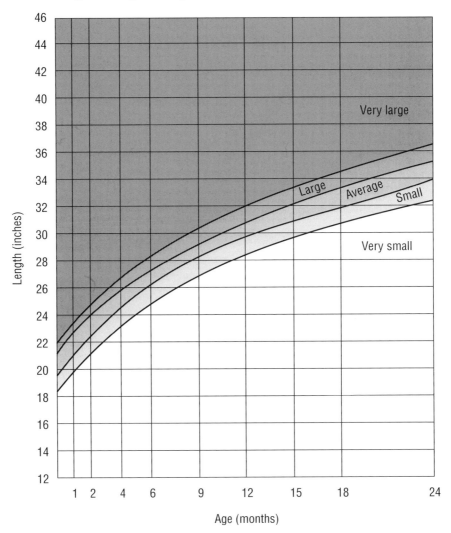

Weight for Age—Boys

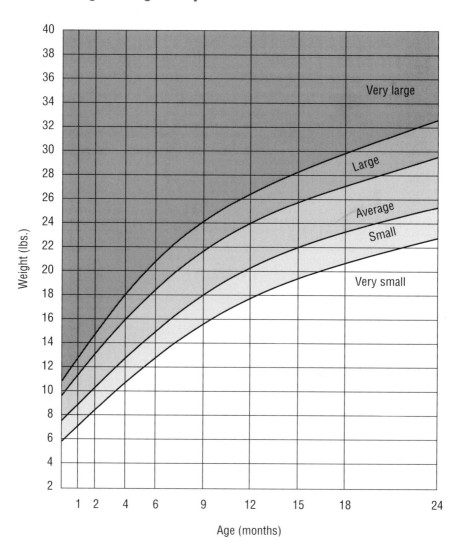

Length for Age—Girls

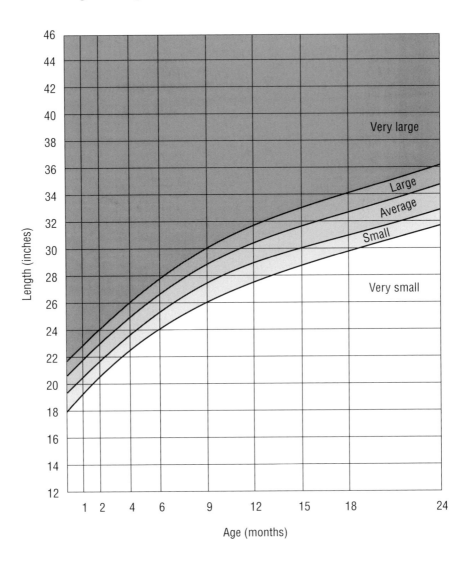

Weight for Age—Girls

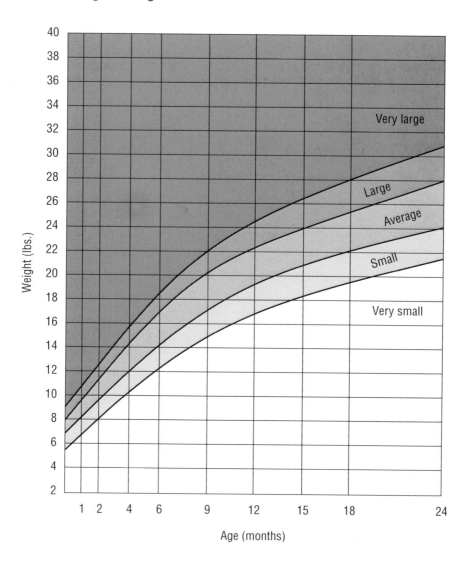

Age (months)

Weight (lbs.)

Adapted from *My Health Diary*, 1992, by the U.S. Department of Health and Human Services, Health Resources and Services Administration, Washington, DC.

Glossary

Abruptio Placentae: A condition in which the placenta has begun to separate from the inner wall of the uterus before the baby is born.

Alpha-fetoprotein (AFP): A protein produced by a growing fetus; it is present in amniotic fluid and, in smaller amounts, in the mother's blood.

Amniocentesis: A procedure in which a small amount of amniotic fluid is taken from the sac surrounding the fetus and tested.

Amniotic Fluid: Water in the sac surrounding the fetus in the mother's uterus.

Amniotic Sac: Fluid-filled sac in the mother's uterus in which the fetus develops.

Analgesia: Relief of pain without total loss of sensation.

Anencephaly: A type of neural tube defect that occurs when the fetus's head and brain do not develop normally.

Anesthesia: Relief of pain by loss of sensation.

Antibiotics: Drugs that treat infections.

Antibody: A protein in the blood produced in reaction to foreign substances, such as bacteria and viruses that cause infections.

Antigen: A substance, such as an organism causing infection or a protein found on the surface of blood cells, that can induce an immune response and cause the production of an antibody.

Apgar Score: A measurement of a baby's response to birth and life on its own, taken 1 and 5 minutes after birth.

Areola: The darker skin around the nipple.

Auscultation: A method of listening to the fetal heartbeat during labor, either with a special stethoscope or the use of a Doppler ultrasound device.

Biophysical Profile: An assessment of fetal heart rate, fetal breathing, fetal body movement, fetal muscle tone, and the amount of amniotic fluid. Heart rate is determined by the nonstress test. Ultrasound is used for the other four measurements.

Braxton Hicks Contractions: False labor pains.

Breech Presentation: A situation in which a fetus is positioned buttocks or feet down, at the top of the birth canal, ready to be born first.

Carrier: A person who shows no signs of a particular disorder but could pass the gene on to his or her children.

Cephalopelvic Disproportion: A condition in which a baby is too large to pass safely through the mother's pelvis during delivery.

Chancre: An infectious sore caused by syphilis and appearing at the place of infection.

Chloasma: The darkening of areas of skin on the face during pregnancy.

Chorioamnionitis: Inflammation of the membrane surrounding the fetus.

Chorionic Villi: Microscopic, fingerlike projections that make up the placenta.

Chorionic Villus Sampling (CVS): A procedure in which a small sample of cells is taken from the placenta and tested.

Chromosomes: Structures that are located inside each cell in the body and contain the genes that determine a person's physical makeup.

Colostrum: A fluid secreted in the breasts at the beginning of milk production.

Congenital Disorder: A condition that affects a fetus before it is born.

Contraction Stress Test: A test in which mild contractions of the mother's uterus are induced and the fetus's heart rate in response to the contractions is recorded using an electronic fetal monitor.

Corticosteroids: Hormones given for arthritis or other medical conditions.

Cystitis: An infection of the bladder.

Dilation and Curettage (D&C): A procedure in which the cervix is dilated and tissue is gently scraped or suctioned from the inside of the uterus.

Down Syndrome: A genetic disorder caused by the presence of an extra chromosome and characterized by mental retardation, abnormal features of the face, and medical problems such as heart defects.

Ectopic Pregnancy: A pregnancy in which the fertilized egg begins to grow in a place other than inside the uterus, usually in the fallopian tubes.

Edema: Swelling caused by fluid retention.

Electronic Fetal Monitoring: A method in which electronic instruments are used to record the heartbeat of the fetus and contractions of the mother's uterus.

Endometriosis: A condition in which tissue similar to that normally lining the uterus is found outside of the uterus, usually on the ovaries, fallopian tubes, and other pelvic structures.

Epidural Block: Anesthesia that numbs the lower half of the body.

Episiotomy: A surgical incision made into the perineum (the region between the vagina and the anus) to widen the vaginal opening for delivery.

Estrogen: A female hormone produced in the ovaries that stimulates the growth of the lining of the uterus.

Fetal Alcohol Syndrome: A pattern of physical, mental, and behavioral problems in the baby that is thought to be due to alcohol abuse by the mother during pregnancy.

Fibroids: Benign (noncancerous) growths that form on the inside of the uterus, on its outer surface, or within the uterine wall itself.

Follicle-Stimulating Hormone (FSH): A hormone produced by the pituitary gland that helps an egg to mature and be released.

Forceps: Special instruments placed around the baby's head to help guide it out of the birth canal during delivery.

Gene: A DNA "blueprint" that codes for specific traits, such as hair and eye color.

Glucose: A sugar that is present in the blood and is the body's main source of fuel.

Human Chorionic Gonadotropin (hCG): A hormone produced during pregnancy; its detection is the basis for most pregnancy tests.

Hydramnios: A condition in which there is an excess amount of amniotic fluid in the sac surrounding the fetus.

Insulin: A hormone that controls the levels of glucose (sugar) in the blood.

Jaundice: A buildup of bilirubin that causes a yellowish appearance.

Lanugo: Fine hair that sometimes grows on a baby's back and shoulders at birth; it goes away in 1 or 2 weeks.

Laparoscopy: A surgical procedure in which a slender, light-transmitting instrument, the laparoscope, is used to view the pelvic organs or perform surgery.

Linea Nigra: A line running from the navel to pubic hair that darkens during pregnancy.

Lochia: Vaginal discharge that occurs after delivery.

Luteinizing Hormone (LH): A hormone produced by the pituitary glands that helps an egg to mature and be released.

Macrosomia: A condition in which a fetus grows very large; this problem is often found in babies of diabetic mothers.

Maternal Serum Screening: A group of blood tests that check for substances linked with certain birth defects.

Meconium: A greenish substance that builds up in the bowels of a growing fetus and is normally discharged shortly after birth.

Miscarriage: The spontaneous loss of a pregnancy before the fetus can survive outside the uterus.

Multiple Pregnancy: A pregnancy in which there are two or more fetuses.

Neural Tube Defect (NTD): A fetal birth defect that results from improper development of the brain, spinal cord, or their coverings.

Nonstress Test: A test in which fetal movements felt by the mother or noted by the doctor are recorded, along with changes in the fetal heart rate, using an electronic fetal monitor.

Oxytocin: A drug used to help bring on contractions.

Paracervical Block: The injection of a local anesthetic into the tissues around the cervix to relieve pain during childbirth.

Perineum: The area between the vagina and the rectum.

Pica: The urge to eat nonfood items during pregnancy.

Pituitary Gland: A gland located near the brain that controls growth and other changes in the body.

Placenta: Tissue that connects woman and fetus and provides nourishment to and takes away waste from the fetus.

Placenta Previa: A condition, usually discovered during late pregnancy, in which the placenta lies very low in the uterus, so that the opening of the uterus is partially or completely covered.

Postterm Pregnancy: A pregnancy that extends beyond 42 weeks.

Preeclampsia: A condition of pregnancy in which there is high blood pressure, swelling due to fluid retention, and abnormal kidney function.

Preterm: Born before 37 weeks.

Progesterone: A female hormone that is produced in the ovaries and matures the lining of the uterus. When its level falls, menstruation occurs.

Pudendal Block: An injection given in the perineum that relieves pain during delivery but not labor.

Pyelonephritis: An infection of the kidney.

Quickening: The mother's first feeling of movement of the fetus.

Respiratory Distress Syndrome (RDS): A condition of some preterm babies in which the lungs are incompletely developed.

Retracted Nipple: A nipple that has pulled inward.

Spina Bifida: A neural tube defect that results from improper closure of the fetal spine.

Spinal Block: A form of anesthesia that numbs the lower half of the body.

Stillbirth: Delivery of a baby that shows no sign of life.

Sudden Infant Death Syndrome (SIDS): The sudden death of any infant or young child that is unexpected and in which the cause of death is unknown.

Teratogens: Agents that can cause birth defects when a woman is exposed to them during pregnancy.

Transducer: A device that emits sound waves and translates the echoes into electrical signals.

Trimester: Any of the three 3-month periods into which pregnancy is divided.

Tubal Sterilization: A method of female sterilization in which the fallopian tubes are closed by tying, banding, clipping, or sealing with electric current.

Ultrasound: A test in which sound waves are used to examine internal structures. During pregnancy, it can be used to examine the fetus.

Umbilical Cord: A cordlike structure that forms normally during pregnancy and connects the baby's bloodstream to the mother's.

Vacuum Extraction: The use of a special instrument attached to the baby's head to help guide it out of the birth canal during delivery.

Vasectomy: A method of male sterilization in which a portion of the vas deferens is removed.

Vernix: The greasy, whitish coating of a newborn.

Vibroacoustic Stimulation: The use of sound and vibration to wake the fetus during a nonstress test.

Index